Sculptures for the
Emperor

Explorer Challenge

Find out who has this
moustache …

OXFORD
UNIVERSITY PRESS

Anneena and her mum had started going to a pottery class. Anneena enjoyed the class and was quite good at making little pots. After a few weeks, she tried making little figures out of clay.

"I really like making figures," she said. "This one is going to be a girl with an umbrella."

"The figure looks like Biff," laughed Anneena's mum.
"She even has a big umbrella like Biff's."

"You're right. It does look like Biff," said Anneena.

"It's good," said the teacher, "but the legs are too wide.
Let me show you how to work on some of the details."

A week later, Anneena's teacher said, "Your little figure has been in the kiln and it didn't crack in the heat. You can paint it with glaze now. That will give it beautiful shiny colours."

"I'll paint the umbrella to look just like Biff's," said Anneena.

When it was finished, Anneena wrapped the figure up and gave it to Biff.

"I made it," said Anneena shyly. "I hope you like it."

Biff unwrapped the figure and gasped. "It's me with my umbrella!" she exclaimed. "It's lovely. It's one of the nicest presents I have ever had."

Biff ran downstairs and fetched her umbrella. She began to open it when Anneena stopped her.

"Hey!" said Anneena. "Be careful with that. You might break something! Like the little figure I just gave you!"

At that moment, with Biff still holding the
umbrella, the key glowed and they were whisked into
an adventure.

The key took them back in time. They were in China over two thousand years ago. They found themselves in a large hall. At the end of it were six men.

Anneena's eyes widened. "Those men are wearing armour," she whispered. "Perhaps they are soldiers."

The soldiers were standing completely still. Not one of them moved.

"Er … hello," said Biff nervously. "Um … can you tell us where we are?"

"They aren't moving," gulped Anneena. She took a few steps towards them. "In fact, I can't see them breathing."

As the girls went closer, they saw the soldiers were life-size models, beautifully made of clay and painted in bright colours.

"Amazing!" exclaimed Biff. "They are so lifelike."

Biff leaned forward to touch one when she heard footsteps behind her and a voice shouted, "Stop!"

"Please do not touch the sculptures for the Emperor," the voice called.

Two boys came into the hall. They were carrying vases of herbs.

"These figures have been made with special care," one of them said. "The Emperor is coming today to inspect them. These herbs are to make the room smell sweet."

"The figures are amazing," said Biff. "What are they for?"

"Don't you know?" gasped the smaller boy. "The Emperor needs thousands of clay warriors like these to protect him."

"Even though there are thousands of them, each one is different," said the bigger boy.

"All the people in our village make the figures," said the bigger boy. "Every so often the Emperor comes to inspect them."

"Come with us and we will show you how they are made," said the smaller boy.

The boys took Biff and Anneena into a huge
workshop. The girls gasped when they saw it. In front
of them were rows of legs.

"The figures are made in parts," explained the
smaller boy.

On a long bench were rows of clay heads.

"These are the head shapes ready for the most skilful artists to create the faces," the bigger boy said.

"Our father is very skilled," said the smaller boy. "He makes the warriors' faces. Come and see how he does it."

The boys took the girls to see their father.

"I add more clay to the head shape. Then I can carve eyes, noses, mouths, ears, hair and even make hats for the warriors," said the boys' father. "Each face is different."

"It's just fantastic," said Anneena.

"It takes many years to learn to do this," he went on.

Suddenly a gong sounded.

"It's time to put on clean clothes. The Emperor is coming," said the boys' father. "You can sweep the workshop floor again first."

"But we swept it just now," protested the boys.

"We'll do it," said Biff. "We don't mind."

The boys and their father left the girls to get on with sweeping the floor.

"I'm just amazed to see how they make these clay warriors," said Biff. "Whoops!"

When Biff and Anneena went outside, people were standing along the street of shops and houses.

"Look at all these people waiting for the Emperor," said Anneena.

Then a whisper ran along the crowd like a breath of wind: "The Emperor is here!"

The Emperor was seated on a richly decorated chariot pulled by horses. Above him was a canopy fixed to slim poles.

"The Emperor looks very grand," said Anneena. "Imagine having all those clay warriors made just for him."

As the Emperor passed by, people bowed in respect.

"We'd better do the same when he gets to us," whispered Biff.

Then, something terrible happened. It began to pour with rain.

The rain came down in torrents. Biff and Anneena
had never seen rain like it. Biff put up her umbrella and
they both huddled under it. Some people had umbrellas
made of silk and cloth but they soon collapsed.

And then the rain stopped as suddenly as it had begun. Everyone was soaked except the Emperor. Then Biff noticed the canopy over the Emperor's head was bulging with water. It looked as if it was about to burst.

Biff rushed forward and handed her umbrella to the Emperor. At that moment, the canopy split and a gush of water cascaded down. Everyone breathed a sigh of relief. Biff had saved the Emperor from getting soaked.

The Emperor nodded at Biff and the procession moved on with the Emperor holding Biff's umbrella.

"Well," laughed Biff, "it looks as though I might not get my umbrella back. But I don't mind."

"I hope the key glows soon," said Biff. "I got soaked doing that!"

Anneena smiled. "Well, at least you kept the Emperor dry," she said.

Then, two of the Emperor's attendants ran up.

"Come quickly!" one of them panted. "The Emperor wishes to see you at once, and here is your umbrella."

The Emperor had finished inspecting the clay warriors. He was pleased with the superb workmanship. He had been given six perfect models of the figures.

The girls were taken to the Emperor. "Bow down and only speak if you are spoken to," they were told.

"You did well," the Emperor told Biff. "In future, my chariot will have an umbrella even bigger than yours."

"Would you like to keep my umbrella, Your Greatness?" said Biff.

The Emperor laughed loudly. "I would!" he cried. "And you can have a small warrior in return."

At that moment, the key glowed. It was time to go.

"That was an amazing adventure," said Biff. She put the terracotta warrior next to the little figure Anneena had made. "This clay warrior is great," she said, "but I like your model of me even more."

She gave Anneena a big hug.

Retell the Story

Look at the pictures and retell the story in your own words.

Look Back, Explorers

What were in the vases that the boys were carrying?

When Biff and Anneena arrived, they saw six men. Why didn't the men move?

Biff says that the figures are *amazing*. What other words would you use to describe them?

Can you describe what happened to the Emperor and his chariot when it rained?

What happened to Biff's umbrella in the end?

Did you find out who has this moustache?

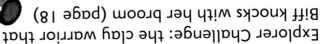

Explorer Challenge: the clay warrior that Biff knocks with her broom (page 18)

What's Next, Explorers?

Now you've been on a magic key adventure to see the Emperor's sculptures, find out about different sculptures of people …

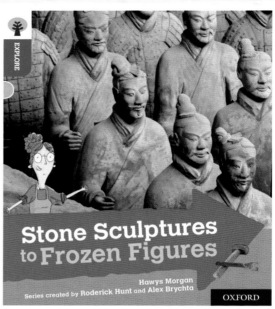

Stone Sculptures to Frozen Figures

Hawys Morgan
Series created by Roderick Hunt and Alex Brychta

OXFORD

Explorer Challenge
for *Stone Sculptures to Frozen Figures*

Find out where this sculpture is …

The BP exhibition
Indigenous Australia enduring civilisation

The BP exhibition

Indigenous Australia enduring civilisation

Gaye Sculthorpe
John Carty
Howard Morphy
Maria Nugent
Ian Coates
Lissant Bolton
Jonathan Jones

The British Museum

The BP exhibition *Indigenous Australia: enduring civilisation*
Supported by BP

Logistics partner IAG Cargo

Published to accompany the exhibition at the British Museum organised with the National Museum of Australia, from 23 April to 2 August 2015.

Some information in this book derives from 'Engaging Objects: Indigenous communities, museum collections and the representations of Indigenous histories', a major research project involving the British Museum, the Australian National University and the National Museum of Australia, funded principally by the Australian Research Council.

Australian Government
Australian Research Council

This exhibition has been made possible by the provision of insurance through the Government Indemnity Scheme. The British Museum would like to thank HM Government for providing Government Indemnity and the Department for Culture, Media and Sport and Arts Council England for arranging the indemnity.

First published in 2015 by The British Museum Press
A division of The British Museum Company Ltd
38 Russell Square, London WC1B 3QQ
britishmuseum.org/publishing

A catalogue record for this book is available from the British Library.
ISBN   978 0 7141 2694 4

Designed by Will Webb Design
Printed and bound in Italy by Printer Trento srl

MIX
Paper from responsible sources
FSC® C015829

The papers used by The British Museum Press are recyclable products and the manufacturing processes are expected to conform to the environmental regulations of the country of origin.

Frontispiece: Mask, See fig. 78, p. 200

Warning
Aboriginal and Torres Strait Islander people are advised that this book may contain names and images of recently deceased Indigenous Australians.

Contents

CLARENCE HOUSE

I was touched and delighted to have been asked to be Patron of the 'Indigenous Australia: Enduring Civilisation' exhibition at the British Museum. This remarkable exhibition is the product of collaboration between the British Museum, the National Museum of Australia, the Australian National University and Indigenous Australian communities, drawing on the unique collection that has been amassed over the past two hundred years.

The exhibition celebrates the extraordinarily rich culture of the Indigenous peoples of Australia, which has endured for tens of thousands of years, despite periods of great upheaval, social dislocation and change. I am always so struck by the reverence that Aboriginal and Torres Strait Islanders' communities have for the land, for "country" and for their natural environment, which is intrinsic to so many of the precious objects on display.

These artefacts and artworks also serve as vessels of cultural meaning and intergenerational learning, which form part of what I understand to be the longest unbroken cultural tradition in the world. They are rich in spiritual teachings and lessons of cultural customs, laws and norms, and have enabled Aboriginal communities to pass down knowledge, wisdom and skills from one generation to the next.

I hope you are as moved as I am by this truly remarkable collection and can perhaps be inspired to regain that sense of reverence for land, country and the natural environment which is so much a part of the innate wisdom of all indigenous communities around the world.

Sponsor's foreword

In our business, time and place are very significant. They determine where we look and where we operate to produce the energy the world needs. The age and locations of rocks reveal a great deal of information about what may lie within them. But we are also conscious that there are other dimensions of time and place that we need to consider before we even think of sending seismic vibrations into the earth in search of oil and gas.

These cultural dimensions – the ideas, stories, art and customs of communities – may be less tangible than geological formations, but they are a powerful and significant consideration. And these dimensions are perhaps even longer and deeper in Australia than anywhere else in the world.

The Aboriginal and Torres Strait Islander peoples of Australia can trace their history back over 60,000 years and represent one of the oldest continuing cultures in the world. So it is a great pleasure for BP to support an exhibition that reveals the unique and enduring relationship between these peoples and their lands, waters and environment.

The extraordinary objects that form this exhibition connect us with the hundreds of individual language groups that shaped the land for many millennia before the arrival of British colonists in the late 1700s transformed the country. And while the treasures of some of those groups have been tragically lost over the years, this exhibition brings together many objects of great quality and significance to continue the story of Indigenous Australia into the present day.

This contemporary angle is hugely important for BP. We have a proud history of supporting Aboriginal and Torres Strait Islander communities throughout nearly a century of operations in Australia, and we embrace the spirit of reconciliation through the support of several programmes promoting Indigenous education and employment. It is my strong belief that we are a better company the more closely our workforce respects and resembles the cultural diversity of the countries, such as Australia, in which we operate.

BP is very pleased to continue our long-standing relationship with the British Museum by supporting this exhibition, which we hope will inspire an interest in Australia's Indigenous peoples and culture in many thousands of visitors.

Bob Dudley
Group Chief Executive BP

Director's foreword

Australia and the United Kingdom have enduring ties dating back to the voyages of exploration made by Captain James Cook in the eighteenth century and the subsequent British colonisation of Australia from the 'First Fleet' in 1788. The links today remain strong through the relationship with the Crown as the Head of State of Australia and strong family, sporting and cultural ties. Yet despite this apparent familiarity, the rich and diverse cultural history of Indigenous Australia remains little known and appreciated within the United Kingdom. I am delighted that the British Museum can present a major exhibition and publication on Indigenous Australia in 2015.

The objects from Indigenous Australia in the British Museum are immensely significant. Many were collected at a time before museums were established in Australia: they represent tangible evidence of some of the earliest moments of culture-contact between Aborigines, Torres Strait Islanders and Europeans. As a result of collecting made through early naval voyages, many objects originate from coastal locations rather than the arid inland areas often associated with Indigenous Australians in the popular imagination.

As the collections date from the time of early contact in 1770 until the present, the objects provide evidence of the cultural continuity of Indigenous Australia and of the significant challenges faced by Indigenous Australians from the colonial period to the present. This history shows why issues about Indigenous Australia are still often so highly debated in Australia today.

In late 2015, many of the objects in this exhibition will travel to Canberra for a related exhibition at the National Museum of Australia. This will be the first time that these objects have been exhibited there since they were collected. The British Museum acknowledges that for Aboriginal and Torres Strait Islander peoples, this return will be of high cultural and symbolic significance.

In developing the exhibition and the research behind it, the British Museum has partnered with colleagues at the National Museum of Australia and the Australian National University with the support of the Australian Research Council. We have particularly benefited from the input of many Indigenous Australians who have been consulted and engaged throughout the project. We also thank Dr Mathew Trinca, Director of the National Museum of Australia, and National Museum of Australia Council member Peter Yu, for their leadership and support throughout this project.

All of us are grateful to HRH The Prince of Wales for his patronage of the exhibition, testimony of his long engagement with the culture and traditions of Indigenous Australians. This exhibition is made possible with support from our logistics partner IAG Cargo, the Australian High Commission who have supported the public programme and through the extraordinary generosity of our long-term partnership with BP. We are most grateful to them all for their support that enables the achievements and knowledge of Indigenous Australians to be appreciated at large: a civilisation that has endured for millennia and that, having endured colonisation, remains to be celebrated today.

Neil MacGregor
Director, British Museum, London

A

PAPUA NEW GUINEA

SOLOMON ISLANDS

Torres Strait

inset below

• Yirrkala

Groote Eylandt

*Gulf of
Carpentaria*

*Cape
York
Peninsula*

VANUATU

•Cairns

•Cardwell

GREAT DIVIDING RANGE

QUEENSLAND

New Caledonia

PACIFIC OCEAN

Lake Eyre

GREAT DIVIDING RANGE

•Brisbane

USTRALIA

Norfolk Island
(Aus.)

NEW SOUTH
WALES

Darling River

•Lake Mungo

•Sydney

•Adelaide

Murray River

Canberra
A.C.T.

VICTORIA

•Lake Condah

•Melbourne

Flinders Island

TASMANIA

•Hobart

PAPUA NEW GUINEA

Saibai

Erub

Tudu

Mabuiag

Iama

Mer

Badu

Torres   Strait

Moa

N

Muralag

Zuna

*Cape York
Peninsula*

0   50 miles

0   80 km

Introduction

Gaye Sculthorpe, Lissant Bolton and Ian Coates

1.

Shield (front and reverse)
The shimmering designs, including rare hand stencils, made by blowing pigment over hands placed on the wood, indicate the rich cultural life in the Shoalhaven region in the mid-1800s.

Attributed to Shoalhaven region, New South Wales, before 1862
Kurrajong (*Brachychiton populneus*) wood, natural pigment
L. 890 mm, W. 340 mm, D. 70 mm
British Museum, London
Oc.1809 Exh. BM

When Europeans first made contact with the peoples of the great southern continent – Australian Aboriginal people and Torres Strait Islanders, or 'Indigenous Australians' – they were often perplexed. Australian Aboriginal society, one of the most long-standing and successful civilisations in world history, was composed so differently to their own that Europeans of the time found it hard to comprehend what they were seeing. In 1688 the English explorer William Dampier (1651–1715) voyaged along the north-west coast of the continent. He described the Aboriginal people he saw as 'the miserablest People in the World'[1] because as far as he could see they had no houses, did not till the soil, possess iron or 'worship anything'.[2] Although later observers were more positive, outsiders have often misunderstood Indigenous Australian societies as comprehensively as did Dampier.[3] They were not able to understand the unfamiliar Australian landscape or recognise such a radically different way of living. They were unable to grasp that for more than 60,000 years Aboriginal people have successfully modified and managed the landscape to ensure the food and other resources they need. Equating civilisation with buildings, writing and metals, these visitors failed to appreciate a civilisation based on skilled land management techniques with a profoundly philosophical religion and a rich artistic and ceremonial life (figs 1–2).

This book accompanies the British Museum's exhibition *Indigenous Australia: enduring civilisation*. The exhibition explores Indigenous Australia in its own right as well as its engagement with British colonisation from 1788. Early settlers and visitors collected objects from Aboriginal people and Torres Strait Islanders, many of which became part of the British Museum collection. The exhibition and this book use some of these, and more recently-acquired objects, to explore the resilient story of Indigenous Australia.

Aboriginal people and Torres Strait Islanders have a complicated relationship with museums. Until the late 1970s, museums in Australia and elsewhere collected and displayed their objects and human remains often without respecting Indigenous perspectives on that process, reflecting many of the attitudes of the wider settler society. In recent decades, however, the engagement between Indigenous Australians and museums has become multifaceted and wide-ranging. Indigenous Australians are now often employed in museums and many communities have been able to reconnect with important sources of cultural and historical information housed in museum collections. Collections of historical objects are being researched, interrogated and reinvigorated with new meanings through digital media, exhibitions and contemporary art.

In the context of these transformations in 2011 the British Museum, the National Museum of Australia and the Australian National University initiated a four-year research project entitled 'Engaging Objects: Indigenous communities, museum collections and the representations of Indigenous histories' funded principally by the Australian Research Council.[4] The project built upon a curatorial exchange programme between the National Museum of Australia and the British Museum, which brought NMA curator Ian Coates to London to study the British Museum's Australian collection. The ambition of the project was to reconnect this collection with contemporary Australian Indigenous communities, and to understand more about what that collection can mean. As a result, British Museum and National Museum of Australia curators have taken information about the collection back to Aboriginal and Torres Strait Islander communities in Australia, seeking their perspectives on those objects and on museums in general. A number of Indigenous artists were also given creative fellowships to visit London and respond artistically to objects in the collection.[5] The research project has fed into the development of two linked exhibitions: the one at the British Museum in London (April–August 2015), which this book accompanies, and one at the National Museum of Australia in Canberra (November 2015–March 2016).

The Australian objects in the British Museum continue to be significant for many Aboriginal and Torres Strait Islander people: connecting to specific remembered people, to certain events or, as for June Oscar (b. 1962), emphasising a different sense of value: 'I think museums, as buildings of bricks and mortar, are reflective of western culture and western thinking. For us, the museum of ours is out in the landscape, it's out in the country. It is the important places we visit at every chance we get. On a daily basis, we're stepping out into our museum.'[6]

'Country' is a term used widely by Indigenous Australians to refer to a particular area of land or water from which a person's primary identity and sense of spiritual association and belonging derives. The first chapter of the book, 'Understanding country', explores Indigenous ways of knowing about and using 'country', both past and present. Objects here become a set of keys

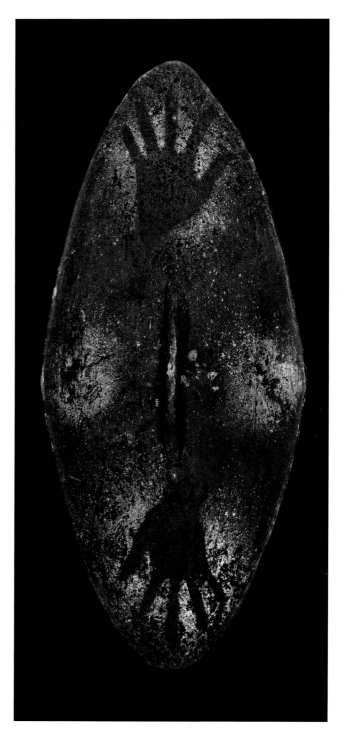

stoviglie = crockery
sleep = sonno
vasca = bath (tub)
note (message) = biglietto
arredare = to furnish
perhaps? = per caso

(una persona) alla mano

an informal person

intesa / agreement/
understanding

solito = usual
insolito = unusual
di solito = usually

affatto = not at all !

metterci = to take (time)

figurati = just immagine ;
" think

c'e qualcosa che non va = ?

that unlock stories of country, such as creation beliefs, trade and exchange, land use and management, technology, art and ceremony.

What happened when Indigenous Australia as confronted with British colonialism is explored in the second chapter, 'Encounters in country', which outlines some of the challenges Indigenous Australians have had to negotiate from 1788 until the present. Some groups met the first British arrivals in the late eighteenth century; a few did not have significant contact until the early 1960s when their land was used for the testing of atomic weapons. The latter's experiences are still within living memory.

No matter when contact occurred, Indigenous Australians across the continent have had to find ways to deal with the new colonial order. While Australia's colonial history is often seen through the prism of Britain's incursions and impact on Indigenous people, it is also worth contemplating Indigenous Australians' ideas about and engagement with Britain – and what it has stood for and represented to them. This has involved persistently seeking redress for dispossession and recognition of their rights, often appealing to ideas of British justice and fairness, and taking their grievances to British governments and institutions, including the monarch.

The third chapter, 'Out of country', briefly considers the range of ways in which objects (and sometimes Aboriginal people) reached Britain and the British Museum. These stories reveal varied forms of diplomacy and engagement between Indigenous peoples, colonists, collectors, other intermediaries and the Museum, both in Australia and in Britain. The book ends with a consideration of some of the ways in which museum objects are being given fresh values and meanings by Indigenous Australian artists today, who draw on knowledge contained in museum objects in developing new works and critique, or reflect on past museum practice.

Ideas of civilisation

The concept of 'civilisation', referring to a highly developed society, entered the English language in the mid-eighteenth century around the time the British Museum was founded in 1753.[7] The term 'civilisation' was often used to describe complex societies that had major monuments, used systems of writing and engaged in agriculture, such as the ancient cultures of Mesopotamia, Egypt, Greece or Rome. In the nineteenth century, influenced by new ideas about natural selection, the theory that humankind could be divided into hierarchicalised races was developed. The concept of 'civilisation' facilitated hierarchy by contrasting 'advanced' Western societies to those deemed lacking in technology – for example, those without metal were often labelled 'primitive' and thus in need of 'civilisation'. Much historic discourse, even in the twentieth century, referred to Aboriginal people as having a 'primitive society' or as being 'stone age' people.[8]

2.
Shield (reverse)

Attributed to Shoalhaven region, New South Wales, before 1862
Kurrajong (*Brachychiton populneus*) wood, natural pigment
L. 875 mm, W. 355 mm, D. 70 mm
British Museum, London
Oc.1808 Exh. BM

Although such perspectives have been held by many who arrived after Dampier, they have also been contested.[9] While it was useful for settlers to characterise Indigenous Australians as a lesser and primitive 'race' who would inevitably fade away before the 'more civilised', there have always been exceptions, such as Lieutenant William Dawes (1762–1836), who worked with Aboriginal people around the Sydney region to record the local language (Darug) between 1790 and 1791. A number of the people who made collections of objects over the decades did so as part of their engagement with and desire to understand and better represent Indigenous Australia. Aboriginal and Torres Strait Islander knowledge and practice, developed over more than 60,000 years of settlement, have subtleties that Europeans continue to take time to understand.

It was not until the late nineteenth and early twentieth centuries that studies by English anthropologists such as A.C. Haddon (1855–1940) in the Torres Straits and W. Baldwin Spencer (1860–1929) along with Australian ethnologist Frank Gillen (1855–1912) in central and northern Australia began to reveal the complexity of Indigenous Australian societies to outsiders.[10] In the 1920s and 1930s, the Australian explorer George Hubert Wilkins (1888–1958), the American anthropologist W. Lloyd Warner (1898–1970) and Australian anthropologist Donald Thomson (1901–1970) lived for periods of time with Aboriginal people in northern Australia and published works that described complex social, economic and ceremonial systems.[11] With the development of archaeology in Australia from the 1950s and use of radio-carbon dating, the antiquity of Aboriginal Australia began to be understood. From the 1970s, through the work of archaeologists, linguists, anthropologists and historians (both Indigenous and non-Indigenous), understandings of the achievements of Indigenous Australians and their place in the world have been transformed.

Archaeologist Scott Cane has described the revolution in knowledge of the ancient past in Australia over the past forty years in this way:

> The first settlers [Indigenous Australians]… had in fact made
> the first oceanic crossing in the history of humankind, performed
> the oldest human cremations on earth, revered the afterlife
> before anyone else, dug the oldest mines in continuous use,
> painted the largest art galleries on the planet, and were the first
> to… depict the human face, paint battle scenes, make axes and
> invent the returning boomerang. Australia's first settlers recall
> the longest oral histories and belong to the oldest continuing
> culture on earth.[12]

Archaeologists believe that the first people to settle Australia came by water from the area now known as Indonesia, over 60,000 years ago.[13] The continent of Australia was then still joined to New Guinea and Tasmania, which were not separated as islands until the sea level rose about 8–10,000 years ago. Artefacts from Malakunanja and Nauwalabila in northern Australia indicate Aboriginal people were living in those places more than 50,000 years ago.[14] About 42,000 years ago, at a time when Neanderthals were still living alongside *homo sapiens* in Britain, a man and a woman, fully modern people (*homo sapiens*), died at Willandra Lakes in western New South Wales. The man's bones were covered in red ochre suggesting a funeral rite and the young woman cremated in what may be the earliest evidence of human cremation.[15] In a society without writing, galleries of rock art throughout the continent record changing artistic and social systems through millennia.

The continent of Australia is larger in size than the whole of Europe. At the time of British colonisation, in the region of 250 different languages were spoken across Australia. Land was owned by particular social groups governed by established bodies of customary law that varied regionally. Indigenous people lived in all the continent's diverse environments: tropical rainforests, arid regions and, in the south-east, highlands with annual snow. As today, rainfall was a key influence on the way of life. In arid regions, some groups owned and used areas of land hundreds of square kilometres in size, whereas in well-watered regions, such as the tropical rainforests of north Queensland or along the Murray River, groups lived within smaller but resource-rich areas.

It has been estimated that in 1778 the Indigenous population of Australia was about 1 million. This quickly declined due to diseases brought by the colonists, violence between settlers and Indigenous people on the frontier, social dislocation as traditional lands were taken over by settlers, and what historian Janet McCalman has termed 'ecological imperialism' caused by the introduction of new animals and plants.[16] By the early twentieth century, with the Indigenous population declining, regional governmental policies were generally based on the assumption that Indigenous Australians were dying out. For those with a mixed genetic heritage, Australian policy intended that they would be gradually assimilated into 'white' society. In 1973 when the British Museum mounted an exhibition entitled *The Australian Aborigines* at the Museum of Mankind, it noted that 'in parts of the east, south-east, south and south-west Australia the aboriginal culture has been extinct for more than a century… the assimilation of the aborigines is proceeding, but with varying degrees of success'.[17] This was far from the truth, but it is a perspective still held in some quarters of Australian society today, as it was at the onset of colonisation. The colony that became Australia was founded on the mistaken notion of *terra nullius*: that there were not pre-existing societies with pre-existing rights and laws that governed them and the lands they inhabited. It took until 1992 for the Australian legal system in the High Court's *Mabo* decision[18] to overturn the assumption that the land belonged to no one.

The Australian collection at the British Museum covers the history of the encounter between British colonisers and Indigenous Australians, from the initial confrontation of Lieutenant James Cook's (1728–1779) landing at Botany Bay in 1770 to the present engagement of Indigenous Australians with others on a global stage. Ethnographic collections are often seen either as a record of a past way of life of people before colonisation or as a record of the colonial project itself – material objects brought back as trophies from the frontier. Both perspectives run the risk of creating an absolute divide between the past and present, denying the continuities in people's lives and their ongoing connections to a deep past. Indigenous people survived the encounter and continue to build their lives into the future, and the colonists themselves have changed through the process of history. Museum collections are a resource for a much more subtle understanding of the past that contains the seeds of a new history. The British Museum celebrates the achievements of many of the world's societies. The exhibition *Indigenous Australia: enduring civilisation* affirms the rich and diverse contribution of Indigenous Australian societies to world history.

A note on terminology

This book uses the term 'Indigenous Australians' to refer to both Aboriginal people and Torres Strait Islanders who today comprise about 3 per cent (almost 700,000 people) of the total Australian population of about 23 million. In the last Australian census in 2011, 606,200 people identified as being of Aboriginal origin only, 38,100 of Torres Strait Islander origin only and 25,600 as both Aboriginal and Torres Strait Islander origin.[19]

Torres Strait Islanders live both on the islands of Torres Strait and on mainland Australia, particularly but not exclusively in Queensland. Although culturally related to peoples of Melanesia, they maintain a strong separate identity. The Torres Strait Islands were annexed to the then colony, now state, of Queensland in 1879. Torres Strait Islanders generally associate with their particular island of origin, wherever they live.

Aboriginal people commonly use the name of their group or language to refer to themselves, such as 'Yolngu', 'Wiradjuri' or 'Gunditjmara' and such group and language names are used in the text (fig. 3). Throughout the book, cultural practices are described using both the present and past tenses. This reflects the fact that some practices are ongoing in some areas and may have ceased in others.

3.
Language groups across Australia
The shaded areas on this map indicate the hundreds of Indigenous language groups across Australia. Only a few, which are significant in the text, are labelled here. Within each language group dialects exist. Many of the languages are endangered with only about 20 being spoken regularly. Locations are approximate.

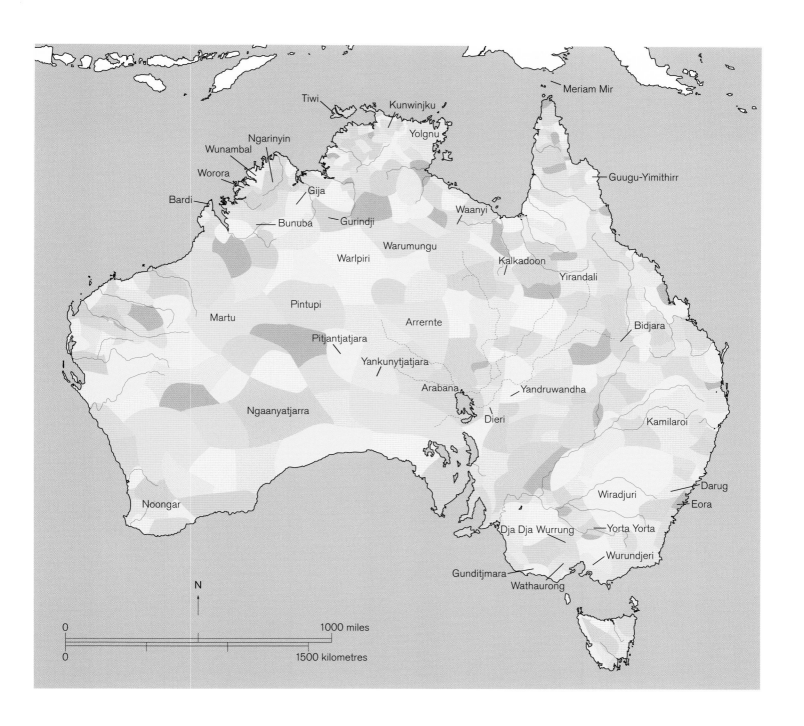

Introduction

Understanding country

Howard Morphy and John Carty

Nobody knows about our culture. You go to England ask people on the street if they know about our culture and they know nothing. These things held by the museums… if they're in the possession of the museums, they should be used to educate people overseas and anywhere about our culture…. If museums are serious about respecting Aboriginal culture, these are the things which need to be told along with these items… the way Aboriginal people lived.
Neil Carter, Gooniyandi and Kidji

The country we now call 'Australia' was not always so. Australia only became a federated nation in 1901. The first British prison ships had arrived in 1788, and during the first half of the nineteenth century the continent saw a series of fledgling British colonies – such as New South Wales or Van Diemen's Land – invaded, settled and ultimately made home by Europeans. But these are the last pages, still being written and rewritten, in a much longer story.

Australia is home to some of the oldest landscapes, and longest continuous cultural traditions, on our planet. Its first explorers, its first people, arrived here from the north at least 60,000 years ago. Over time the environment changed, transformed in turn through droughts, ice ages and changing sea levels, and was inhabitable in different places and at different times. People occupied the continent as a whole, adapting to the various environments and modifying them in turn.

The biggest human intervention in changing the shape of the landscape was the controlled use of fire. The land was subject to cool season burning, which prevented catastrophic fires, encouraged certain food-bearing species, resulted in new growth and improved access to resource-rich places. In some cases these practices promoted the development of grasslands, and transformed forested areas into open woodlands, which aided the hunting of game. The first Europeans stood upon landscapes that were shaped in part by human intervention, not only in the galleries of rock art but more so in these artfully managed environments.

The first Europeans arrived, then, on a continent that had been domesticated by millennia of continuous human habitation. This complexity, and the evidence for it, was invisible to newcomers who, in looking for other evidence of civilisation – agriculture, iron, animal husbandry, property, fences – failed to see the evidence of an enduring civilisation that was everywhere inscribed in the country before them. So they gave new names to it all – Victoria, Queensland, Port Arthur – that rendered it familiar, more like home. But every inch of it was already named in one of the 250 languages being spoken. Every inch of it was already home, already someone's country.

European history has been based largely on the written record, but for most of Australia's history that is absent. Until recently the history of Aboriginal society has relied on accounts from the European side of the frontier. In some places ethnographic accounts help to fill in the picture, but in most parts of Australia those accounts are absent; the frontier moved forward too rapidly, utterly transforming people's lives. Trade routes and ceremonial exchange patterns were disrupted, and the annual seasonal cycle of food harvesting and religious performance became impossible as people's freedom of movement was curtailed. From written accounts we know far more about Aboriginal societies that were colonised late than those that bore the brunt of the initial invasion. Aboriginal oral histories are becoming an increasingly important and prominent part of Australia's mainstream historical narratives. But other kinds of record exist and their potential is also now beginning to be realised.

Australia has among the richest and most diverse bodies of rock art anywhere in the world. Rock paintings and rock engravings stretch back in places up to 40,000 years. They record centuries of changing climate, changing regional fauna and flora, a great range of objects and ceremonial regalia and encounters with outsiders (fig. 1 and endpapers). Rock art traditions continue in some areas right up to the present and provide a means

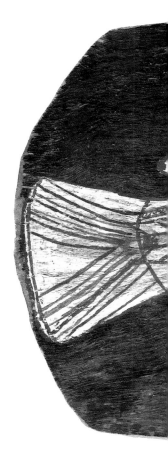

1.
Paintings of fish and other animals on a rock shelter

Injalak Hill, Gunbalanya, western Arnhem Land, dated variously between 100 and 8,000 years old Northern Territory
Photograph: M. Gebicki

2.

Bark painting depicting a barramundi
The barramundi (a species of fish) is painted in the 'X-ray' style of western Arnhem Land. In some areas painting on rock continues alongside painting on bark.

Gunbalanya, western Arnhem Land, Northern Territory, *c.* 1961
Natural pigment on bark; H. 295 mm, W. 615 mm
British Museum, London
Oc1961,02.1 Exh. BM

of linking people to past generations and earlier practices (fig. 2). The landscape itself is a record of the way in which Aboriginal people had managed the land by using fire as a means of increasing the food resource. The patterned burning is still present in many places as a memory in the landscape, with its almost park-like structure of open forests. The remains of stone weirs that were once part of elaborate fish traps can be found in tidal reaches and river estuaries. Archaeologists digging beneath the surface can find much evidence of past lives. But, in addition, museum collections provide an almost unparalleled resource when we pay proper attention to them.

Museum collections trace the encounters with colonists but they also contain a vast reservoir of information about the people who made the objects. Material objects reveal people's knowledge of the resources of the environment, their techniques of manufacture, regional variations in types of material culture, art and design, and their religious beliefs and practices. They provide information about trade and relationships between groups. They give evidence on how outsiders were perceived and the ways in which Indigenous Australians tried to establish relationships with those who threatened to take over their country. More than that, material objects connect directly with the actions of people in the past and bring them forward in time. In this way the objects in the British Museum continue to speak to the silences in Australia's recent history. Most importantly they speak of the very particular genius of Australia's first peoples: as expressions of their enduring mastery of a continent, and of their ongoing struggle and creativity in navigating their place within it.

European colonisation

The European colonisation of Australia was a slow process. It was not until the 1980s that the last of the people of the Western Desert moved to dwell permanently in one of the settlements that had been developed on the perimeter of their lands. When they moved into the settlement, they were welcomed, feted, the last of the desert people to leave their hunter-gatherer life. Their treatment was very different from what it might have been had they been encountered by Europeans in earlier days. In the nineteenth century, on the mobile frontier of the pastoral industry as it stretched out into marginal lands, there was violent conflict.

The colonial frontier moved from south to north from the eighteenth century through the nineteenth and into the twentieth. But colonial times were not linear and Aboriginal people encountered Europeans with very different motivations for being on their land. From early on agencies were set up and legislation was enacted to protect the Aboriginal people whose lands were being appropriated and who were subject to violence and diseases introduced by the Europeans. Missionaries in particular played a significant role early on, but the refuges they provided were temporary and the missions were often then closed and the reserve lands taken away. Missionaries continued to play an important role as the frontier moved on. In some cases their policies entailed the separation of children from their families and the repression of cultural and religious practices; in others they were far more sympathetic to Indigenous beliefs and ways of life and became advocates for Indigenous rights in the face of the invasion of their land.

The encroachment of the pastoral industry almost inevitably resulted in initial conflict and competition for the land and its resources. Aboriginal rights and interests in land had limited recognition under European–Australian law, but the rights of the owners of cattle and sheep were protected from early on. Stock killing became the main Aboriginal 'crime' and the reason for 'dispersal',[1] arrest and incarceration.

After the initial invasion, in some regions a way of life was established between cattle stations and Aborigines. The cattle industry needed Aboriginal people as labour on the stations and in many areas they were able to remain on their lands by fitting in with station life. But they did so with few legal rights and when circumstances changed, as they did with the granting of award wages in the 1960s, they could quickly be excluded from their country.

At the end of the nineteenth century the discovery of gold brought the sudden influx of people into Pine Creek in the Northern Territory, Kalgoorlie in Western Australia, and Palmer River in north Queensland. This disrupted people's lives, bringing violence and disease. As Australia moved into the twentieth century from an economy based on primary industry to one in which mineral exports played an increasingly important role, conflict over the ore-rich country moved to the fore. The myth that, at the time of European colonisation, Australia was *terra nullius* – a land belonging to no one – denied Aboriginal people any rights in law that should have flowed from their prior ownership of the land (see pp. 200–6).

The view from the north

At the time European colonisation began in the south-east corner of Australia, Aboriginal people along the north coast had long been in contact with people from outside the continent. The impact of the colonisers moved ahead of the frontier with the spread of disease and feral animals, through the passage of exploring expeditions and visits by traders and missionaries. Indigenous Australians would have been aware of European advance, and responded to it.

When Lieutenant Cook landed in Botany Bay on 29 April 1770 we have a good idea what people in Arnhem Land, across the continent on the northern coast, were doing around the same time, although we have no historical records. April was the end of the wet season and people all along the coast had been bidding farewell to the traders who came every year from Sulawesi in eastern Indonesia.

Aboriginal people along the coast of northern Australia from the Kimberley region to the Gulf of Carpentaria had a long history of interaction with people from further north. Much of the early evidence comes from archaeological excavation and chance finds of objects – coins and pottery – that originate from as a far away as China and the east coast of Africa. Many of the encounters were brief, the result of exploratory visits. Northern Australia was on the edge of the expanding trading systems of South-East Asia, which in turn were becoming increasingly integrated within global networks extending to Europe and China.

Trade between the people of eastern Indonesia and northern Australia intensified in the 200 years before European colonisation. The trade centred on *trepang* (sea cucumber). The shallow bays off the northern coast provide an excellent environment for the growth of trepang, which is a valued commodity in Chinese cuisine and medicine. The trade was organised through the port of Makassar in Sulawesi. Each year a fleet of *praus* (fishing boats) left from Sulawesi at the beginning of the monsoon season to spend the wet season on the Arnhem Land coast. The traders established relationships with different Aboriginal communities and returned on a regular basis depending on the abundance of trepang. The processing of trepang was a long and complex one requiring them first of all to be gutted and boiled and subsequently smoked and dried. Evidence of the Makassan trade is abundant in the remains of camp sites, pottery and the hearths for trepang boiling.

The trepang industry was flourishing when British colonists first mapped the north Australian coast. In early February 1803 Captain Matthew Flinders (1774–1814) met six praus in what he subsequently named the Malay Road on their way south to Blue Mud Bay. H.S. Melville's (1824–1894) engraving (fig. 3) provides a superbly detailed image of trepang processing in 1845 at the short-lived British settlement of Victoria, Port Essington, that indicates its scale. The trade however came to an abrupt end in 1907 when the Australian government introduced customs and excise requirements that prevented the fleet returning. At that time much of Arnhem Land remained beyond the colonial frontier. Mission stations had yet to be established along the Arnhem Land coast. One can only imagine the effect the ending of the Makassan trade had on the communities they visited.

The Makassans had a considerable impact on the life and economy of Aboriginal people along the northern Australian coast. The places where they

THE TREPANG FISHERY ON THE NORTHERN COAST OF AUSTRALIA.

3.
The Trepang Fishery on the Northern Coast of Australia
Makassan fishermen prepare *trepang*, or sea cucumber, most likely in Port Essington, Northern Territory, *c.* 1842–6.

Woodcut after H.S. Melville (1824–1894),
born London, England
Reproduced in *The Queen*, London, 8 February 1862
British Library, London
MFM.m66108 [1862]

set up their temporary settlements became the fulcra of relationships with the Indigenous population. Aboriginal people worked with the Makassans for trade goods: cloth and iron were particularly important. They established social relationships with the captains and crew and some people travelled back in the boats with them to Makassar. The earliest ceremonial spears from eastern Arnhem Land are in the collection of the British Museum (fig. 4) and are likely to have been the result of trade with the Makassans. The spears were collected by Carl Alfred Bock (1849–1932), a Norwegian naturalist and anthropologist, on a trip to Makassar in July 1879. Bock visited a market in which he saw large quantities of trepang prepared for sale and later travelled to Pare-Pare to the north. He paid a visit to the Rajah and bargained for knives and lances from the men and fibre items from the women. The spears are not documented but are similar to the ceremonial spears (*bathi*) that continue to be made today in eastern Arnhem Land by Yolngu people. They are called hook-spears in English, which refers to the structure of barbs cut into the wooden spearhead. The configuration of barbs identifies them as belonging to a particular social group. The spears are primarily used in ceremonial contexts and as objects of exchange. Whether they travelled to Makassar with an Aboriginal visitor or were traded before the boats left Australia, they are signs of the network of trade that extended northwards.

There is evidence that the Makassans brought new technology in the form of dugout canoes and harpoons in addition to introducing people to the habit of smoking tobacco. Certainly the words for these items in local languages can be traced to outside contact. In Yolngu, the word for dugout canoe is *lipalipa* and for a smoking pipe *bamutaka*, both Makassarese words. But perhaps the strongest evidence of the close nature of the relationship with the Makassans lies in the area of art, religion and oral tradition (fig. 5). The rock paintings from the Kimberley coast in the west to Groote Eylandt in

4.
Ceremonial spears
The earliest known ceremonial spears from eastern Arnhem Land were collected in Makassar, Indonesia in 1879. Some Yolngu people travelled to Makassar with the *praus*, but the spears could have also been gifts or trade items.

Eastern Arnhem Land, Northern Territory, before 1879
(left) Cooktown Ironwood (*Erythrophleum chlorostachys*), gum; L. 2430 mm, W. 20 mm, D. 25 mm
British Museum, London
Oc,BK.132 Exh. BM
(right) Mulga wood (*Acacia multisiliqua*), gum; L. 2390 mm, W. 23 mm, D. 25 mm
British Museum, London
Oc,BK.131 Exh. BM

the Gulf of Carpentaria include many with Makassan themes. The predominant images are of the praus with their distinctive sails, sometimes including the ship's crew working on the deck. There are images of people smoking pipes or holding guns, and details of attire: men wearing uniforms and women draped in fabrics. The rock paintings feature other vessels too, some of European origin, as well as images of people in European dress, even riding bicycles. The fisher-traders from Indonesia mediated relationships with European colonists, in particular the Portuguese and Dutch, before the arrival of the British.

The most detailed oral history of the Makassans comes from eastern Arnhem Land where themes from the Makassan era are woven into Yolngu myth and ritual practices. Yolngu provided anthropologists Lloyd Warner, Donald Thomson and Ronald (1916–1990) and Catherine Berndt (1918–1994) with detailed accounts of their relationships with the Makassans.[2] The Makassans developed close connections with particular clan leaders exchanging names with them. For example, a Yolngu leader named Wirrpanda living at the turn of the eighteenth century is said to have exchanged his name with PoBassu, the captain of the fleet of praus encountered by Flinders in 1803. In 1947 Yolngu created maps of their country for Ronald Berndt and one of them covered the journey along the Arnhem Land coast to the islands of eastern Indonesia. At the same time Mugurrawuy Yunupingu (190?–1975) made a crayon drawing of the Port of Makassar illustrating the quarter of the town where Aboriginal people stayed. Yolngu produced detailed paintings on bark of Makassan life during their wet season visits. Mawalan Marika's (c. 1908–1967) crayon drawing of Yalangbara (Port Bradshaw), in his clan estate, shows the location of the Makassan settlements, trepang processing places and where they moored their praus. His brother Mathaman's (c. 1920–

5.
Bag
The design references the annual visits of Makassan fishermen to the northern coast of Australia. The white rectangular forms, with horizontal red stripes, are the sails of Makassan *praus*. The white diagonal crosses against a red background refer to women's breast girdles, which represent the blooming clouds of the wet season, when the Makassan ships would arrive.

Port Essington, Northern Territory, before 1912
Fibre, human hair, natural pigment; H. 473 mm,
W. 210 mm, Diam. 86 mm
British Museum, London
Oc1939,08.37 Exh. BM
Donated by Gregory M. Mathews

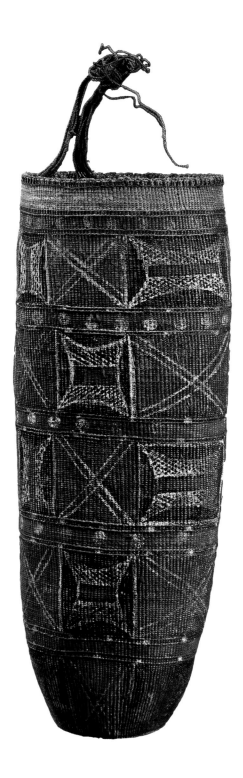

1970) painting, *Makasar Boiling down the Trepang*, 1964 (fig. 6), illustrates the trepang boilers, the paddle-shaped stirring spoons and the containers of processed trepang in the hulls of the boats. Today, a hundred years after the boats stopped coming, the Makassans remain an important part of Yolngu tradition. This is a reflection not only of the impact that they had on society in the years of active trading but also the way in which the voyagers have been integrated within Yolngu ceremonial life and material culture across Arnhem Land (see p. 95).

Across the Gulf of Carpentaria from Arnhem Land, Cape York Peninsula has always been linked to Papua New Guinea by the island chain of Torres Strait. Until 8,500 years ago, Australia and Papua New Guinea were joined together. The majority of the Torres Strait Islands were formed between 6,500 and 8,500 years ago as a result of the Holocene sea level rise. The connections across Torres Strait have been curiously played down in most studies of Australian prehistory. The reason is not hard to discern. Culturally, the Torres Strait Islanders are in many ways distinct from Aboriginal Australians. The Torres Strait Islanders practised agriculture as well as hunting and gathering with a strong emphasis on fishing. Their religious beliefs and practices differed as did their settlement patterns, which centred on permanent villages connected by trading networks. However, current research demonstrates that interaction across Torres Strait was clearly continuous, and there were strong social, religious and trading links with the people of the Australian mainland. The main language of the eastern islands is a Papuan language, Meriam Mir, which is related to the languages of the Trans-Fly region along the southern coast of Papua New Guinea. The remaining Islanders spoke dialects of an Australian Aboriginal language, Kala Lagaw Ya. Early accounts indicate close and friendly relationships between people of the western Torres Strait and the Aboriginal populations of Cape York Peninsula. The marine technology of the region overlapped, with Aboriginal groups using single and double-outrigger canoes. While Aboriginal groups emphasised the gathering of wild foods there is clear

6.
Makasar Boiling Down Trepang
At the top Makassan fishermen use large pots and paddles (also depicted above their heads) to boil the trepang. Below the trepang is loaded into the hulls of Makassan *praus*, with their distinctive rectangular sails.

Mathaman Marika (*c.* 1920–1970), Rirratjiŋu clan, Dhuwa moiety, Yolngu
Yirrkala, northeastern Arnhem Land, Northern Territory, 1964
Natural pigment on bark; H. 1350 mm, W. 575 mm
National Museum of Australia, Canberra
1985.0259.0095 Exh. BM

evidence that on occasions they cultivated yams and were well aware of the agricultural methods of their northern neighbours. Archaeologist Melissa Carter's summary of the region concludes: 'the islands formed the central geographic core of a trans-Strait socio-economic maritime network.... Linkages though formal trade, warfare, intermarriages and regular, less informal inter-island and island-mainland movements fostered a degree of cultural continuity across the Strait and between the islands and the adjacent coasts.'[3]

In addition to their integration within regional trading systems Torres Strait Islanders and their mainland neighbours have had a long history of trade with people from further afield (figs 7–8). The historical sources are not as extensive as they are in the case of the Makassan connections further west. However, by the second half of the nineteenth century sea traffic through Torres Strait had intensified, and the region's resources were soon reaching global markets. Lucrative markets in pearls and pearl shell opened up and the island population was soon joined by an influx of Japanese, South Sea Islander and European traders and divers.

7.
Pipe
Pipes and tobacco first came to the Torres Strait via trade with New Guinea.

Erub, Torres Strait, Queensland, *c.* 1842–6
Bamboo, incised and pigmented; L. 425 mm, Diam. 58 mm
British Museum, London
Oc1846,0731.2 Exh. BM
Donated by J.B. Jukes

8.
Drum
Drums like this were traded from New Guinea to Torres Strait. Many traded items were adapted for local use.

Erub, Torres Strait, Queensland, *c.* 1842–6
Wood, incised and pigmented; H. 750 mm, Diam. 100 mm
British Museum, London
Oc1846,0731.1 Exh. BM
Donated by J.B. Jukes

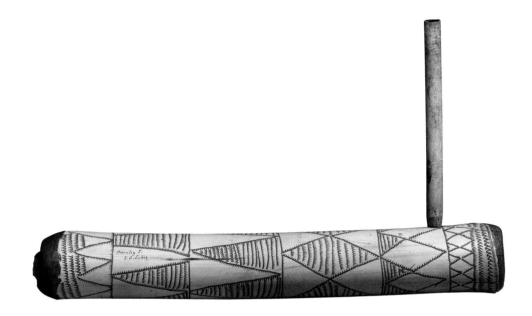

Trade and ceremonial exchange

When the Makassans and others first negotiated their relationship with the Aborigines along the coast of northern Australia they encountered people who were already deeply enmeshed in networks of trade and exchange. While many of those systems of trade were focused on particular regions others required extensive journeys by people and material goods across great distances. Trade involved scarce or highly prized raw materials but also had a ceremonial dimension in which goods were exchanged to cement relationships and create new alliances.

The best-documented regional trading system is the Wunan that operated in the Kimberley region of Western Australia. The Wunan involved the movement of trade bundles across the region through a network of exchange partners. The bundles would include traditional objects such as spearheads, pearl shell ornaments, balls of string and, as the pastoral industry encroached on people's country, European goods such as blankets and wool. When the Norwegian anthropologist Johannes Falkenberg (1911–2004) studied the system in the 1950s the unit used to value the items in the trade bundle was an iron or stone spearhead.[4] The value of the individual items changed according to their scarcity as the bundle moved across the region. One type of item included was pearl shell ornaments that were sourced and manufactured on the north-west Kimberley coast by groups including the Bardi and Djawi (fig. 9, and figs 20–23, p. 42). In the Kimberley they were used as pubic coverings or worn around the neck, and were sometimes elaborately engraved with designs associated with a group or individual. As they moved beyond the region and away from the coast their scarcity increased and they gained in value, often becoming ceremonial objects. Today the trade bundles are no longer a part of everyday life but partnerships are still forged that connect across the region, and the ceremonial performances, or *junba*, that often provided the context for trade continue in a changed environment.

It is likely that the trading system was stimulated by the goods obtained from the Makassans, which gave coastal peoples access to important new resources. Certainly the anthropologist Donald Thomson argued for the importance of iron, cloth and tobacco obtained from the Makassans on the northern coasts of Arnhem Land. Iron was cold hammered by Yolngu into lethal spearheads often referred to as 'shovel nose spears' because of their size. Thomson records that the trade in such spears extended as far as the Roper Valley in the south. Such introduced materials were simply added to pre-existing trading networks often based on redistributing locally abundant but regionally scarce raw materials. The main source of stone spearheads in Arnhem Land was the stone quarry of Ngilipidji located in the Mitchell Ranges a long way inland to the south in the country of the Wägilak people. Thomson provided detailed documentation of the manufacture and trade of the stone blades as he observed it in the 1930s.[5] The blocks of stone were quarried

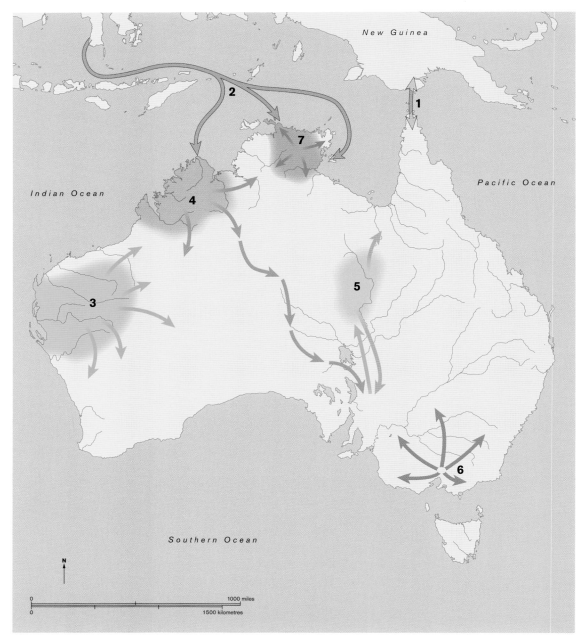

New Guinea

Indian Ocean

Pacific Ocean

Southern Ocean

N

| 0 | | | | 1000 miles |
| 0 | | | | 1500 kilometres |

9.

Major trade routes across Australia

This map gives a general indication of some of the major trading routes that existed across Indigenous Australia.

1 Pearl shell from Torres Strait was traded north and south; Islanders received drums, canoe hulls and other goods from New Guinea.

2 Metal and other goods were exchanged with Makassan fishermen who came to the northern coasts to collect *trepang*.

3 Red ochre from Wilgie Mia in the Weld Ranges was traded widely.

4 Pearl shell from the Kimberley coast was traded inland and across the continent.

5 Pituri was traded from the Channel country, often in exchange with red ochre from the Flinders Ranges to the south.

6 Stone for axes was traded from Mount William in the south-east.

7 Stone for spearheads from Ngilipidji quarry was traded widely in the Arnhem Land region.

10.
Spearhead wrapped in paperbark

Collected Groote Eylandt, Arnhem Land, *c.* 1923–5
Stone, paperbark (*Melaleuca*), fibre, resin; L. 210 mm,
W. 45 mm
British Museum, London
Oc1925,1113.41 Exh. BM

11.
Axe head

Mount William, Victoria, before 1932
Greenstone; L. 140 mm, W. 52 mm, D. 35 mm
British Museum, London
Oc1932,0702.1 Exh. BM
Donated by W. Rodier

from beneath the surface and left to harden before the spearheads were struck from them. The spearheads were then carefully wrapped in paperbark (fig. 10), packed into woven baskets and subsequently traded throughout the Arnhem Land region.

Along with spearheads, the material for making spear shafts was also the subject of trade. Arnhem Landers distinguished between spears on the basis of weight, with the flight of the light spears being likened to a shower of fine rain and that of the heavier spears to the monsoonal downpours.[6] The lightest spears were made from reeds from the Arafura swamp and Thomson records in his field notes that the true makers of the spears were the people from that region.[7] The archaeologist Harry Allen concludes: 'This alerts us to the importance of trading relations in this part of Australia…. *Bambusa arnhemica* grows only in the wetter parts of the Northern Territory and… access to this shaft material in Arnhem Land was entirely through trade'.[8]

Stone technology was vital in Aboriginal Australia and high-quality materials were scarce commodities. Stone was used in the manufacture of everything from grindstones to axes and spearheads, implements for working wood, knife blades, construction of dwellings, fish traps and for many other purposes. Different objects required material with quite different properties. Major quarries existed across Australia and became nodes of trading networks. In north-central Queensland the Kalkadoon people shaped axes from igneous rocks quarried in the Mount Isa-Cloncurry region and traded them extensively across the Gulf region. One of the most renowned axe quarries was at Mount William in Victoria, where evidence of stone working activity extends for over a kilometre along a ridge. Axes were being manufactured at the time of European colonisation (fig. 11). In the 1880s the Wurundjeri leader and artist William Barak (1824–1903) described the process of extraction and manufacture, which he had witnessed as a young man, to the anthropologist A.W. Howitt (1830–1908). The hard greenstone blanks were shaped *in situ* and then taken to suitable locations where they could be ground down, shaped and polished to be ready for trade. Studies by Isabel McBryde and others have shown the widespread distribution of these axes extending over Victoria and western New South Wales.[9]

Kimberley spear points[10]
John Carty

I sent some biface points made by the Worora
tribe to the British Museum and the reply came
back that they were the most beautiful spear-
points made by any natives in the world.[11]

Of over approximately 6,000 Australian items in the British
Museum, almost one third of these are stone flakes,
spearheads, tools and knives deposited by various
collectors. Stone tools are of interest to collectors and
archaeologists as evidence for the prehistory of Aboriginal
Australia and of human societies more generally. This was
often stimulated by the belief that Aboriginal Australians
represented a living example of Stone Age society and
could provide insight into the ways of life and technological
systems of early stages of human society. It has long been
recognised that there is no simple relationship between
technology, dynamism and the complexity of human cultures
and societies.

In the absence of metals, stone was a core material
that Australian people worked, refined and mastered. It was
painstakingly shaped by flaking, pecking or grinding into
many types of tools: knives, scrapers, chisels, axes and
spear points. Research into Australian stone tools has
shown continuing changes over time in stone technology
and the development of regional artefact types. Kimberley
spear points are perhaps the most celebrated example of
these processes of technological change: pressure-flaked
and serrated with extraordinary skill, they were highly valued
articles of trade among Aboriginal people,[12] and remain
widely regarded by archaeologists,[13] collectors and museum
curators as some of the finest achievements in Australian
stone work (fig. 12).

The unique form and process of manufacture of
Kimberley points captivated and intrigued early European
visitors. Lieutenant Phillip Parker King (1791–1856)
documented one of the first encounters with these points,
collected in a punitive raid in retaliation against the spearing
of his ship's surgeon in Hanover Bay in August 1821.

12.
Spear points
A group of spear points crafted from various
types of stone, glass (including from coloured
bottles) and the cream-coloured ceramic
insulators from telegraph poles.
Kimberley region, Western Australia,
c. 1885–1940

Stone, glass, ceramic, gum or resin; L. 40–163 mm
British Museum, London
From left to right from top:
Oc1943,03.14 Exh. BM Donated by A.F. Bohman
Oc1943,03.12 Exh. BM Donated by A.F. Bohman
Oc1933,0315.99 Exh. BM Bequeathed by William Leonard
Stevenson Loat
Oc1899,-.466 Exh. BM Donated by C.H. Ord
Oc1911,-.142 Exh. BM Donated by J.M. Creed
Oc1898,0519.2 Exh. BM Donated by W.O. Mansbridge
Oc1981,Q.2144 Exh. BM
Oc1981,Q.2148 Exh. BM
Oc1943,03.15 Exh. BM Donated by A.F. Bohman
Oc1936,0310.16 Exh. BM Donated by J.R.B. Love
Oc1935,0413.10 Exh. BM Donated by Gordon Milver
Oc1936,0310.23 Exh. BM Donated by J.R.B. Love
Oc1936,0310.32 Exh. BM Donated by J.R.B. Love
Oc1898,0519.4 Exh. BM Donated by W.O. Mansbridge
Oc1943,03.17 Exh. BM Donated by A.F. Bohman
Oc1935,0413.11 Exh. BM Donated by Gordon Milver
Oc1936,0310.34 Exh. BM Donated by J.R.B. Love
Oc1950,07.11 Exh. BM Bequeathed by Mrs F.G. Latham
Oc1935,1016.6 Donated by B.B. Grey
Oc1943,03.6 Exh. BM Donated by A.F. Bohman
Oc1953,03.21 Exh. BM Donated by Mary Montgomerie
Bennett
Oc1936,0310.29 Exh. BM Donated by J.R.B. Love
Oc1943,03.10 Exh. BM Donated by A.F. Bohman
Oc1973,04.1 Exh. BM
Oc1943,03.5 Exh. BM Donated by A.F. Bohman
Oc1936,0310.37 Exh. BM Donated by J.R.B. Love
Oc1933,1214.1 Exh. BM Donated by Mrs Munday
Oc1907,-.193 Exh. BM Donated by Frederick Glyn
Montagu Powell
Oc1943,03.16 Exh. BM Donated by A.F. Bohman
Oc1981,Q.2147 Exh. BM

[There] was a small bundle of bark, tied up with more than usual care; upon opening it we found it contained several spear-heads, most ingeniously and curiously made of stone; they were about six inches in length, and were terminated by a very sharp point; both edges were serrated in a most surprising way; the serratures were evidently made by a sharp stroke with some instrument, but it was effected without leaving the least mark of the blow: the stone was covered with red pigment, and appeared to be a flinty slate. These spear-heads were ready for fixing, and the careful manner in which they were preserved plainly showed their value, for each was separated by strips of bark, and the sharp edges protected by a covering of fur.[14]

Careful wrapping of fragile spearheads preserved them from damage. Such parcels of points (see fig. 10, p. 33) were also traded with other Aboriginal groups, although as a result of this particular encounter they were removed from circulation along the exchange routes that existed throughout the region. With the other objects seized that day, they travelled instead along new pathways of exchange and value. In the possession of various members of King's expedition, among whom they had been divvied up, they made their way to England and Europe, with some ending their travels in the collection of the British Museum.

After colonisation, Kimberley points became objects of great interest for collectors and museums, and other visitors to Australia sent ever more information about them to the British Museum. Where King was perplexed at how the points were produced, J.R.B. Love (1889–1947), a missionary in the Kimberley (see p. 230), made detailed studies of Worora men's process of manufacture, and sent examples of the points at various stages of production (and the tools used in each stage) to the British Museum.[15]

The Worora man, in his hunting, always keeps his eyes open for useful bits of stone that will make spearheads.… A walk through one of the camps, at any hour of the day, is almost certain to give the sight of a man busy on the making of a stone spearhead. For an anvil he uses a slab of sandstone, on which he places 'a cushion' consisting of several layers of paperbark. With a blunt-point stick of hardwood, a foot in length, he presses on one edge of the small stone… and breaks off a flake. Turning the stone, he continues this till he has roughed out the shape of a spear-head. He next takes a piece of kangaroo thigh bone, ground to a point on a rough stone, and presses flakes away from the edges of the spearhead, till it has reach the finished shape. The final stage is now to take a thin bone, ground to a fine edge, and serrate the edges of the spearhead by pressing out the tiny flakes from the sharp edges. This is a very delicate operation, and a careless pressure will break a spearhead that has taken much labour to bring to the desired shape. The whole work of making stone spearheads is a highly skilled art. Some of the stones used are semi-precious, as agates and crystals. The completed spearhead is a really beautiful object, with a needle-point and wonderfully symmetrical edges.… Yet all this labour is for one throw of the spear! The stone points are very brittle, and consequently break off when thrown, unless the spear should pierce a soft part of the beast and be retrieved unbroken. More often than not, the point is broken off in the Kangaroo that is has struck…. The wonder is that such care is lavished on an article destined to have such a short life.[16]

Love's appreciation for the skill and technical mastery of the process provided a welcome de-mystification of the object. But he is equally concerned to highlight that, above and beyond its function as a spearhead, the elegance of design, the perfection of the form – however short-lived – were equally as important to the men who made them: 'When the stone is finally shaped, serrated and complete, the artist (for artist is the proper name for him) puts his new spearhead in his mouth, wets it, and holds it up to appraise its beauty and keen point. If it is a translucent stone, he holds it up to the light and lovingly ponders over its colour.'[17]

In most parts of Australia spearheads, knives and chisels were quickly fashioned out of metal found or traded with white people. Some enterprising Aboriginal men near Port Essington had even enlisted the local blacksmith to beat out iron spearheads for them (see p. 137). But Kimberley points, delicately chipped and flaked into their serrated state, could not be created from metals. They could, however, be fashioned from other materials that were central to the colonial endeavour. The explorer David Carnegie (1871–1900) noted in the record of his travels in the 1890s:

> Since the white man has settled a portion of the Kimberley, glass bottles have come into request among the natives. When first the telegraph line from Derby to Hall's Creek and thence to Wyndham was constructed, constant damage used to be done to it by the natives who climbed the poles and smashed the insulators for spear head making. So great a nuisance did this become that the Warden actually recommended the Government to place heaps of broken bottles at the foot of each pole, hoping by this means to save the insulators by supplying the natives with glass.[18]

Glass and ceramics, more workable than iron (and many stones) but with a lustre (and an increasing availability), became favoured materials for Aboriginal men in the Kimberley in the late nineteenth and early twentieth centuries, as the spear collected by C.H. Ord (1856–1923) in 1899 attests (fig. 13). They also quickly became prized articles of trade along both Aboriginal and colonial networks of exchange that often terminated in museums around the world.[19]

But museums were not alone in collecting and showing off their acquisitions. Bowerbirds in the Kimberley were also notorious for 'collecting' these spear points to dress their bowers and impress their potential mates. Anthropologist Kim Akerman notes that in 1973 two spear points made from glass identifiable as Lea and Perrins Worcestershire Sauce bottles (manufacture dated to c. 1885–90) were recovered from a bower in the Kimberley.[20]

Whether in the bowers of birds or museums, made of stone or colonial telegraph insulators or British glass, these artefacts continue to point to broader questions about the British Museum's collection. The meaning of these points, their efficacy and use, changed as they moved through the world. All of the objects in the Museum's Australian collection, by virtue of having been collected post-1770, are expressions of changes occurring in Australia. Whether through the introduction of new materials or new trade networks, all such objects – properly understood – continue to illuminate a dynamic and still-changing world as much as any imagined 'traditional' one.

13.
Spear point

Kimberley region, Western Australia
Glass, resin; L. 108 mm
British Museum, London
Oc1899,-.466 Exh. BM
Donated by C.H. Ord

14.
Grindstone with residue of red ochre

Swan River, Western Australia, *c.* 1838
Stone, red ochre; H. 30 mm, W. 100 mm, D. 58 mm
British Museum, London
Oc1839,0620.28 Exh. BM
Donated by Samuel Neil Talbot

15.
**Feather ornament decorated
with red ochre**

Swan River, Western Australia, *c.* 1838
Feather, wood, fibre, red ochre;
L. 280 mm, W. 120 mm, D. 40 mm
British Museum, London
Oc1839,0620.23 Exh. BM
Donated by Samuel Neil Talbot

Grindstones were another important trading commodity and were employed throughout Australia for a multiplicity of purposes. They were used in creating the polished surface of axe heads, for grinding earth pigments into powder (figs 14–15), for crushing fruits and berries and making them into cakes, and for grinding different seeds and nuts into flour. In many areas grinding surfaces are readily available. In some places grooves or depressions can be seen worn into the surface of exposed rocks as a result of centuries of grinding. Grindstones are vital to desert economies where flour made from the seeds of grasses and shrubs provides the vegetable staple of the economy. However, across much of central Australia sources of good quality portable grindstones are scarce and needed to be traded in.

One of the great ancestral stories of the Pitjantjatjara/Yankunytjatjara peoples of the Western and Central Deserts is the journey of the Ngintaka or Perentie Lizard Man from his home country west of the Mann Ranges to Walyatjatja in the east.[21] The Ngintaka man began his journey when he heard the distant sound of a grindstone emanating from the east. The grindstones in his country produced only coarsely ground flour and the beautiful smooth sound he heard hinted at something better. The story relates how the Ngintaka man arrived at Walyatjatja after a long journey and found a large group of Nyintjiri people camping there, grinding woollybutt grass seed on a special grindstone. The story goes on to record how the Ngintaka man stole the grindstone and after many adventures returned with it to his country in the west where he was finally killed by the Nyintjiri ancestral people and was transformed into features of the landscape.

Excellent quality grindstones are indeed scarce across Pitjantjatjara lands where the Ngintaka man came from. Grindstones are conserved and carried over long distances and are passed on from mother to daughter down

16.
Jakayu Biljabu carrying her mother's grindstone on her head
Grindstones were particularly important in arid regions where seeds were a significant source of food. In some areas grindstones are still used.

Near Bidu on the Canning Stock Route, August 2009
Photograph: Diana James

the generations (fig. 16). The fine grindstone the Ngintaka man stole from Walyatjatja would have been traded in from further east. One of the finest sources of good-quality grindstones is in the country of the Arabana people at Palthirri Pirdi west of Lake Eyre. The archaeologist Mike Smith has estimated that more than 100,000 grindstones have been quarried from the fine sandstone deposits and traded over the vast distances of central Australia.[22]

Pigments, in particular red and yellow ochre, white clay and manganese (black), were also traded widely. In some parts of Australia sources of ochre are abundant. The ochres differ in their quality and shade. In many cases their significance is enhanced by their spiritual association; ochres are seen as manifestations of ancestral substance, in particular blood and fat. In some cases the qualities combine and enhance the value of the ore, which is sought for trade and ceremonial purposes. In eastern Arnhem Land ochres mark the division of the moieties:[23] the Dhuwa moiety is closely associated with red ochre and the Yirritja moiety with yellow. In each case there are preferred sources. The Dhuwa moiety ochre *ratjpa* is a heavy rock, which produces a

rich pinkish-red colour that is naturally burnishing; in the case of the Yirritja moiety, a pure brilliant yellow ochre is quarried from Gururrunga on Caledon Bay. Rights in those ochre sources are carefully protected and the rights-holders control the initial distribution of the ores.

While the majority of trade was carried on through fairly local exchanges some trade routes required travel over great distances. One of the longest and best-documented trading routes was centred on the Lake Eyre region and involved red ochre from the south being exchanged for pituri (a mild narcotic) from the north. The source of the red ochre was the renowned quarry of Pukardu at the northern end of the Flinders Ranges. The Pukardu ochre 'with its dark pink hue and silvery sheen'[24] has similar aesthetic qualities to *ratjpa*. The ochre was seen by different groups respectively to be the transformation of the blood of an ancestral dog or emu. The ochre was highly friable and could be brushed from the walls and collected from the floor of the mine. It was made into solid cakes by mixing it with water or urine. According to Samuel Gason (*c.* 1842–1897), a policeman stationed at Lake Hope, the cakes weighed 20 pounds (9 kilos). The cakes were then traded both south and north. Groups of men left from the region surrounding Lake Eyre in July or August to travel the 300 kilometres or more south to the mine. The trade journey was also linked to the ceremonial cycle and the initiation of young men into adulthood. The group increased in size as the journey progressed and could eventually build up to 300 people. The trade items people carried with them included pituri, manganese, baskets, boomerangs and flour ground from wild seeds. The exchanges are likely to have been organised between partners who had established long-term relationships. Gason records that on their return people were carrying loads of up to 70 pounds (32 kilos) of ochre on their heads supported by a circular pad of human hair string.[25]

17.
Pituri bag

Gregory River region, Queensland, *c.* 1891
Pituri leaf (*Duboisia hopwoodii*), human hair, fibre;
H. 250 mm, W.130 mm, D. 105 mm
British Museum, London
Oc1897,-.637

18.
Pituri bag

Gregory River region, Queensland, *c.* 1891
Pituri leaf (*Duboisia hopwoodii*), fibre, wool, human hair;
H. 200 mm, W. 290 mm, D. 30 mm
British Museum, London
Oc1897,-.634 Exh. BM

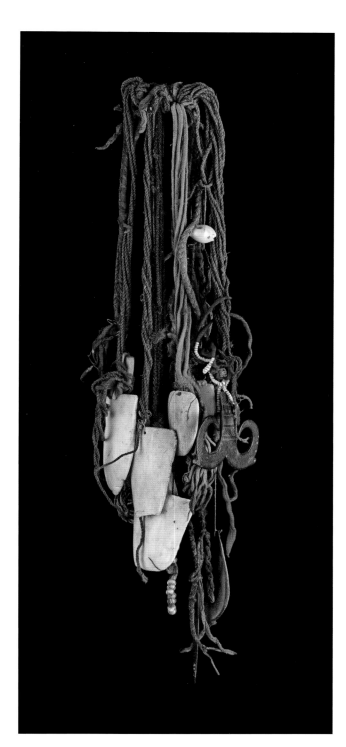

Pituri (*Duboisia hopwoodii*) is a plant with narcotic properties that grows in dunes on desert margins. The dried leaves and stems are chewed, sometimes mixed with ash from a fire. The active ingredient is nicotine. The toxicity of the plant varies according to the growing environment. The most valuable pituri grew in the area of the Mulligan and Georgina Rivers in western Queensland. The pituri was cured by being placed in holes dug in the hot sand, covered and left until all the moisture had evaporated. It was traded north to the Flinders River, which flows into the Gulf of Carpentaria, and south as far as the Flinders Ranges. Gason recorded that an expedition of men would annually leave the Lake Eyre region to travel the 250 kilometres or more north to obtain pituri.[26] The cured leaves were tightly packed into string or wallaby skin bags for the return journey (figs 17–18). A man who took part in both the quest for red ochre and pituri would have travelled a distance of well over 1,000 kilometres on foot across the Central Desert.

The raw material that travelled farthest through its incorporation in regular trading systems was the pearl shell from the Kimberley and Cape York Peninsula. In the north pearl shell from Cape York Peninsula and the Torres Strait Islands entered into exchange systems along the Papuan coast and into the interior of New Guinea. In Australia pearl shell found its way to the far southern coast and was a valued commodity across the continent. It was traded both as manufactured objects and as raw material (fig. 19).

19.
Marriage ornaments
Worn by married women or hung around the necks of brides, the individual elements are made from various types of shell, which were traded widely.

Mer, Torres Strait, Queensland, before 1889
Turtle shell, pearl shell, ceramic, cotton hair cord; L. 440 mm
British Museum, London
Oc,89+.57 Exh. BM
Donated by A.C. Haddon

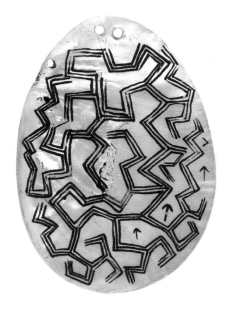

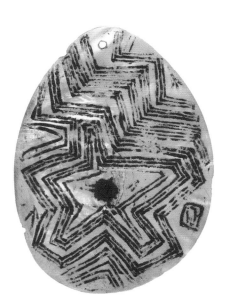

20.
Pearl shell pendant

Aubrey Tigan (1945–2013), Bardi
and Djawi
Broome, Western Australia, c. 2012
Pearl shell, natural pigment;
H. 165 mm, W. 135 mm
British Museum, London
2012,2030.1 Exh. BM

21.
Pearl shell pendant

Attributed to Cossack, Pilbara region,
Western Australia, before 1896
Pearl shell, natural pigment;
L. 174 mm, W. 122 mm
British Museum, London
Oc1896,-.1041 Exh. BM

22.
Pearl shell pendant
The design includes plants
and animals and a human
figure, possibly European,
with a pipe and 'billy' can.

Kimberley region, Western Australia,
before 1954
Pearl shell, natural pigment, human
hair; L. 166 mm, W. 115 mm
British Museum, London
Oc1954,06.377 Exh. BM
Donated by Wellcome Institute
for the History of Medicine

23.
Pearl shell pendant

Attributed to Cossack, Western
Australia , before 1896
Pearl shell, natural pigment;
L. 165 mm, W. 120 mm
British Museum, London
Oc1896,-.1039 Exh. BM

Pearl shell (figs 20–26) was prized for its iridescent qualities – its capacity to shine – which spoke to Indigenous aesthetic sensibilities. It was incorporated into decorative forms for personal adornment or ritual purposes as is evidenced by the beautiful pearl shell belt that has survived from Melbourne's colonial days (fig. 24). The meanings attached to pearl shell changed as it moved south and its value increased according to its scarcity (see fig. 9, p. 32). But one widespread association was its connection with rain and lightning. Whether this reflected its place of origin in the monsoonal regions of northern Australia or its glistening aura is a matter of speculation.

24.
Belt with pearl shell pendants

Melbourne, Victoria, before 1870
Bark, hair, pearl shell;
L. 660 mm, W. 96 mm
British Museum, London
Oc.6014 Exh. BM
Donated by Thomas Rupert Jones

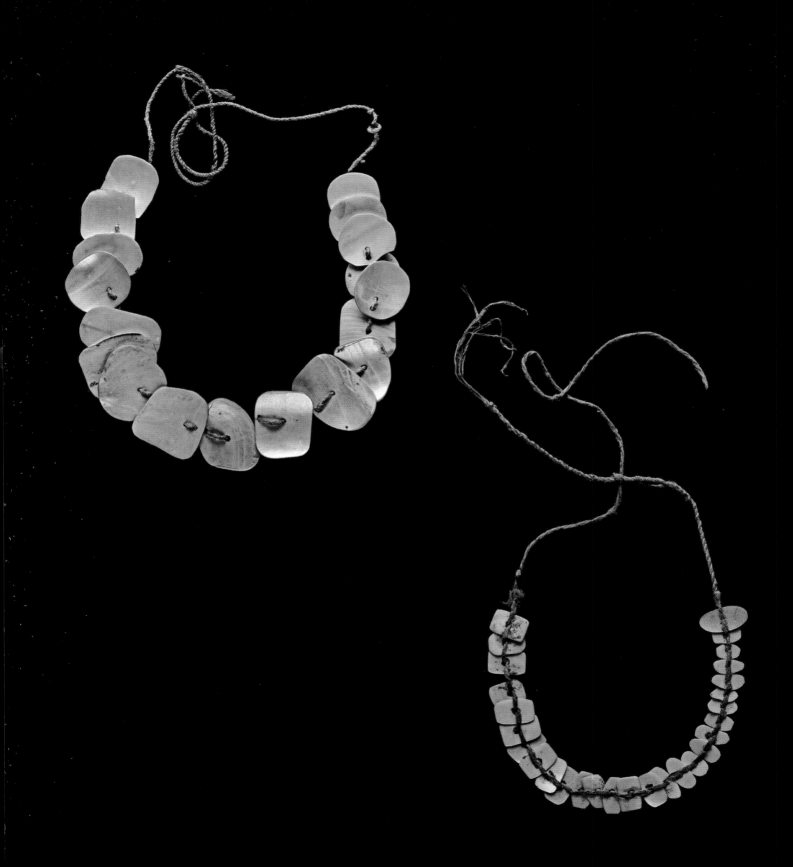

Living off the land and sea

Australian Aboriginal people lived predominantly as hunters and gatherers off the natural resources harvested from the land and sea. Today in many areas hunting and gathering continues to be a significant component of people's lives. It is important to stress the harvested nature of their economy and the extent to which Aboriginal Australians managed the resources of the land and were involved in the shaping of the landscape. Aboriginal people were in long-term contact with agricultural people across the Torres Strait and unquestionably remained hunters and gatherers by choice as opposed to a lack of knowledge or technological capacity. In some parts of Australia along the north coast and in better watered regions in the south-east and west, Aboriginal people occupied rich environments that could sustain relatively large populations. In contrast, in much of central Australia they occupied some of the harshest environments on earth. Yet in both they managed to develop sustainable economies adapted to the demands of the environment in ways that enabled them to occupy almost every niche of a vast continent.

In the Torres Strait Islands the hunter-gatherer economy of Aboriginal Australians existed side by side with the horticultural practices of Melanesia. The natural resources of the different islands varied greatly and, accordingly, so did the balance of economic activities. Melissa Carter writes that prior to European colonisation the 'population of the Eastern Islands was sedentary and relied heavily on fishing and gardening, while the populations on the other islands were more mobile, subsisted on hunting and fishing, and relied to varying degrees on plant collection and cultivation.'[27] People hunted sea creatures, harpooning dugong (a large sea mammal, like a manatee) and turtle. Fishing was central to the economy, with methods ranging from nets, lines (fig. 27) and spears to fish traps set up in the intertidal zone. Harvesting these resources of the sea remains an integral part of life for many Islanders today. Land animals, including marsupials, cassowaries (a large flightless bird), goannas and bush turkeys were hunted on islands where they occurred but their numbers were much smaller than on the mainland. Shellfish provided an important component of the diet on many islands. People harvested and nurtured a diversity of wild food resources as they did on the mainland but in addition planted crops in gardens. The main subsistence crops grown were yams, coconuts and plantains.

The hunter-gatherer way of life varied enormously across the continent. Hunter-gatherers, no less than agriculturalists, have to take account of the seasons and a range of different environments. Aboriginal people have occupied a continent through periods of major climatic and environmental variation and have adapted to changing conditions and developed new technologies. Their relationship with the environment has always been an active one. They developed practices of managing the land over centuries

25.
Shell ornament
Nautilus shell was traded extensively in Cape York Peninsula and northern Queensland.

Nautilus shell, fibre; L. 820 mm
Mulgrave River region, near Cairns, Queensland, c. 1900
British Museum, London
Oc1933,0403.46 Exh. BM
Donated by Florence M. Walker

26.
Shell ornament

Mulgrave River region, near Cairns, Queensland, before 1895
Nautilus shell, fibre; L. 630 mm
British Museum, London
Oc1895,-.250 Exh. BM
Donated by Sir Augustus Wollaston Franks

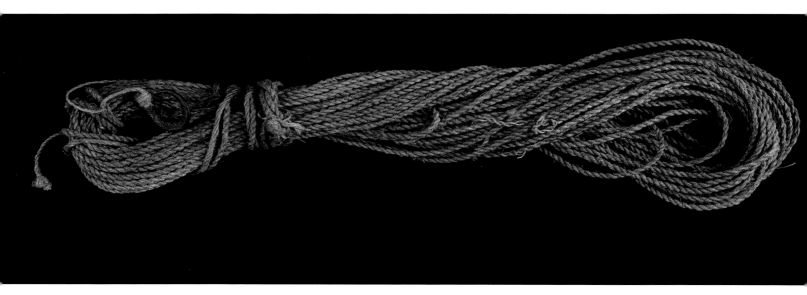

that had long-term consequences on regional ecologies and the shape of the landscape.

One of the most important instruments in managing the land has been fire. In the 1970s archaeologist Rhys Jones coined the phrase fire-stick farming to refer to the many different ways in which fire was used to gain a livelihood from the land (fig. 28).[28] Fire was an integral part of hunting and gathering: for clearing areas of land to allow access to places, burning grasslands to encourage new shoots to grow, producing new crops of seeds and attracting kangaroos, masking the smell of the hunters or screening them from their prey. The timing of fire varied according to the local environment and rainfall. In desert regions the pattern of rainfall was irregular, but people nonetheless carried out systematic burning by monitoring areas of rainfall and firing the vegetation after harvesting the food produced. Even so there was a preference to burn in summer months if at all possible. In areas of marked seasonal rainfall across northern Australia firing the land took place in the early dry season when the undergrowth was high and the ground drying out. Lighting fires at that time of year ensured that they could be kept under control and be of limited extent. Each year different areas of country would be burnt creating a mosaic of land in various stages of regeneration, and providing periods of time for the land to recover. The regular burning of country ensured that catastrophic fires resulting from the build up of fuel could be avoided, protecting people and animals and allowing trees to regenerate rather than be killed by the severity of the flames. In other places regular burning was conducted to create and preserve areas of grassland. Over the centuries it is argued that the regime of fire created a

27.
Fishing line with turtle-shell hook

Zuna, Torres Strait, Queensland, c. 1844
Fibre, turtle shell; L. 300 mm, W. 70 mm,
D. 50 mm (coiled and tied)
British Museum, London
Oc1978,Q.331 Exh. BM

28.
Hamzah Taylor lighting a hunting fire near Parnngurr community

Western Desert, Western Australia, 2009
Photograph: Jenny Chang

Understanding country

particular balance in the environment, favouring certain plants and animals over others. When that fire regime changed, as happened in many places after European colonisation, the land often became impoverished with a significant reduction in species diversity.

The writer Dick Kimber and the archaeologist Mike Smith provide an excellent summary of the factors involved in firing the country in central Australia:

> Everyone understood this fire technology, but they still needed to talk about it. The women debated matters with their husbands, telling them which vegetables and fruits they favoured for the next season. Different patches of country were chosen sometimes to protect certain trees, such as quandong (*Santalum acuminatum*) with its plentiful fruit, or to promote those plants that increase their productivity after fires, such as the 'bush raisin' (*Solanum*); sometimes to clear in order to find goannas and small game or to promote green shoots favoured by kangaroos and wallabies. The hunters were chiefly concerned to ensure a suitable pattern and temperature of firing. The senior men also decided when it was time to protect sacred sites by using fire to burn breaks.[29]

Not every area was burnt with equal frequency and some areas were protected from fire. In Arnhem Land today people avoid burning areas of jungle and small patches of rainforest. These are associated with deeper soils and contain a range of botanical resources. They are also the places where certain species of yam grow in abundance that provide a major staple food in the early dry season. The growth of yams is encouraged by replanting the vine with the top part of the tuber attached ensuring a large crop the following year. Similar practices occurred across Australia. In Noongar country in the Swan River region of Western Australia, occupied today by the suburban outskirts of Perth, the surveyor William Snell Chauncy (1820–1878) noted patches of yams growing in dogwood thickets.[30]

The regular controlled burning of the land affected the shape of the Australian landscape as a whole in creating what the historian Bill Gammage evocatively terms 'the biggest estate on Earth'.[31] Gammage was struck by how the descriptions and images produced by early European colonists of Australia conveyed an impression of a landscape that was managed in a systematic way (fig. 29). The colonists drew comparisons with the European landscapes with which they were familiar, in particular the great parklands associated with country estates. He cites among many others Charles Sturt (1795–1869), the explorer of the Murray River system in the late 1820s, who wrote: 'In many places trees are so sparingly, and I almost said judiciously distributed as to resemble the park lands attached to a gentleman's residence in England'.[32] Gammage argues that the pattern Sturt observed was the result of conscious intent and this thesis has been a rich source of debate in Australia. What is undeniable is that the recurrent pattern of burning practices over generations produced landscapes that were transformed by human agency and favourable to people's ways of life. Aboriginal people created major routes across country linking resources that they accessed seasonally, clearing the pathways regularly. There were established settlement sites where people lived for many months at a time using seasonally abundant resources. There were areas of permanent grassland where kangaroo and wallaby fed, particular hills were kept free of trees for kangaroo hunts, patches of jungle were preserved for their food resources, places were maintained where ceremonies were held as were burial grounds that had been used for generations. In arid regions wells were dug and protected from animals, and in coastal regions people created middens (mounds built up from the remains of shellfish) that enabled people to camp on higher drier ground with protection from mosquitoes.

Knowledge and method

Aboriginal people made and continue to make use of the diversity of their environment. Their knowledge of animals and plants is vast as indicated in elaborate vocabularies that often reflect the different uses to which plants and animals can be put (fig. 30). Plants were employed in the construction of houses, the manufacture of implements, weaving and fibrework, for food and medicine, as stimulants and as sources of poison to stun fish or even emu drinking water from billabongs. Precise terminologies mapping the seasonal cycle in different regions enable people to anticipate the time when they should move to exploit seasonally abundant resources. Plants on land became indicators of the bounty of the sea, the yellow flowers of the kurrajong in Arnhem Land signalling the time to hunt stingray, that is, when the stingray were fat but after they had finished spawning. Donald Thomson, who undertook intensive fieldwork in Cape York Peninsula and Arnhem Land in the 1930s and 1940s, summarised the situation well when he wrote that people 'are familiar with the various botanical (ecological)… [zones]… and distinguish these by special terms. They can name, without hesitation, the characteristic trees, shrubs, and herbaceous plants in every association, as well as the food plants and animals, and raw materials… which they obtain from each'.[33] This summary applies equally well today in many regions. The ethno-botanical knowledge of Indigenous Australians is immensely rich and remains a hugely neglected source of information in uncovering Australia's biodiversity.

The number of food plants available on a seasonal basis is vast. Researchers in central Australia identified 140 species, of which seventy-five

29.
***Aborigines Using Fire
to Hunt Kangaroos***

Joseph Lycett (*c.* 1774–*c.* 1825),
born Staffordshire, England
New South Wales, *c.* 1817
Watercolour on paper; H. 177 mm,
W. 278 mm
National Library of Australia, Canberra
PIC R5689

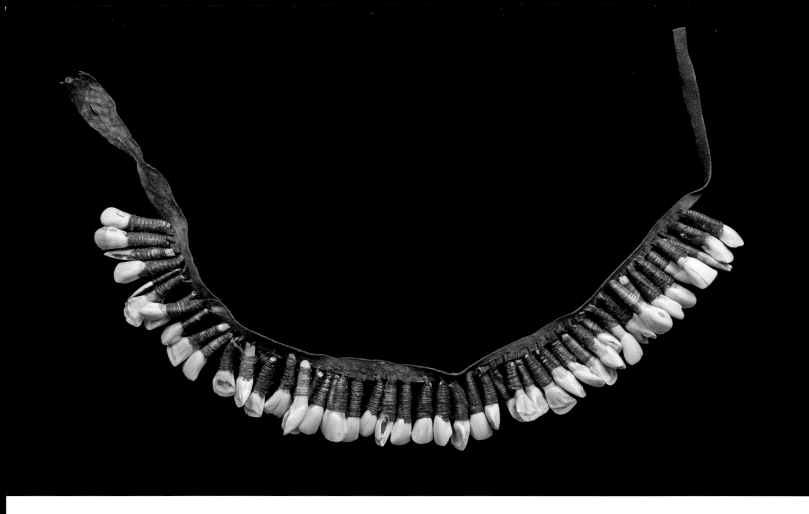

were exploited for their seeds. Seeds required a high labour input. They needed to be collected, winnowed (separated from the chaff) in a *coolamon* (wooden dish) and ground with a mortar before being cooked in the ashes of a fire (fig. 31). Collectively they provided a staple that was obtainable when more favoured foods that grew around a campsite or waterhole had been depleted.[34]

Knowledge of plants and animals included techniques for the preparation and preservation of food. This enabled people to prepare poisonous or bitter yams for eating and to differentiate between pituri plants that could be used as a narcotic and those which could be used as fish poison. The nuts of the cycad palm (*ngatu*) are one of the food staples of northern Australia. In their raw state the nuts are highly poisonous and require complex treatment to make them edible. They are first broken up and placed in dilly bags and immersed in running water for a week or more to leech out some of the poison. The nuts are then pounded on grindstones to make a flourlike paste that is then roasted in the ashes of a fire. The end result is loaves of ngatu bread that until recently provided one of the main staples

30.
Necklace of wallaby teeth

Warrnambool District, western Victoria, before 1847
Plant fibre, animal skin, swamp wallaby (*Wallabia bicolor*)
tooth; L. 630 mm
British Museum, London
Oc1847,0413.1 Exh. BM
Donated by Augustus Strong

when large groups congregated for ceremonial gatherings. Along the southern Queensland coastal region the bunya pine (*Araucaria bidwillii*) provided a staple for ceremonial gatherings. The trees produced abundant cones and the nuts were prepared in many different ways, being eaten raw, roasted or after they had been soaked in water or in the mud at the bottom of flowing streams. Burying them in mud was both a method of storage and added to their flavour.

The Snowy Mountain region of New South Wales and Victoria is one of the harshest environments in Australia but it has one surprising seasonally abundant food resource, the Bogong moth. Each summer vast numbers of the moths that have bred in the broadleaved woodlands of New South Wales and southern Queensland aestivate (summer hibernation) for months in the caves and crevices of the mountains. The archaeologist Josephine Flood who researched the 'moth hunters' records that upwards of 17,000 have been counted on a square metre of surface.[35] The moths were harvested in large numbers by men and after feasting themselves they brought back quantities roasted and made into cakes, which together with the smoking used in the collecting process preserved them for some time.

Knowledge of techniques for preserving food was, and in some regions remains, widespread. In desert regions the fruit of *Solanum* (bush tomato) either in their raw state or dried were threaded onto sticks for later consumption. Dried fruits, berries, seeds and cakes made from them were sometimes wrapped in leaves and stored in the branches of trees away from animals. In the majority of cases food was preserved for the specific purpose of building up large supplies for ceremonial gatherings or, as with the moth hunters, enabling the sharing of a desired food on return to the community. Foods such as Bogong moths, cycad nuts and bunya bunya kernels were both seasonally abundant and capable of being preserved in the short term and hence provided the ideal food to support large gatherings. There are,

31.
Vessel
This vessel stands out among others for its elegant form and the fineness of the carving and decoration.

Derby, Kimberley region, Western Australia, before 1896
Wood, natural pigment; L. 1070 mm, W. 220 mm
Pitt Rivers Museum, University of Oxford
1896.50.4 Exh. BM
Donated by William Saville Kent

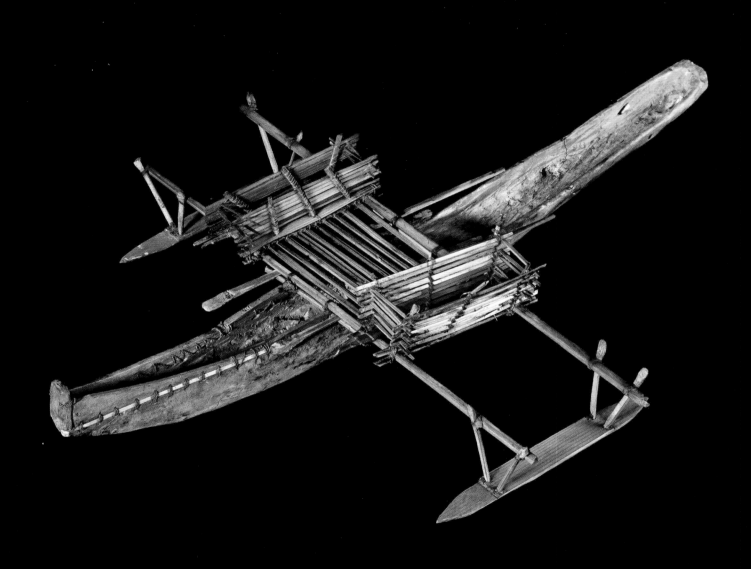

32.
Model outrigger canoe
In the Torres Strait canoes were vital for trade, fishing and for hunting dugong and turtle. This model has two outriggers, which support a platform, and crates for stowing provisions. As wood was scarce on the islands, the large hulls were trade items in themselves, being procured from the Fly River estuary in Western Province, Papua New Guinea.

Torres Strait, Queensland, before 1870
Wood, fibre; L. 560 mm
British Museum, London
Oc.6933.a Exh. BM
Donated by Sir Augustus Wollaston Franks

however, some examples of foods that were preserved in the longer term for domestic consumption. The best-documented example is again from Arnhem Land where *mundjutj* (wild plum) in addition to being eaten raw, which it generally is today, was preserved for future use. The fruit, which matures in the wet season, was initially dried in the sun before being rubbed in ochre and then further dried until it was hard and brittle. The prepared fruit was then wrapped in paperbark parcels and stored in baskets. When the time came to eat it the dried fruit could either be soaked in water or pulverised on a grindstone and mixed with water.

Food staples varied greatly according to environment. Across most of Australia the major proportion of the diet consisted mainly of vegetables, with fish and game being significant supplements to the diet. However, in coastal regions fish and shellfish can provide a significant year round resource as is also the case with the major river systems. Betty Meehan's ethnographic study of the Anbara people of central Arnhem Land demonstrated the importance of shellfish to coastal marine economies, a fact testified by the large number of shell middens that are evidence of past lives.[36] Aboriginal and Torres Straight Islanders have well-developed fishing technologies. Watercraft range from the dugout canoes of northern Australia to the outrigger canoes of the Torres Strait and north Queensland (figs 32–33), widely distributed bark canoes, and many different kinds of rafts, including the distinctively shaped mangrove tree vessel of the Worora people of the western Kimberley region and the unique Tasmanian raft made from bundles of reeds or stringy bark (fig. 34). Some highly specialised canoes were developed for particular environments (fig. 35). In the region of the Arafura

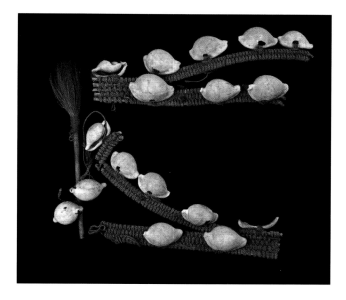

33.
Canoe prow ornament

Dauar, Torres Strait, Queensland, before 1889
Wood, fibre, cowrie shell, cassowary feather;
L. 400 mm, W. 420 mm
British Museum, London
Oc,89+.197 Exh. BM
Donated by A.C. Haddon

34.
Model canoe
Full-size bark canoes were renowned for their
stability, transporting people and animals.

Probably Oyster Cove, Tasmania, c. 1850–1851
Melaleuca bark, Leptospermum bark; H. 80 mm,
L. 745 mm, W. 155 mm
British Museum, London
Oc1851,1122.3 Exh. BM
Donated by Joseph Milligan

Swamp, people constructed a flat-bottomed bark canoe with a sharply
pointed nose that could be manoeuvred easily through the dense grasses
that covered the surface of the water. The canoes were used in expeditions
to hunt magpie geese and collect their eggs as they nested in the swamp
towards the end of the wet season. The goose hunters were the subject of an
iconic series of photographs by Donald Thomson (fig. 36) that became the
inspiration for a series of paintings by the Ganalbingu artist Milpurrurru
(1934–1998; fig. 37) and subsequently for Rolf de Heer's 2006 film
Ten Canoes.

People fished and continue to fish with spears, lines and hooks, in
addition to deploying many different kinds of net. Men usually fish with spears
and women with lines. Fish-spears were generally composite and multi-
pronged and directed with the aid of a spearthrower. The prongs were
fashioned from wood with barbs carved in or made from bone or stone
cemented in with different forms of gum. In Arnhem Land some fish-spears
were created from naturally barbed stingray prongs. The right to produce
them was vested in a particular clan and the spears were an important trade
item. In the north of Australia specialised harpoons were made for hunting
turtle and dugong. Today pointed iron prongs have largely replaced wooden
and composite ones, often being tied onto the spear shaft with wire rather
than being hafted or joined together with string and gum or resin.

35.
Canoe with punting pole

Wimmera River, northwestern Victoria, before 1906
River red gum (Eucalyptus camaldulensis) bark;
L. 3500 mm
British Museum, London
Oc1906,1015.1-2
Donated by John Walter Gregory

36.
**Ganalbingu and Djinba men use bark
canoes while hunting magpie geese and
their eggs in the Arafura Swamp**
From left to right: Djarrdi 1, Marrakaywarra,
Gunyirrnyirr, Ngulang 2, Ngulmarmar, Mangan,
Guminydju, Dhulumburrk 1, Kikirri and
Dhunipirri.

Central Arnhem Land, May 1937
Photograph: Donald Thomson
Museum Victoria, Melbourne
TPH 1090

37.
Magpie geese in the Arafura Swamp

George Milpurrurru (1934–1998),
Gurrumba Gurrumba clan, Yirritja moiety, Yolngu
Ramingining, central Arnhem Land,
Northern Territory, 1988
Natural pigment on bark;
H. 2370 mm, W. 780 mm, D. 25 mm
British Museum, London
Oc1989,05.1 Exh. BM

Understanding country

In addition to fishing with lines and spears, the use of fish traps, dams and weirs was widely adapted to the particular environment and to seasonal factors. Stone fish traps were constructed all around the coast to take advantage of tidal flows. In many cases the main structure was semi-permanent with boulders placed across the intertidal zone, the gaps in between being filled when the time came to operate the trap. Traps were also set up in inland waterways. Henry King (1855?–1923) photographed a series of fish traps far inland on the Darling/Barwon River at Brewarrina (fig. 38). The traps usually combined different hunting technologies, with the fish stranded by the outgoing tide or caught in the flow of the river being netted or speared.

Fish traps reached one of their highest stages of development in the inland waters and estuaries of Arnhem Land, which experience extreme seasons. During the wet season from December to March the rivers flood and the surrounding country is inundated. Fish breed prolifically but are dispersed across the flooded plains. With the onset of the dry season the waters recede and the fast-flowing rivers are filled with an abundance of fish. Many different types of fish trap are constructed according to the characteristics of the watercourses. In the majority of cases one or more dams are set up to allow the water and fish to build up. Sometimes the fish are caught as they try to leap the dam; elsewhere fish traps are placed in the walls of the dams, or poison is used to stun the fish. Perhaps the most

38.
A series of fish traps on the Darling/Barwon River

Brewarrina, New South Wales, 1889–1900
Photograph: Henry King
Powerhouse Museum, Sydney

39.
Gorl **fish trap**

Milingimbi, Arnhem Land, Northern Territory, *c.* 1950s
Bark, natural pigment; L. 800 mm, W. 470 mm
Museum der Kulturen, Basel
Va 960

40.
Raywala (right) and Tjam Yilkari Kitani (left) using *gorl* fish traps

Glyde River, eastern Arnhem Land, 1937
Photograph: Donald Thomson
Museum Victoria, Melbourne
TPH 740

remarkable fish trap is the *gorl* (fig. 39), which was described in detail by Donald Thomson.[37] This trap involves the building of a weir by placing a long pole across the river that forms the frame for a palisade of stakes driven into the mud. The stakes are then packed in with grasses from the flood plain and plastered with mud to seal the surface. One or more conical cylinders made from sheets of stringy-bark sewn together at the edges are pushed through the upper section of the weir with the narrow end downstream. A platform is built on the downstream side with a floor of sticks that form a grating through which water can drain. Semicircles of bark are then placed on the platform where the end of the funnel protrudes from the dam wall so that as the waters flow through the bark funnel the fish become trapped inside the container (fig. 40). This form of trap is set up towards the mouth of the Glyde River into which the waters of the Arafura Swamp drain in the early dry season. The trap operates through the night as the fish travel with the receding floodwaters downstream to the river mouth. The right to produce gorl fish traps is vested in two clans, the Liyagalawumirri and Ngaladarr, and is sanctioned by religious law that enables the distribution of the catch to be controlled. The vesting of the right to use a particular technology in the membership of the 'originating'

41.
Fish trap

Barron River region, near Cairns, Queensland,
c. 1900
Fibre; L. 840 mm, W. 100 mm
British Museum, London
Oc1933,0403.51 Exh. BM
Donated by Florence M. Walker

42.
Wet tropical rainforest
In far north Queensland, the
rainforests are home to incredibly
diverse species of plants and animals.
Rainforest people use materials from
fig trees and lawyer cane to make
objects, such as fish traps, shields
and baskets.

Cathedral fig tree
Altherton Tablelands, Queensland
Photograph: Ashley Cooper

clan both ensures cooperation between groups in the region and encourages innovation – each clan has rights over its own fish trap.

The majority of fish traps used people's knowledge of the flow of water and the annual cycle of the fish to boost their catch at particular times of year. In the regions of Lake Condah and Mount Eccles in south-west Victoria people managed the riverine environment to maximise the harvesting of eels. George Augustus Robinson (1791–1866) in the early days of European colonisation recorded the extensive nature of the system.[38] An elaborate network of weirs, stone races, trenches and eel traps was created that enabled people to manage the seasonal migration of eels that took place in autumn to their greatest advantage (see figs 80–81, p. 91). They linked adjacent wetlands together increasing the number of eels in the system and facilitating trapping. The traps were in the form of elongated open-ended tapered baskets that could be placed in the weir, the eels being caught when they emerged from the far end. In the rainforest region of north Queensland, men used elongated fish traps of lawyer cane in receding rivers to catch fish (figs 41–42).

Dwellings

We weren't nomads. We didn't wander aimlessly all over the
bloody place and go walkabout. We had an existence here.
Ken Saunders, Gunditjmara (b. 1943).[39]

Aboriginal Australians constructed very different types of dwellings according to the nature of the environment, the availability of raw materials and the seasonal pattern of movement. Paul Memmott's book, *Gunyah Goondie and Wurley: The Aboriginal Architecture of Australia*, provides an overview of regional styles of housing.[40] In the more arid parts of Australia where mobility was high people would camp in the open for much of the year, clearing the ground and making windbreaks from available grasses and bushes. During the dry season in northern Australia when people moved away in small groups from wet season camps, they also spent much of the time camped in the open. However, for much of the year people lived for long periods of time in semi-permanent settlements associated with major food resources such as fish, shellfish, water chestnuts or yams, and in the wet season when much of the land was inundated, people lived in more substantial houses that provided protection from the elements. In Arnhem Land shelters made from sheets of stringy bark on wooden frames were built either at ground level or on platforms raised above the ground to provide protection from animals and flooding. Large round huts covered in paperbark were built for the wet season, with a smouldering fire filling the house with smoke to keep out mosquitoes.

Similar substantial structures were found across Australia to keep people warm and dry in winter. In south-west Tasmania domed houses covered with layers of paperbark and thatched with grass kept out the cold, and the Gunditjmara eel trappers of Victoria built semi-permanent dwellings of circular stone walls with timber-framed roofs. These structures had interconnected rooms, some of which were used to house possessions; the homes themselves were clustered into domestic villages (fig. 43).

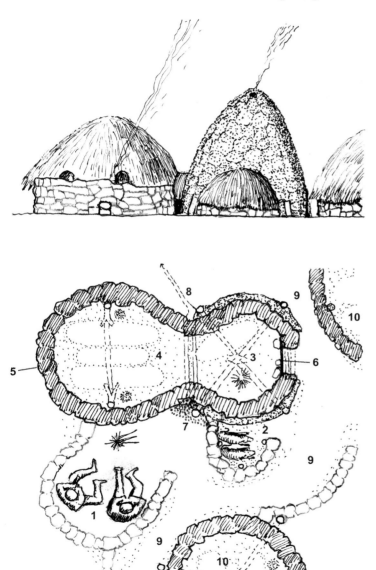

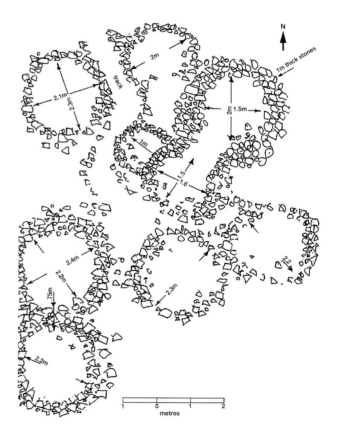

43.

(left) A hypothetical reconstruction of a Gunditjmara village house with stone wall and timber-framed, domed roof clad in peat sods

1 Diurnal windbreak made of stone wall
2 Dog shelter as attached dome
3 Main shelter, outer room; structure of lean-to curved poles with sapling or reed substructure, peat sod cladding, and chimney in apex
4 Main shelter, inner nocturnal room; structure of two curved posts with ridgepole, curved rafters that span between ridge and stone wall, reed and grass cladding
5 Stone wall, 200 mm wide and 900 mm high
6 Door of rigid bark sheet
7 Sullage pit
8 Surface drain
9 Pathway
10 Adjacent structures
Drawing: Paul Memmott

(right) Sketch plan of the remains of stone walls in the vicinity of Darlots Creek, western Victoria
It is hypothesised that the circular spaces contained a combination of dwelling and storage spaces in part of a village complex.

Drawing: Heather Builth

44.
A house on Saibai, Torres Strait, Queensland, 1888

Photograph: A.C. Haddon

Although the physical form of houses was relatively simple, the structural organisation of both temporary and semi-permanent settlements was complex. Settlements were divided on the basis of gender and marital status: family units, a young men's camp, a widows' camp and so on. At gatherings when large numbers of people came together for funerals and religious ceremonies, people distributed themselves according to the country from which they came, so mapping out the geographical relationships between their clan territories. The area was often divided into different zones: closed places where restricted parts of the ceremony were performed and ritual objects were made, huts where objects were kept or initiates were secluded, and major public arenas where different groups performed in turn. Such ceremonial spaces were often structured around sand or ground sculptures deriving from the creative acts of dreamtime ancestral beings.

Torres Strait Island architecture was much more substantial, durable and larger in scale. The economy, combining fishing with agriculture, was associated with permanent village settlements. There were many different styles of housing that varied regionally and often shared features in common with Melanesian forms. Houses on Saibai, for example, one of the northernmost islands, were built on elevated frames of wood and bamboo with woven palm frond panels and high gabled roofs (fig. 44). These provided protection from storm flooding and king tides, and defence from the ubiquitous mosquito.

Fibrecraft
Lissant Bolton

Indigenous Australians were and are masters of fibrecraft, creating a wide range of objects from an equally large array of plant and animal sources. The commonly held misapprehension that the items made by Aboriginal people were limited in scope can be entirely disproved by reference to fibrecraft alone. The number of fibre objects that have been and are still produced across the continent is enormous. From cane, grass, spinifex, sedges, rushes, reeds, flax, vines, leaves and bark, and also animal fur and human hair, people spun threads, twined cords and ropes, split cane, and treated leaves, vines, rushes and reeds in specific ways to extract and use the fibres. They looped, knotted, coiled, twined and plaited the fibres: different techniques for different fibres, and for making a variety of items. These include hunting and fishing nets, fishing lines, fish and eel traps, ropes, sails, bags, baskets, mats, sandals, clothing and ornaments (figs 45–53). Fibre objects were also made as games, not least the loops of string for cats' cradles in northern Australia and the Torres Strait.

The harvesting of the fibres was and is based on detailed knowledge of plants and seasons, so that the fibres could be extracted at the optimum time for each purpose. That knowledge continues to be put to new purposes as people develop new kinds of objects to make. Women in central Australia, in the Ngaanyatjarra Pitjantjatjara Yankunytjatjara (NPY) lands, have recently based novel work on old fibre skills (such as in making the traditional women's padded head ring, used for carrying). NPY women are now employing a wide range of grasses as well as introduced yarns and raffia to create baskets and figure sculptures for sale. As Nellie Patterson (b. 1943) explains: 'We women have always used many different fibres in our daily work, and we handle many different plants and grasses and bark each day in our foraging for food. Each plant has

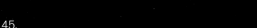

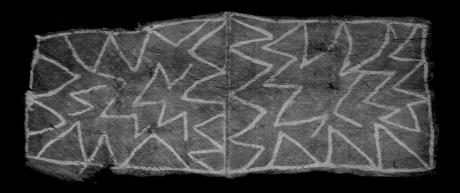

46.
Bark blanket
A rare blanket made from the bark of the fig tree, common in the rainforest of north Queensland. Such blankets were used for warmth and sometimes in mortuary practices.

Atherton/Tully/Cardwell region, Queensland, before 1900
Fig tree (*Ficus pleurocarpa*) bark, natural pigment;
H. 1145 mm, W. 485 mm
British Museum, London
Oc1900,0723.1 Exh. BM

45.
Biting bag (or spirit bag)
Men wear these string bags around their necks and bite into them in spiritual contexts.

Arnhem Land, Northern Territory, before 1896
Fibre, cotton; Diam. 75 mm
British Museum, London
Oc1896,-.118 Exh. BM
Donated by Sir Augustus Wollaston Franks

different stems and barks and prickles and fibres. Our mothers introduced us to all the plants that we use in our daily lives.'[41]

It is not only women who had such knowledge and produce these objects. Men often made string, rope and nets, and in some places they were also responsible for making bags and baskets. Great skill and flair went into creating these items, and people took pleasure and pride in them. A dictionary of the Diyari language, published at the turn of the twentieth century, records the phrase *billieli pankina*, meaning 'to make a great fuss about one's fine dillybag'.[42]

Men produced the sculptural baskets of the Queensland rainforest (figs 47–48). Variations in these highly distinctive rigid baskets, made from split lawyer cane and known as bicornual baskets, reflect the diverse range of purposes to which they were put, from food-gathering to carrying babies. Small bicornual baskets, sometimes with painted designs, were used for transporting men's personal and ceremonial belongings. Abe Muriata (b. 1952), from Cardwell in north Queensland, is continuing this tradition today, accurately characterising himself as a master craftsman (see pp. 246–7).[43]

The British Museum collection includes fibre objects made across the continent, and collected from some of the earliest moments of encounter (fig. 49) until the present, perhaps the first being a string bag from Sydney before 1844 (fig. 50). Some of the objects are no longer made. In the southern parts of Australia, where it is often very cold in the winter, people sometimes made possum-skin cloaks, the skins being sewn together with kangaroo sinews; others made and wore mats. During the winter in the Coorong region of southern South Australia, people used large sedge and bark fibre mats as cloaks to protect them from the bitterly cold winds. Early in the settlement of South Australia diarist and poet Mary Thomas (1787–1875) recorded that Aboriginal people on the Adelaide Plains had

47.
Bicornual basket

Mulgrave River region, near Cairns, Queensland, before 1900
Lawyer cane (*Calamus*); H. 310 mm (excluding handle), W. 330 mm
British Museum, London
Oc1933,0403.56 Exh. BM
Donated by Florence M. Walker

48.
Bicornual basket

Mulgrave River region, near Cairns, Queensland,
before 1900
Lawyer cane (*Calamus*); H. 300 mm, W. 330 mm
British Museum, London
Oc1933,0403.57 Exh. BM
Donated by Florence M. Walker

'some mats of grass… of their own manufacture' and that the 'women usually had mats fastened to their shoulders, in which they carry their young children and provisions'.[44] Sometimes these mats had pockets created in them by means of a smaller mat, sewn to the centre of the larger, in which other things could be carried, an example of which was collected by George Augustus Robinson between 1839 and 1849 (fig. 51).

The making of fibre objects was often a mainstay of Aboriginal communities after the European incursion (fig. 52). Constrained to live in missions and other types of reserve, baskets became a significant component of early Aboriginal enterprises, with forms being adapted to suit the taste of European purchasers. Europeans also sometimes brought new techniques, as the missionary Greta Matthews did in 1922 in introducing the coiling technique (which she apparently learnt from Aboriginal communities on the Murray River) to women in Arnhem Land. Traditional Arnhem Land baskets are made with the twining technique. Women across that region have taken up coiling, developing new forms and, in another innovation, dyeing the pandanus (screw pine) fibre with natural dyes to make beautiful baskets and bags.

Today people continue to make fibre objects for ritual and for personal purposes, but also for the art market (fig. 53). As well as making baskets, women in the NPY lands produce humorous fibre objects, not least a life-size coiled grass and jute string Toyota truck, which won the National Aboriginal and Torres Strait Islander Art Award in 2005. In Arnhem Land, people also make fibre sculptures.

49.
Basket for carrying clubs

Encounter Bay region, South Australia, before 1855
Fibre; H. 540 mm, W. 390 mm
British Museum, London
Oc1855,1220.176 Exh. BM
Donated by the Lords of Admiralty/ Haslar Hospital

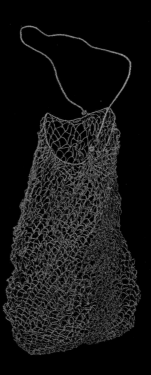

50.
String bag

Port Jackson region, New South Wales, before 1844
Illawarra flame tree (*Brachychiton acerifolius*) bark fibre;
H. 410 mm, W. 350 mm
British Museum, London
Oc.4061 Exh. BM
Donated by Henry Christy

While some such works are humorous in intent, others reference animals and spirits that are important in Dreaming stories. The significance of the new fibre objects reaches into millennia-deep understandings about the world. The endless uses and possibilities of fibre are being explored today as throughout Indigenous Australian history.

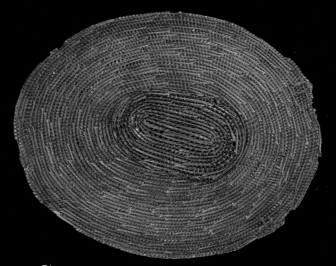

51.
Coiled mat with pocket

Southeast Australia, 1839–49
Spiny-head mat-rush (*Lomandra longifolia*) fibre;
L. 652 mm, W. 541 mm
British Museum, London
Oc,+.4674 Exh. BM
Donated by Sir Augustus Wollaston Franks

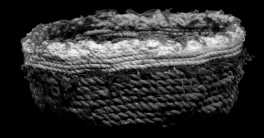

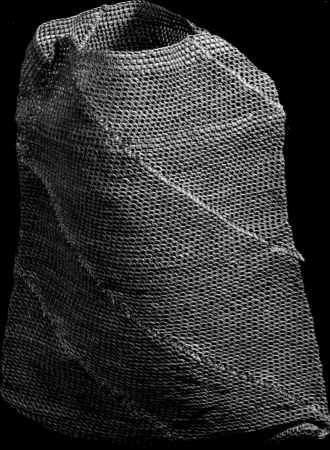

52.
Looped and knotted bag

Cleveland, Queensland, late 19th century or
early 20th century
Fibre; H. 560 mm, W. 420 mm
British Museum, London
Oc1954,06.386 Exh. BM
Donated by Wellcome Institute for the History of Medicine

53.
Ghost net basket
Discarded commercial fishing nets pose hazards to fish and mammals in the Torres Strait. Mahnah Angela Torenbeek collects these ghost nets from beaches and makes them into baskets. By removing the nets Torenbeek, a committed educator, upholds her responsibility to care for the sea.

Mahnah Angela Torenbeek (b. 1942), Wagalgai
Moa, Torres Strait, Queensland, 2010
Synthetic fibre; H. 120 mm, Diam. 250 mm
British Museum, London
2011,2017.1 Exh. BM

An industrious life

Donald Thomson, who spent two years living with Yolngu people in Arnhem Land in the 1930s, provides the most detailed account and a rich photographic record of the daily life of Aboriginal hunter-gatherers. He wrote that:

> The first impression that any stranger must receive… is of industry. He cannot fail to see that everybody, man or woman, works hard and that the work is well organised and runs smoothly.… Neither men nor women are idle for long, and even in camp as they sit around their fires they may be seen to pick up a basket, a fish net, a spear or other weapon, and work on this as they talk.[45]

Thomson notes people's appreciation of skill in manufacture and the fact that they would seek out work of renowned craftsmanship. 'Not every man is skilled in the weaving of *bäti* (baskets), of which many types are recognised, each with his own name and each of which is made for a special purpose. A man with special skill in weaving becomes known… [as]… *kong mainmäk*, a "good hand".[46] But although appearance and finesse are important, an object's value is enhanced by past association with a particular person or previous success, and by the spiritual power (*marr*) it has gained.

Europeans were blind to the complexities of Aboriginal life and long held a view of hunter-gatherer society that was distorted by the lens of nineteenth-century evolutionary theory. They failed to understand the complex nature of relationships between people and land that had maintained a favourable way of living for most of humanity's existence. There was a tendency to overstate the mobility of hunter-gatherer societies and a failure to recognise that the very viability of these societies depended on long-term relationships with the land, which entailed forms of ownership. Mobility varied enormously according to seasonal and environmental factors but the majority of Aboriginal Australians moved between a small number of settlement sites within their estates. The stability of Aboriginal populations enabled them to monitor long-term relationships between people and environment, helping to maintain a balance between population and resources. Dependence on natural resources for food, transport, clothing and shelter required a detailed knowledge of the properties, characteristics and distribution of plants, and the behaviour of animal species. That knowledge remains a profound resource for understanding the world.

The fact that the land was managed also provides a context for understanding the inevitable conflict with the Europeans who came to occupy the land as farmers. Aboriginal people in the well-watered regions had created the ideal environment for the migratory pastoralism of the incoming European settlers who drove their cattle across the country, establishing their own estates on the way. The plains that provided the excellent grasslands for kangaroo were pre-adapted for pastoralism. Conflict became inevitable since people were competing for the same resource, exploited in different ways. For much of Australia's history those areas that were the ideal places for European settlement were the places where Aboriginal people had established their long-term seasonal camps for countless generations.

Form, function and aesthetics

With minimal trading relationships outside the mainland, relationships to land in Australia were mediated by the very materials that the land, and its waters, produced locally. From wood, stone, fibre and animal products, Aboriginal and Torres Strait Islander people were able to fashion toolkits of great economy and efficiency. Aboriginal material culture has some core objects – such as spears, stone knives, wooden dishes, shields and baskets – that are common to most groups, in slightly different forms, across the continent. These vary noticeably according to the natural resources available, and the unique cultural orientations and aesthetic preferences of the people who make them.

In the desert regions of central and Western Australia there is a more limited range of raw materials than elsewhere and a premium is placed on mobility. People moving through the desert had to carry much of their material world with them and this in part explains the multifunctional nature of the objects they made. Spearthrowers (see p. 80) provide an excellent example.

54.
Bark container

Kunmunya Mission, Kimberley region,
Western Australia, c. 1931
Bark, gum, resin, fibre, spinifex fibre, cane fibre, boxwood,
natural pigment; H. 160 mm, Diam. 220 mm
British Museum, London
Oc1953,03.6 Exh. BM
Donated by Mary Montgomerie Bennett

55.
Coconut water containers

Mer, Torres Strait, Queensland, c. 1892
Coconut, fibre; (left) H. 130 mm,
Diam. 130 mm; (right) H. 140 mm,
Diam. 140 mm
British Museum, London
Oc1922,1024.7.a-b Exh. BM
Donated by Tom Roberts

In contrast in the better-watered regions there was less of a need for multifunctionality and longer-term seasonal residence enabled material objects to be stored. Gunditjmara stone houses even had store rooms for such purposes (see fig. 43).

In many regions of Australia material culture was extensive with people using a considerable number of techniques to exploit a wide range of the resources of the environment. Containers were required for infinite purposes: from drawing water from a source, to carrying and storing fruits, seeds and honey, storing personal possessions, and for use in trade as objects of ceremonial display. They were made from bent, folded and sewn bark (fig. 54), carved and hollowed out wood, bamboo, coconuts (fig. 55) and large shells, and string and woven fibres. Different regions of Australia had multiple types of baskets, and basketry techniques and weaving were used to produce objects for a variety of purposes, including manufacturing components of fish traps and woven mats and sails. However, the diversity of forms of Australian material culture can only be partially explained by what they were used for. Barry Cundy in his detailed study of Australian spears argued convincingly that much of the variation in their form and in their complexity of manufacture can be explained not in functional terms but in sociological terms reflecting and objectifying the skill and individuality of the maker and factors such as clan identity.[47]

Shields, for example, vary significantly across Australia. The broad rainforest shields of Queensland are painted with striking totemic designs (fig. 56). These are in contrast to the smaller wunda shields of the Pilbara, their narrow hardwood forms deeply incised with geometric patterns (figs 57–58). In turn, these are noticeably different in form and design from the engraved shields of south-east Australia (fig. 59). Yet there is arguably as much variation between these south-eastern shields as there is between them and the engraved shields of the north-west.

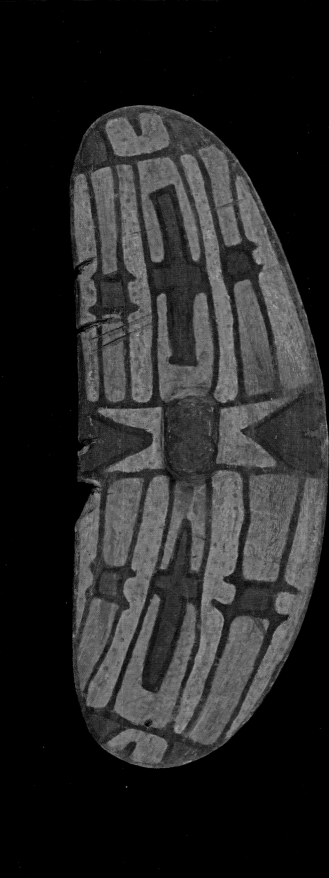

56.
Rainforest shield
The distinctive shape results from the curve of the buttress roots of the fig tree. The maker may have used Reckitts Blue, a laundry whitener, which is bright blue in its concentrated form.

Mulgrave River region, near Cairns, Queensland,
c. 1900
Wood, natural pigment, Reckitts Blue; L. 1000 mm,
W. 375 mm
British Museum, London
Oc1933,0403.9 Exh. BM
Donated by Florence M. Walker

57.
Shield

Cossack, Western Australia, before 1896
Wood, natural pigment; L. 1010 mm, W. 222 mm, D. 45 mm
British Museum, London
Oc1896,-.1025 Exh. BM

58.
Shield

Broome region, Western Australia, c. 1885
Wood, natural pigment; L. 920 mm, W. 160 mm, D. 50 mm
British Museum, London
Oc,+.2419 Exh. BM
Donated by Frederick Napier Broome

59.
Shield

South-east Australia, before 1950
Wood; L. 1125 mm, W. 230 mm, D. 50 mm
British Museum, London
Oc1950,04.10 Exh. BM

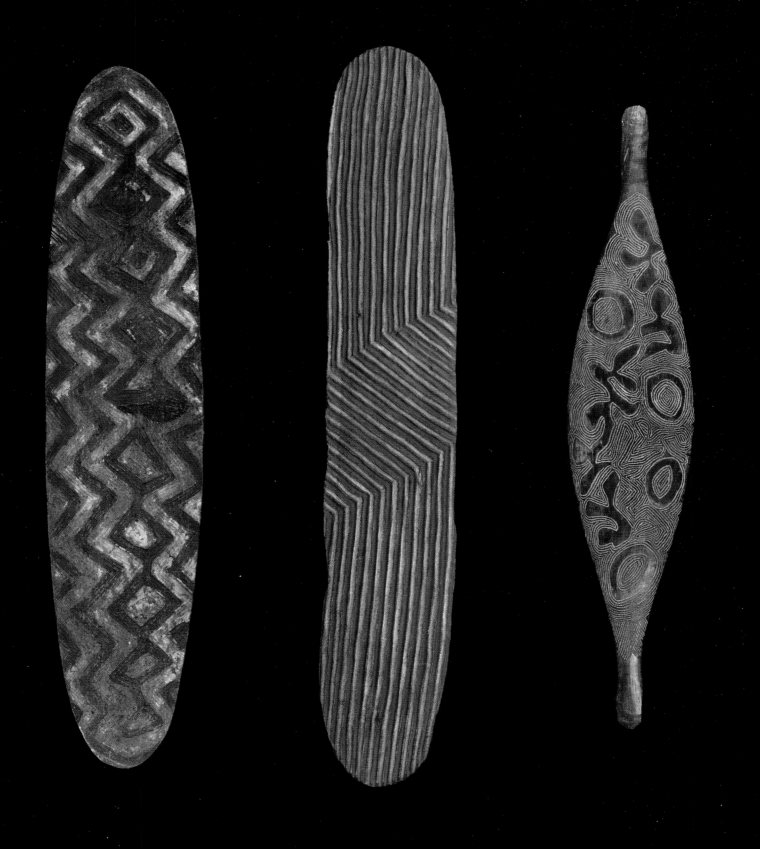

A symphony of lines: reading south-east shields
Jonathan Jones

Engraved with a symphony of lines, the shields of south-east Australia best exemplify the region's artistic cultural traditions. Both hardwood parrying shields and bark broad shields feature a celebration of diamonds, zigzags, squares, bands, circles, criss-crosses and dots that are scored and interwoven with the occasional figurative form. As with Western Desert acrylic painting or Arnhem Land bark painting, these iconic designs represent country and the actions of ancestors. In the superbly crafted broad shield (fig. 60) this idea of mapping country and tracing the arc of ancestral energy is witnessed – the face, divided down the centre by a recessed line, has been cloaked on one side with a series of meandering lines and spiralling circles and squares, and on the other with a rounded chevron design, which, together, speak unmistakably of a river landscape. The work can be read both geographically and symbolically, and to Rodney Carter (b. 1965), a Yorta Yorta and Dja Dja Wurrung man, 'the shields or the symbols upon the shields represent identity. You can liken them to what we use now as titles for our houses. The lines, the colours, the carvings – they tell people who you are, and, more importantly, they tell people where you come from.'[48]

The skill and time involved in creating shields, and the inherent cultural importance of their designs, saw the objects play a central role in south-east ceremonies and performances. Indeed, conflict was a highly ceremonial and organised activity and when used in this context shields and their designs would have assisted the bearer, calling up the power of their country and ancestors. National Museum of Australia researcher Carol Cooper stresses the communicative role of shields, which, she argues, 'had the power to create optical illusions during battle, a quality enhanced by the dexterity of the warriors'.[49] In an 1898 ceremony along the Macquarie River in central-western New South Wales, shields were documented by photographer Charles Kerry (1857–1928) in a series of rare images. Boomerangs create arches, clubs pierce earthen mounds and shields are caked in ochre, all playing an active part. Ochre remnants from these types of activities can still

60.
Broad shield

Attributed to Victoria, before 1857
Wood; L. 940 mm, W. 203 mm
British Museum, London
Oc.1814
Donated by Royal Botanic
Gardens, Kew

61.
Broad shield

South-east Australia,
mid-19th century
Wood, natural pigment;
L. 1015 mm, W. 210 mm
British Museum, London
Oc1921,1014.79 Exh. BM

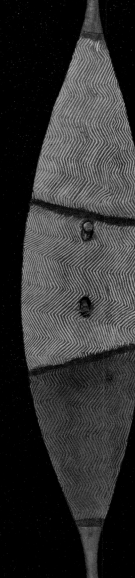

be seen on many shields today (figs 61–63). Ultimately, shields were an important part of funerary practices: 'a warrior is usually wrapped in his opossum rug, tied tightly, and buried with his weapons and all his worldly possessions',[50] and notably this important tradition was performed for the Wiradjuri warrior and hero Windradyne (*c*. 1800–1829) in 1828. In these ways, shields and their designs are communicative ceremonial objects existing as part of a complex cultural and social fabric.

It was these designs that unwittingly captured the attention of outside audiences, with shields, clubs, boomerangs and woomeras (spearthrowers) collected en masse as part of the larger colonial and imperial project. As frontier violence swept across south-east Australia a handful of colonists amassed collections and traded objects as exotic souvenirs. This scavenging in the frontier aftermath saw material culture used as a tool of propaganda to justify popular scientific and museological theories of the day. Men's weapons dominated colonial collections, and achieved the dual purpose of manufacturing the image of the noble savage while disarming south-east nations, rendering them vulnerable. This acquisition process was first established by Australia's 'founders', Captain James Cook (1728–1779) and Sir Joseph Banks (1743–1820), who in a pre-emptive strike in 1770 fired on a group of Gweagal men, including one man remembered as Cooman or Goomun,[51] that resisted their landing in Kamay, known today as Botany Bay. Once the Gweagal had been dispersed the first-known collection of Aboriginal material was made, including spears described as lances and a broad shield described as a 'target' by Cook[52] for its painted design of a white background with symmetrical red lines, characteristic to Sydney and neighbouring coastal regions. South-east shields have remained targeted ever since.

A significant south-east shield was collected by Sir Thomas Mitchell (1792–1855) during his time as Surveyor General of the New South Wales colony from 1827 to 1855 (fig. 64). This stout parrying shield with its mixture of carved radiating diamonds, chevrons, criss-crosses and entwined lines speaks of a complex local cultural knowledge. As with many other south-east objects in museums, little is known about the context in which this object was collected even though it comes from a distinguished collector. It can be assumed that the shield was acquired on one of Mitchell's

62.
Broad shield

Attributed to Murrumbidgee River, New South Wales, before 1868
Wood, natural pigment;
L. 845 mm, W. 220 mm
British Museum, London
Oc.5180
Donated by Sir Augustus Wollaston Franks

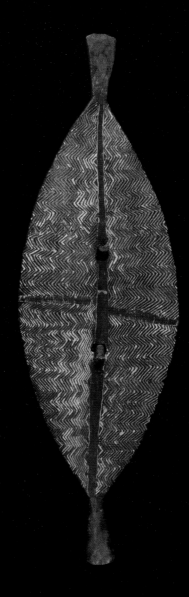

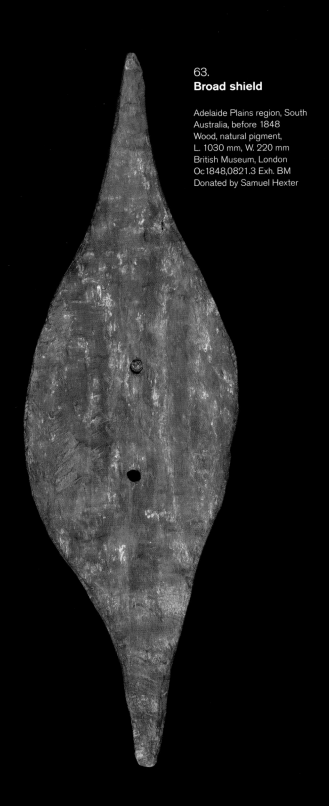

63.
Broad shield

Adelaide Plains region, South
Australia, before 1848
Wood, natural pigment,
L. 1030 mm, W. 220 mm
British Museum, London
Oc1848,0821.3 Exh. BM
Donated by Samuel Hexter

journeys into the south-east, where he was often the first European to venture. As such, this shield, along with the handful of other objects collected by Mitchell, represents one of the earliest known objects of material culture collected from the region. In a brief description in Mitchell's published diaries there is no mention of the shield's acquisition, leaving doubt over the object's origin. It is known that during his journeys Mitchell was engaged in a number of skirmishes that resulted in the murder of Aboriginal people, and so the discrepancies between his published and unpublished diaries raise a number of issues.[53] In light of this one cannot help but wonder if this shield is a trophy of Mitchell's conquest.

Within the turmoil of colonisation a handful of stalwart carvers continued to practise. Their engagement with introduced steel tools, including hatchets and knives traded along the frontier, played a significant part in this continuation. While Mitchell actively gifted many steel tools to ease his passage across country, the introduction of steel preceded the frontier, along with knowledge of the invaders and their diseases, by following traditional trade routes. Mitchell recalls a meeting on the Bogan River in central New South Wales with two men who he believed had never seen a European before but were already in possession of steel axes and knives.[54] For carvers, steel tools provided a new artistic freedom and enabled shields and their designs to take on different forms and elements. This is best seen in, the work of a Wiradjuri master carver from the Macquarie River (fig. 65). In this parrying shield harmony is created through the delicate rendering of concentric rectangles and squares and parallel straight lines, made possible by the new tool in the artist's hand. Not only did shield designs develop with steel tools, but also the use of hatchets and knives shows an adept understanding and ability of makers to Aboriginalise new tools.

Whether the shields they hold are trophies of war or were marketed and bartered, institutional collections weigh heavy on Aboriginal hearts. The removal of objects from country echoes the removal and dispossession of community from country, and the relocation to fringe camps and mission reserves. One of the key issues facing both south-east communities and institutions is the lack of documentation and provenance for most south-east material, including shields. Yet, as representations of our

64.
Parrying shield

South-east Australia, before 1839
Wood, natural pigment;
L. 815 mm, W. 150 mm
British Museum, London
Oc1839,1012.3
Donated by Thomas Mitchell

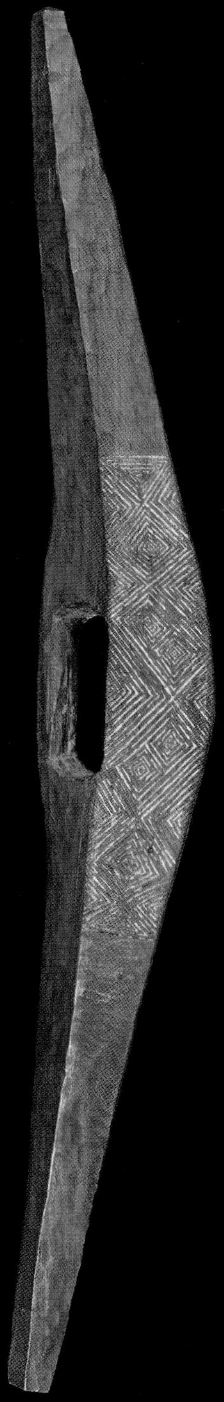

65.
Parrying shield

Attributed to Macquarie River, New
South Wales, before 1894
Wood, natural pigment;
L. 815 mm, W. 150 mm
Oc1894,-.279 Exh. BM
Donated by Sir Augustus Wollaston
Franks

ancestors and their knowledge, shields are like sheets of music waiting to be sung. Their unique markings tell us about the artists and their country, and by engaging with these objects and their histories it is possible to restore some of the cultural information that was lost by the colonial collecting project.

Along with identifying regional styles it is also possible to match master carvers' hands. For instance, the broad shield (fig. 66) has a unique design of interlocking bands of concentric diamonds and triangles with rounded corners threaded together by a series of zigzagging lines. This design bears a striking resemblance to a shield photographed with a man known as Guangnurd or Redman of the 'Goulbourne tribe', which refers to the Taungurung people whose land includes part of the Goulburn River in central Victoria. This photo was taken in collaboration with Guangnurd at the Victorian Aboriginal station of Coranderrk in 1866 by photographer Carl Walters (1831–1907), and begins to contextualise this beautiful shield[55] while conceptually relocating it from museum storeroom to country.

Making these connections can help to provide an insight into the artists, their families and their country. Today, museum collections can act as storehouses so that south-east communities can begin to reconstruct our past, connect with our ancestors and instruct the next generation. These actions begin to undo the acts of colonialism. Uncle Sandy Atkinson (b. 1932), a Moidaban elder, explains: 'These artefacts and this artwork, that's what we've got to learn from, from the past where art was an important way of life, where art was… a recording of history, it was a responsibility that the community gave to a person to record its stories. Our stories, everybody's stories.'[56] Shields and other objects in collections are gifts; gifts from our ancestors left to aid us on our new journeys and to become the springboard for many contemporary practices and understandings.

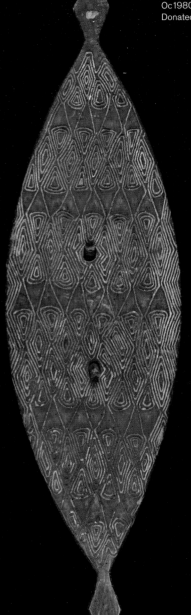

66.
Broad shield

Attributed to Goulburn River, Victoria, before 1872
Wood, natural pigment; L. 890 mm, W. 240 mm
British Museum, London
Oc1980,Q.721
Donated by Sir Augustus Wollaston Franks

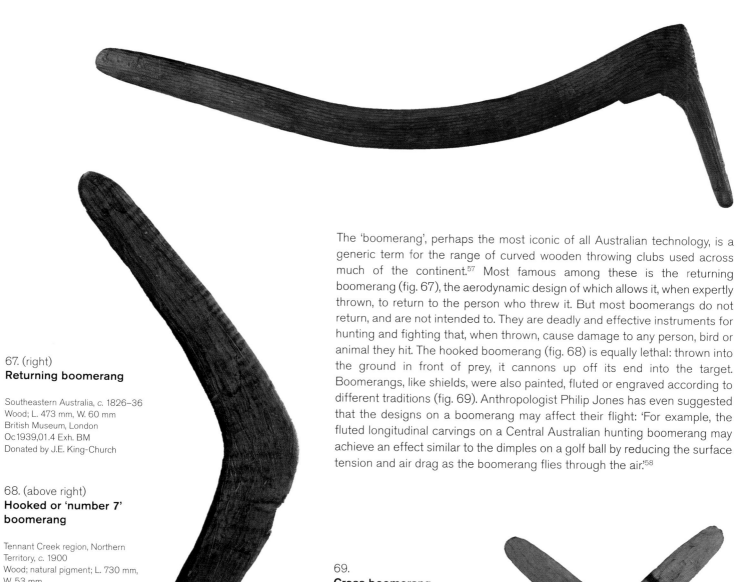

67. (right)
Returning boomerang

Southeastern Australia, c. 1826–36
Wood; L. 473 mm, W. 60 mm
British Museum, London
Oc1939,01.4 Exh. BM
Donated by J.E. King-Church

68. (above right)
Hooked or 'number 7' boomerang

Tennant Creek region, Northern
Territory, c. 1900
Wood; natural pigment; L. 730 mm,
W. 53 mm
British Museum, London
Oc1903,0404.73 Exh. BM
Donated by W. Baldwin Spencer
and Francis James Gillen

The 'boomerang', perhaps the most iconic of all Australian technology, is a generic term for the range of curved wooden throwing clubs used across much of the continent.[57] Most famous among these is the returning boomerang (fig. 67), the aerodynamic design of which allows it, when expertly thrown, to return to the person who threw it. But most boomerangs do not return, and are not intended to. They are deadly and effective instruments for hunting and fighting that, when thrown, cause damage to any person, bird or animal they hit. The hooked boomerang (fig. 68) is equally lethal: thrown into the ground in front of prey, it cannons up off its end into the target. Boomerangs, like shields, were also painted, fluted or engraved according to different traditions (fig. 69). Anthropologist Philip Jones has even suggested that the designs on a boomerang may affect their flight: 'For example, the fluted longitudinal carvings on a Central Australian hunting boomerang may achieve an effect similar to the dimples on a golf ball by reducing the surface tension and air drag as the boomerang flies through the air.'[58]

69.
Cross boomerang
This type of boomerang was made only in the rainforest region of north Queensland.

Mulgrave River region, near Cairns,
Queensland, c. 1900
Wood, fibre, pigment; L. 70 mm,
W. 70 mm, D. 15 mm
British Museum, London
Oc1933,0403.10 Exh. BM
Donated by Florence M. Walker

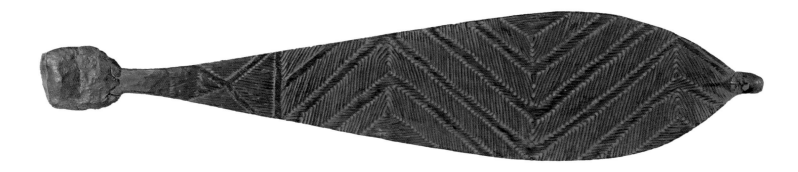

70.
Spearthrower

Victoria River, Northern Territory,
before 1905
Wood, natural pigment; L. 1230 mm,
W. 60 mm
British Museum, London
Oc1905,-.141
Donated by Joseph Bradshaw

71.
Spearthrower

North-west Australia, late 19th or early
20th century
Wood, stone, resin; L. 763 mm
British Museum, London
Oc1980,Q.747 Exh. BM

72.
Spearthrower

Alice Springs region, Northern Territory,
c. 1900
Wood, sinew, porcupine grass resin, flint;
L. 570 mm, W. 110 mm
British Museum, London
Oc1903,0404.54
Donated by W. Baldwin Spencer
and Francis James Gillen

73. (opposite)
Spearthrower
The design depicts a figure
wearing a possum-skin cloak.

Birregurra, Victoria, before 1867
Wood; L. 730 mm, W. 58 mm, D. 11 mm
British Museum, London
Oc.8067 Exh. BM
Donated by Sir Augustus Wollaston
Franks

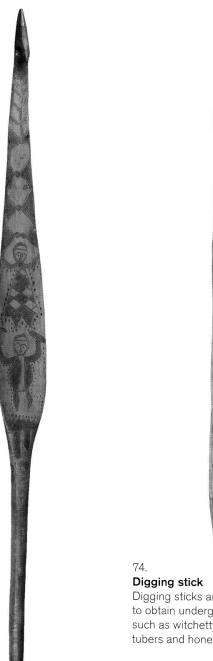

74.
Digging stick
Digging sticks are used
to obtain underground food
such as witchetty grubs, plant
tubers and honey ants.

Adelaide region, South Australia,
c. 1848
Wood; L. 853 mm, Diam. 30 mm
British Museum, London
Oc1848,0821.2 Exh. BM
Donated by Samuel Hexter

While boomerangs remain the icon of Australian engineering, the spearthrower equally encapsulates the genius of Aboriginal people in creating refined, portable technologies that mediate their relationship to specific environments. Spearthrowers operate by improving the natural leverage of the arm. Held in the throwing hand with a spear fixed into its end, the spearthrower enables the spear to be projected with greater velocity and accuracy than by using the human arm alone. While its primary function was common across the continent, its shape and composition varied according to the raw materials available, the form of the spears to be thrown, and the additional purposes for which the object was intended to be used (figs 70–71).

Created and used exclusively by men, a *lankurru* (in Pintupi) or *amirre* (in Arrernte) was arguably the most important part of the male material repertoire (fig. 72). It is the Swiss Army knife of the desert. It is a spearthrower but its broad body hints at its other functions. Its firm edges were used for digging in the desert sand and scraping the ground in preparing a place to sleep. Those same hardwood edges were sawed furiously against softer wood to create the smouldering embers by which desert people made fire. In some parts of Australia stone knives were hafted to its end with natural resins, allowing the spearthrower to be used for butchering animals and also as a chisel for engraving other objects. Extra stone flakes or kangaroo teeth (also used as engravers) were set into the resin and carried as spares in order to make repairs.

The spearthrower itself is often decorated with paintings, engravings or incisions of totemic and personal importance to its owner (fig. 73). This aesthetic aspect is as important as their role in projecting spears. As ceremonial objects, and emblems of the owner's status, skill and authority, spearthrowers perform equally important functions. In this, the spearthrower reminds us that the objects that made life possible also make the world meaningful.

Spearthrowers demonstrate, along with the shields, spear points and baskets already discussed, the principle that everyday material culture provides the basis for the development of ceremonial forms used in religious or political contexts. Boomerangs, brutally efficient as hunting instruments, are equally as important as musical ones: their flat, inverse sides are clapped together to keep time for the singers and dancers in ritual and ceremonial performance. Spears are painted and carved incorporating such complex structures of barbs that almost made them non-functional as weapons. Even the humble digging stick became elaborated in its ceremonial form, elegantly carved, bound in possum-fur string and embellished with feather work – a ceremonial staff that was in turn a testament to the importance of the digging stick in daily life (fig. 74).

The Dreaming: environment, history and art

Just as Australian material culture expresses a range of localised variations from a suite of core objects and technologies, so too do Aboriginal belief and knowledge systems reveal continental variations underpinned by a bedrock of common principles. Australia is governed by localised and environmentally specific belief systems that, however unique to each people and their area, exhibit obvious cosmological and epistemological similarities. Across the continent, ancestral beings – often human or animal, sometimes both – emerged from and moved across unformed landscapes, their actions creating the features of the natural world and the stories of their travels encoding the social, moral and ecological laws that humans were to live by. These ways of understanding the meaningful creation of the world, and how humans fit into it and reproduce that system through meaningful action, is commonly glossed in English as the 'Dreamtime'. It is not possible to begin to understand the Aboriginal worlds that Europeans first encountered in Australia without addressing the meanings of this term.

In Warlpiri and Martu, people refer to the creation period, and its ongoing authority, as *Jukurrpa*. Noongar people of south-west Australia call it *Nyitting*. Yolngu people of Arnhem Land frame their own concept as *Wangarr*, whereas in the Kimberley it is alternatively *Ngarrankarni*, *Waljirri* or *Ungud*, depending on the location and language spoken. In the Tiwi Islands this concept is spoken of as *Parlingari*. For the Eora people around present-day Sydney, and for other language groups in the surrounding regions, *Baiame* is the primary creator. For the Worora, Ngarinyin and Wunambal people of the Kimberley the Wandjina are the creation ancestors (fig. 75). In the Torres Strait Islands, where creator ancestors such as *Tagai* unite seagoing people in shared understandings of their specific histories and environments, cosmology varies from the mainland and notions of the Dreaming are arguably less applicable.

Suffice it to say there are as many terms for the concept of the Dreaming or Dreamtime as there are cultural groups in Australia. The term itself is only a hundred or so years old, having been coined by Frank Gillen (1855–1912) and popularised by his research partner – the anthropologist Baldwin Spencer – in publications at the turn of the twentieth century.[59] In these contexts the concept of 'dream times' was employed to help explain or interpret the Arrernte term for their cosmological system – *Alcheringa* (now written as *Altyerrenge*). In her 2009 book, *Listen Deeply: Let These Stories In*, Arrernte elder Kathleen Kemarre Wallace (b. 1948) explained:

> *Arrernte* people believe that there was a spirit long before anyone or anything existed and that this spirit made the earth first, then the stars, and then people. We call this *altyerrenge*; it's the time which was the beginning.… The *altyerre* beings brought

75.
Wandjina
Wandjina are spirit ancestors for the Worora, Ngarinyin and Wunambal people of the western Kimberley region. The repainting of Wandjina on rock ensures the arrival of the monsoonal rains.

Charlie Allungoy (Numbulmoore) (*c.* 1907–1971), Ngarinyin
Mowanjum, Kimberley region, Western Australia, 1970
Pigment on composition board; H. 1370 mm, W. 1216 mm
National Museum of Australia, Canberra
1985.0173.0012 Exh. BM

the earth into being and gave the *Arrernte* body and spirit
so life could have a form…. 'We'll teach them everything',
the altyerre beings said. That's how people learnt about hunting,
what seeds to gather, how to relate to one another, and how
to keep their bodies and spirits strong through the healing arts
and ceremonies.[60]

Altyerrenge, for Spencer and Gillen, referred to the time of creation, which in Arrernte has a resonance with the human state of dreaming. *Altyerre* is an Arrernte word for dream and the suffix *-enge* signifies possession or belonging to: hence Spencer and Gillen's translation of the term as 'Dream Time'. While the specific relationship between Aboriginal concepts of cosmology and dreaming is not universal across the continent, the term Dreamtime (or Dreaming) has become widely used by both Aboriginal and non-aboriginal Australians as a cross-cultural approximation of an Aboriginal concept such as outlined by Wallace.

The Dreaming or Dreamtime remains useful because Aboriginal concepts such as *Wangarr* or *Waljirri* cannot be easily reduced to existing Western words or concepts. They are not simply words for the creation period, or for religion, or for the moral basis of contemporary action. The Dreamtime cannot be understood in reductive terms, as the anthropologist W.E.H. Stanner (1905–1981) observed, but only as 'a complex of meanings'.[61] The inextricable grounding of religious thought, metaphysics and morality in the landscapes from which it emerged is a defining feature of Aboriginal Australia.

Take the Western Desert concept of *Tjukurrpa* as an example. During the Tjukurrpa, ancestral beings emerged from an unformed land and moved across the desert singing, performing ceremonies and interacting with one another. They left behind their songs, ritual designs and moral lessons for humans to follow. More often than not, much like the Greek gods, their actions provided models for how humans should not act. Jealousy, selfishness, violence, environmental degradation and unregulated sexual behaviour are prominent (and often painful) lessons to be learnt from Tjukurrpa. These lessons are not abstracted into texts, however, but remain written in the forms of the landscape. As ancestral beings travelled, and learnt or failed to learn their lessons, they created the features of the country – including the plants, animals and humans – in which these tales were immortalised. At the end of these journeys, the ancestors returned to the earth, themselves transformed into important waters, hills and rocks, where they reside today in sites of great cultural significance. Other beings, such as the Seven Sisters, ended their journeys in the sky, becoming the stars by which people navigated their world. These ancestral narratives, wherever they end, form an intricate network of Dreaming tracks or 'songlines' that criss-cross the country. In figure 76, it is possible to see the extraordinary density of Dreamings or songlines that

76.
The geography of Spinifex Tjukurrpa
A representation of Dreaming stories passing through Spinifex country.

Drawing: Scott Cane

77. (overleaf)
Spinifex salt pans
The arid lands of the Spinifex people are dotted with clay pans and salt lakes. The traditional owners of this country see it as a sacred geography rich in meaning and crossed by Dreamings, or songlines, of creation ancestors.

North-west of Tjuntjuntjara, Great Victoria Desert, Western Australia
Photograph: Louise Allerton

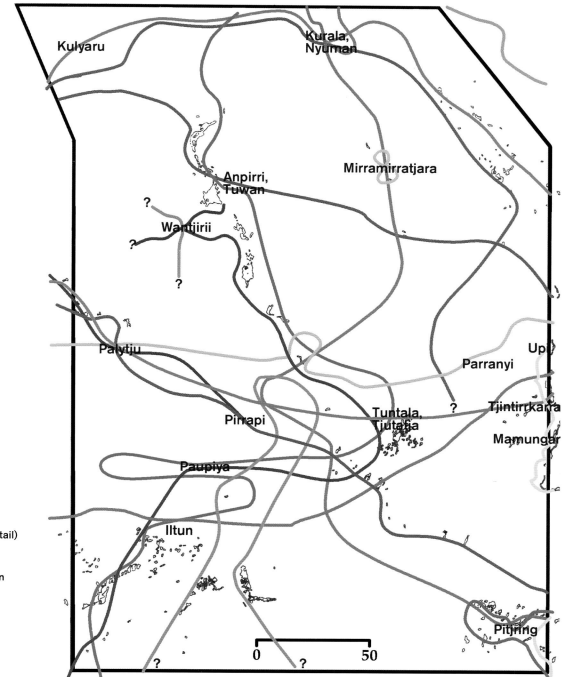

Kulyaru

Kurala,
Nyuman

Mirramirratjara

Anpirri,
Tuwan

?

Wantjirii

?

?

Palytju

Up

Parranyi

?

Tjintirrkarra

Pirrapi

Tuntala,
Tjutatja

Mamungar

Paupiya

Iltun

Pitjiring

███	Bush Turkey
███	Zebra Finch
███	Many Evil Spirits
███	Two Men
███	Seven Sisters
███	Python Man
███	Eagle Hawk (Wedgetail)
███	Woman and Sons
███	Thorny Devil
███	Scrub Kangaroo Man
███	Native Cat Men
███	Water Snake
███	Emu Man
███	Feral Cat Man
███	Dingo Man
███	Old Man

?

0   ?   50

?

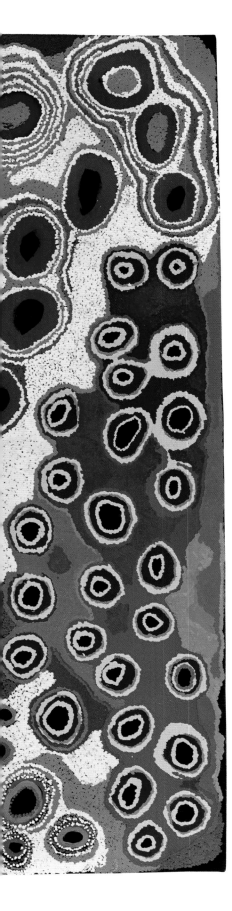

intersect in the country of the Spinifex people (fig. 77). Imagine, then, an entire continent scored by this music.

Just one of the many Dreamings that passes through Spinifex territory is that of the *Kungkarangkalpa*, or Seven Sisters. It involves the travels of a group of women who, in singing and dancing, created aspects of the landscape. The women were pursued by a lustful man, here his name is Nyiiru, who was forever attempting to have his way with the women. The women tricked Nyiiru and escaped into the sky where they became the Pleiades constellation of stars.

The journeys of the seven sisters provide people with pathways through the land, maps to important sites and vital waters, moral lessons, and political structures that ground desert life. No one person can sing the whole songline without the help of other people who are custodians for its different sites and the different verses of the song associated with those sites. Such Dreamings are never held by one person, but are managed by many different people who can speak for the specific sections of the narrative that cross their country, and which link them to the country and people either side of them. Likewise no one individual today can paint the whole story.

In figure 78, six senior Spinifex women have painted country associated with their respective birthplaces and the Kungkarangkalpa (Seven Sisters) songline. The knowledge embedded in these stories is held collectively by senior people. It is passed on from generation to generation through ritual and everyday learning, and increasingly today through artistic practice.

The Seven Sisters is a narrative that emerges across the continent, in various guises, names and places with localised narrative shifts, but the basis of the Dreaming is remarkably consistent. Another Dreaming that manifests in familiar ways across the continent is that of a Rainbow Serpent, the great snake-like creature in the sky whose tongue forks in lightning and whose body arcs away in a rainbow of colour after the rain (fig. 79). In desert languages the creatures have different names such as *Wanyarra* or *Wanampi*; for Noongar people it is *Waugal*; in western Arnhem Land, *Ngalyod*. In the European imagination gigantic flying reptiles breathe fire; in a dry continent such as Australia they are almost universally associated with water or the

78.
Kungkarangkalpa (Seven Sisters)

Kunmanara Hogan (*c.* 1945–2014), Pitjantjatjara;
Tjaruwa Woods (b. 1954), Pitjantjatjara; Yarangka Thomas
(b. *c.* 1939), Pitjantjatjara; Estelle Hogan, (b. *c.* 1937),
Pitjantjatjara; Ngalpingka Simms (b. *c.* 1945), Ngaanyatjarra;
and Myrtle Pennington (b. *c.* 1939), Pitjantjatjara
Tjuntjuntjara, Great Victoria Desert, Western Australia, 2013
Acrylic on canvas; H. 1970 mm, W. 2330 mm
British Museum, London
2014,2009.1 Exh. BM
Donated by BP

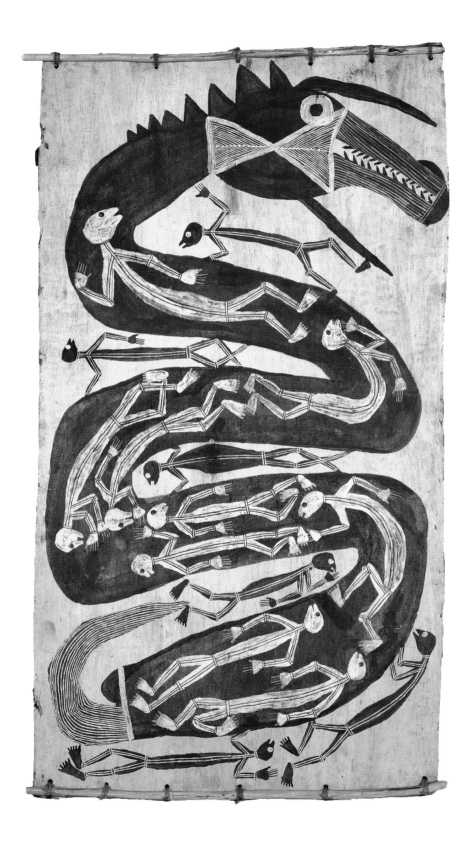

79.
Yingarna, the Rainbow Serpent

Bilinyara Nabegeyo (*c.* 1920–1978), Yirridjdja moiety,
Kunwinjku, late 1960s or early 1970s
Natural pigment on bark; H. 1145 mm, W. 619 mm
Pitt Rivers Museum, University of Oxford
1982.12.1 Exh. BM
Bequeathed by Kenneth Page Oakley

80.
Eel trap

Lake Condah, Victoria, before 1902
Grass fibre; L. 1840 mm, W. 530 mm, D. 550 mm
Museum Victoria, Melbourne
X 016265

81.
Eileen Alberts by a stone eel trap and constructed water channel at Kurtonij, Victoria

Victoria, 2014
Photograph: John Carty

coming of rain. Valleys and rivers reveal the paths these serpents took through the land in the creation period; waterholes and springs are often the sites where they entered the land, and in some cases where they continue to live today.

Dreaming and environment

The Rainbow Serpent and the Seven Sisters are remarkable for the fact that they are found, in similar manifestations, across the continent. But they are also unique in this relative universality: the vast majority of Dreamings are incredibly specific and localised. The ancestors of the Tjukurrpa, in their restless movement from place to place, water to water, provided a blueprint for the way in which desert people would need to live by travelling, to manage relationships and resources, in order to thrive in the harsh climate. The songs these ancestors left behind are maps of their travels, and maps for the travels of the desert people who would follow behind them. Such songs of ancestors who travelled vast distances finding spring waters in desert sands would be unintelligible linguistically, but also unhelpful practically, to Queensland rainforest people.

The Dreaming, unlike many forms of religious thought that have become elaborated into global institutions, remains intimately bound to the specific environments from which it came. The Dreaming as a concept tells us a great deal about what makes Australia unique in global cultures, but it is in the specific Dreamings themselves that the ancestors provide insight into the nature of different kinds of cultural groups within Australia.

Budj Bim

> In the Dreaming, the ancestral creators gave the Gunditjmara people the resources to live a settled lifestyle. They diverted the waterways, and gave us the stones and rocks to help us build the aquaculture systems. They gave us the wetlands where the reeds grew so that we could make the eel baskets, and they gave us the food enriched landscape for us to survive.[62]
> Eileen Alberts, Gunditjmara (b. 1953; figs 80–81)

Perhaps the pivotal Dreamtime ancestor for the Gunditjmara people of south-west Victoria is Budj Bim, who revealed himself in the eruption of a volcano (Mount Eccles) some 7,000 years ago. The eruption of Budj Bim, which was perhaps catastrophic for the people of the time, became a foundation story for the Gundijtmara. From his head came an explosion of cultural ingenuity, as the basalt rocks from the lava flows became the basis for the one of the world's first aquaculture systems. Budj Bim is the ancestor who provided the ecological foundations for the Gunditjmara to remodel their world. Over thousands of years following the volcanic eruptions the lava flows cooled and cracked into the building blocks of a dynamic Gunditjmara culture and society. The basalt rocks that allowed people to redesign, and control, the landscape and its resources, also became the foundations of their domestic permanence in the Budj Bim landscape (see fig. 43, p. 62).

Wati Nyiinyii

Other Dreamings provide insights into the environmental events that shaped the Australian continent and the lives and culture of the people who stood witness to them. Another songline or Dreaming of the Spinifex people is that of *Wati Nyiinyii*. Nyiinyii are Zebra Finches, which are among the most common birds in Australia and particularly in the desert regions. The Nyiinyii Dreaming follows the travels of the Zebra Finch people from north of the Spinifex country, through the sand dunes of the Great Victoria Desert, south across the largely treeless Nullarbor Plain to the Great Australian Bight – the cliffs that run into the Great Southern Ocean at the base of the continent. It is a vast narrative containing detailed social, political and cultural information, much of which is restricted to initiated men. The core itinerary of the Nyiinyii, as held by the Spinifex people, is open knowledge and provides extraordinary insight into environmental aspects of the Dreaming.

> The Nyiinyii were travelling south, through Spinifex country toward the sea, in great numbers and according to finely delineated socio-cultural formations. Within this coherent social group an old man travelling with them causes disorder.
>
> The old man is typically associated with greed – invariably hoarding water for himself. He is also notoriously ruinous to the life of the Wati Nyiinyii. Most significantly, he constantly 'damages' their habitat – ripping up trees and creating general natural disturbance.
>
> In one location, near a beautiful, sacred waterhole in a creek, the old man uproots the 'water trees' (mallee eucalyptus with water in the roots) and this causes scarce water to be lost. The water drains into the ground, creating a huge flood to the south. To regain the water and stop its intrusion over the land to the south, the Wati Nyiinyii are obliged to travel to Eucla to stop the encroaching flood…
>
> Once the Wati Nyiinyii reach the sea they begin bundling thousands of spears to stop the encroaching water. These bundles were stacked very high and managed to contain the

water at the base of what is today the Nullarbor (or Bunda) cliffs and the Hampton escarpment.[63]

It is possible that the Wati Nyiinyii Dreaming encodes ancient historical knowledge about the rise in sea levels when, following the last Ice Age approximately 10,000 years ago, the ice caps melted. At this time the sea levels around Australia rose dramatically, flooding almost a third of the continent. These levels stabilised around 7,000 years ago, when the current coastline reached its present position. The Wati Nyiinyii, like a number of Aboriginal myths recorded across northern and southern Australia in particular, may date back to that ancient and incredible environmental event, their spears holding back the flood for another 7,000 years.[64] If this is the case then the Wati Nyiinii Tjukurrpa is very, very old, and should, as the anthropologist Scott Cane observes, be numbered among 'the oldest extant spiritual traditions on earth'.[65] There are a number of Aboriginal narratives around the continent that appear to date back to, or record, these extraordinary events. It is thought that at one time the Tiwi Islands, now some 80 kilometres off the coast of Darwin, were part of the Australian mainland. Rising sea levels are thought to have cut the Tiwi off from the mainland at least 6,000 years ago. Tiwi origin stories suggest a kindred understanding.

> Long ago there were no people on the earth and darkness covered the land. There were no rivers or billabongs, there was no water in the streams, no hills or valleys. There were no animals living in the sea, no fish, turtles or crocodiles. Above the sky there lived the Yamparriparri, the spirits who roamed around the earth looking for living things that they could devour. Below the earth there was a large cave separating it from the earth by a valley and hills. Here in this land beneath the earth there were some people who roamed about in the darkness. Among these people there lived one old woman. She was really big and bent and her face was lined and wrinkled. Her name was Murtankala. On her back she carried her children, two girls and a boy. One day she dug her way from the cave below and arrived on the earth… Murtankala placed her children in a bark basket and tied it around her neck for she was afraid of the Yamparriparri people because they might want to eat her children.
>
> So then she began to crawl at that place where she had arrived on the earth. When she crawled along she made a large hole behind her and the sea water began to rush in behind her back. She was facing towards where the sun now rises and her face was turned to that eastern side, she crawled on and after a long time returned to where she first started and so she created these two islands.[66]

82.

Barama/Captain Cook

The sculpture represents the Yolngu ancestral being Barama at the sacred water hole of Gängan to the north of Blue Mud Bay. Barama was the great creator ancestor of the Yirritja moiety. However, two heads facing away from each other are painted onto the top of the pole. The artist referred to the two portraits as Barama and 'Captain Cook' without specifying which is which. Both ancestors attempt to imbue the land with law using their sacred objects. In Captain Cook's case it is the flagpole brought to Australia. Barama held two ceremonial staff, which can be seen carved in relief at either side of the pole. The designs on the body refer to events that took place in ancestral times with a fish trap placed in the river and freshwater flowing downstream. The designs and associated songs link the ancestral powers to the seasonal cycle changing from the dry to the wet season. The sacred patterns that flow down the pole show Barama's law to be still in place, holding on to Yolngu land.

Gawirrin 1 Gumana (b. 1935)
Dhalwangu clan, Yirritja moiety, Yolngu
Yirrkala, northeastern Arnhem Land, Northern Territory,
c. 2002
Pigment on wood; H. 3120 mm, Diam. 200 mm
British Museum, London
Oc2003,01.2 Exh. BM
Sponsored by British Museum Friends

The sea water that flowed into Murtankala's tracks became the Apsley Strait, which separates Bathurst and Melville Island today, and the Clarence and Dundas Straits, which divide the Tiwi world from the Australian mainland.

The Dreaming and history

In each of these cases the translated concept of the Dreaming or Dreamtime exists as the creation period. But in localised usage they are far from denoting a mythological past. The Dreaming is a deeply ecological system of knowledge, encoding information about changing environments and climates, changing technologies and changing peoples.

Apart from environmental change, introduced species, such as dogs, and other peoples, have also become absorbed into the Dreaming. Dingoes, thought to have arrived in Australia at least 3,500 years ago,[67] became an integral part of Aboriginal daily life and are woven into the fabric of the Dreaming. Yolngu people incorporated the history of their relationships with the Makassans within their religious system, in ways which made the Makassans themselves part of Yolngu history. A song cycle that recounts aspects of the life of the Makassans is associated with Yolngu mortuary rituals. At the end of the wet season the Makassans set sail back to Sulawesi. Their departure was a time of celebration and sadness – of wishing farewell to the boats at the end of a successful season and anticipating their return in a few years time. Yolngu burial ceremonies centre on saying goodbye to the spirit of the person who has died and ensuring the return of the soul to the spiritual dimension. After the body is buried a ceremony can be performed that re-enacts the departure of the Makassans as an analogue for the departure of the soul. A sand sculpture is made in the form of a Makassan prau or a dwelling, and a pole, from which a flag is flown, is placed in the ground. People perform songs and dances that they would have performed at the departure of the Makassans, waving flags, dancing with 'swords' and eating celebratory meals. They act out life on the ship and sway from side to side, shading their eyes with their hands as they look across the sea for land. The songs provide a detailed account of their experience with the Makassans, long before any of the present generation was born. The Makassans are kept alive through ritual.

More recently, archetypal figures in settler Australian history such as Ned Kelly (1854–1880) and Captain Cook have become ancestral figures in Aboriginal stories and rituals (fig. 82).[68] The Dreaming is not a mythic story that can be opposed to 'history' as it is commonly understood in Western thought. It is a broader system of knowledge in which historical events unfold, and through which the lessons of historical change are absorbed, translated and remembered for future generations. This remembering, in the oral cultures of Australia, is done through song, story and ritual.

Understanding country

Dreaming and ritual: art and ceremony

> Bearing in mind that a performance of a central Australian songline may consist of hundreds of different song texts, the depth of knowledge it embodies and that is required for its decipherment is staggering. Truly the long song series of Australia are among the most impressive monuments of human culture.[69]

The most important accomplishments of Aboriginal and Torres Strait Islander people are not in museums because they are not collectable. Having perfected their daily technologies over thousands of years of refinement, Indigenous people across Australia invested their time and energies heavily in the other core technologies of their existence – religion and the aesthetic practices of painting, singing, dancing, music (fig. 83), sculpture and costume – through which it was constituted. Ritual and ceremonies, epic in scale and operatic in their drama, performed over days and weeks, sometimes over vast distances, are among the great artistic achievements of Australian life.

Nothing in Aboriginal Australia was left to chance. People did not wait for the ancestors, the seasons or the animals to come to them by fortune or fate, but understood themselves as active and necessary agents in the maintenance of social, ecological and cosmological order. Rituals perform many functions, among the most common being those that accompany human beings as they pass from one stage of life to another. Initiations into adulthood, or mortuary rites for those transitioning out of life, were (and remain) prominent features of the ritual calendar.

Also of great importance are rituals that address the seasonal and ecological cycles of life. In parts of Australia even the coming of rain could not be left to chance, and elaborate rituals ensured the delicate balance in dry country. Riji (pearl shell; see p. 42), with their iridescent surfaces, are associated with the rainbow serpent for Bardi people in the west Kimberley. Riji are particularly prized trade items by desert people, for whom the coming of rain could be a life or death proposition.

The great Wandjina beings of the western Kimberley region are also associated with rain. These iconic beings are said to have emerged from the sea and sky, creating features of the earth, before being absorbed into rock walls in their own haloed and mouthless image. The Worora, Wunambal and Ngarinyin people, whose country is populated by these Wandjina paintings, ensured the arrival of the monsoon rains, and the ongoing fertility of the land, by repainting these images in fresh ochre.[70] Donny Woolagoodja (b. 1947) continues this practice of refreshing the Wandjina today (fig. 84).

Fertility or 'increase' ceremonies and practices are targeted at increasing or maintaining the natural resources available to people, but are also an expression of custodians executing their reciprocal responsibilities

83.
Didgeridoo
A didgeridoo is a wind
instrument originally
made and used by men
from Arnhem Land and
neighbouring regions in
northern Australia. The name
didgeridoo derives from the
sound of the instrument.
In Arnhem Land, didgeridoos
are played to accompany
singing.

Groote Eylandt, Northern Territory,
c. 1963
Wood, pigment; L. 387 mm
British Museum, London
Oc1965,03.3 Exh. BM

84.
**Donny Woolagoodja (b. 1947) repainting
a Wandjina in his country**

Photograph: Sahyma Lachman

to the land. Sometimes these involved ceremonies restricted to certain categories of people; at other times they involved public paintings on rock walls.

Just as mainlanders worked to turn the environment into their garden, so too did Torres Strait Islanders seek to do the same with the sea (fig. 85), crafting species-specific charms, such as the dugong charm depicted here (fig. 86), to help in their hunting and fishing endeavours. These modest figures were carved out of stone or wood, and hung on boats or hunting platforms to assist hunters in attracting and killing dugong. Islanders also sought to ensure their own land-based gardens and crops were similarly successful by supplementing their agricultural practices with garden charms, such as figure 87.

85.
Female figure of coral
Such figures embody spirits who roam widely over the island of Mer. Their power is still potent.

Mer, Torres Strait, Queensland, before 1889
Coral; L. 23 mm, W. 190 mm, D. 90 mm
British Museum, London
Oc,89+.185 Exh. BM
Donated by A.C. Haddon

86.
Dugong charm

Tudu, Torres Strait, Queensland, before 1889
Stone, fibre, natural pigment; L. 220 mm, W. 90 mm,
D. 115 mm
British Museum, London
Oc,89+.184 Exh. BM
Donated by A.C. Haddon

87.
Garden charm
This charm is associated with the growth of strong tobacco crops.

Mer, Torres Strait, Queensland, before 1889
Wood, pigment; H. 690 mm, W. 20 mm, D. 125 mm
British Museum, London
Oc,89+.176 Exh. BM
Donated by A.C. Haddon

88.
Lulumu, the ancestral Stingray
Yolngu people maintain the sculpture, which
has been at this site for over a hundred years.

Yilpara, Blue Mud Bay, eastern Arnhem Land
Photograph: Peter Eves

More elaborate sculptural interventions in resource management are observed in Arnhem Land, near Yilpara in the country of the Madarrpa clan. Here there is a remarkable, huge ground sculpture representing the ancestral stingray Lulumu, which has been maintained by Yolngu for over a hundred years (fig. 88).[71] The eyes of the stingray are prominent in the foreground and the long tail can be seen extending into the distance. It marks a place where Lulumu stopped as he raced inland, biting the ground in anger from a spear wound, before returning to the sea where his tail can be seen today transformed into a coral reef extending out from the shore. Where he bit the ground, freshwater wells were created. Today, before going out fishing, Yolngu will sometimes place the bones of a previous meal in Lulumu's eyes: a gesture of benediction, simultaneously of thanks and hope.

Funerals

Australia is home to perhaps the oldest ritualised burial practices in the world. The archaeological discoveries of Mungo Man and Mungo Woman at Willandra Lakes, and the dating of their burials at approximately 42,000 years ago, provide evidence of the world's earliest ritual ochre burial and the first recorded human cremation.[72] The bodies of Mungo Man and Mungo Woman, sprinkled with ochre by those who laid them to rest, locate the spiritual beliefs and practices of Indigenous Australians among the oldest human traditions on the planet. Funeral and mourning rites in many places today continue to use ochre and find diverse expression across various cultural groups. Colonisation and Christianisation resulted in the interruption, or in some cases prevention, of different practices. Many people now observe Christian funeral rites, or adapt and incorporate aspects of Christian traditions into Indigenous mourning practices. Given the enormous social and health issues Indigenous people face in the wake of colonisation, mortality rates are far higher than those of non-Indigenous Australians.[73] As such, funerals and 'sorry business' are rituals of increased regularity and importance across Australia.[74]

Tiwi funerals continue to define Tiwi identity and life. Just as Tiwi creation stories represent the islands as a separate geographic region (see p. 93) from mainland Australia, the same narrative continues, through the children of Murtankala, to explore how Tiwi people came to characterise themselves, through their mortuary practices, as culturally different as well. Purrukuparli was the son of Murtankala, whose creative journeys were described previously:

> Purrukuparli lived with his wife Bima and their infant son Jinani. He was very fond of his son. Every morning when Bima went out food gathering she would take Jinani with her. In the same camp lived a man called Japarra, who persuaded Bima to leave her child asleep under the shade of a tree and sneak into the bush with him. On one very hot day Bima, stayed away from her child too long. The shade moved and she returned to find her infant son dead in the hot sun. When Purrukuparli heard of the death of Jinani he was enraged. Striking his wife on her head with a throwing stick and hunting her into the forest, he decreed that death should come to the whole world. As his son had died, so the whole of creation would die. There was no death before that time. Japarra pleaded with Purrukuparli for the dead body of Jinani, promising to restore him to life in three days. But Purrukuparli got angry and he fought with Japarra using throwing sticks, each wounding the other severely in the face and body. Purrukuparli picked up the body of his son and walked into the sea, calling out loudly – 'you must all follow me; as I die, so must you all die'.[75]

89.
Tunga (bark basket)

Tiwi Islands, late 19th or early 20th century
Bark, pigment; H. 674 mm, W. 507 mm, D. 405 mm
British Museum, London
Oc1913,-.145 Exh. BM
Donated by William Collings Dawson

90.
***Tunga* on top of *Pukamani* (funerary) poles.**
The poles are commissioned by the family of the deceased.

Pularumpi, Melville Island, 1978
Photograph: Margie West

The death of Jinani brought the creation period to a close. This event was marked by the first *Pukamani* burial ceremony, when Purrukuparli organised the funeral rites for his dead son. These rites, and aesthetic elaboration of them, are among the most important events in Tiwi life. The Pukamani ceremony, which appeases the spirits of the dead and ensures the transition of the deceased from life, is performed at a person's burial site, two to six months after burial.

Tutini, the monumental carved wooden grave posts, are central to the Pukamani ceremony (figs 89–90). The poles are carved from local ironwood trees between the burial and Pukamani ceremony, and painted with designs of social and totemic significance to the deceased and their family. The poles are erected around the grave, and incorporated into elaborate dancing and ritual performances as prescribed by Purrukuparli. At the conclusion of the

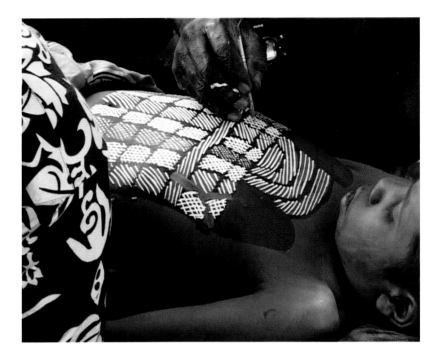

91.
A Yolngu boy is painted with a clan design at a circumcision ceremony
The boy is of the Rirratjingu clan and is being painted with a design from his Märi clan (the clan of his mother's mother). The painting connects him to his ancestral inheritance.

Yilpara, Blue Mud Bay, eastern Arnhem Land, 2004
Photograph: Howard Morphy

ceremony *tunga* (painted bark baskets) are placed over the tops of the poles as gifts for the spirits of the dead and the tutini are left standing to weather and deteriorate as part of the Tiwi landscape. These monumental sculptures are the centrepiece of Tiwi funerals, but are equally at the heart of Tiwi life and art.

Tutini and the Pukamani ceremony are unique expressions of Tiwi culture and identity, but similar forms of funerary sculpture also occur on mainland Australia. The Yolngu of Arnhem Land make *larrakitj*: tree trunks hollowed out by termites, painted with ancestral designs and used as memorial posts or coffins into which the bones of the deceased are interred (see pp. 116–7, 252).

> The larrakitj is like new skin for the bones
> Gawirrin 1 Gumana (b. 1935)

This use of totemic designs to transition people through life is not reserved for funerary rites. It is also a vital part of initiation ceremonies, which move people from one stage of life into another, such as from boyhood to manhood. In Yolngu initiation rituals the boy's torso is painted with designs (fig. 91) relevant to that individual and their family. Such paintings replicate those made on the bodies of the ancestral beings as they performed ceremonies that commemorated their creative acts. These same designs, painted on the chest of an initiate or the larrakitj of the dead, are manifestations of the ancestral journeys that give meaning to the journey through life.

While the initiate, or the deceased, are forever transformed through these experiences, less permanent transformations are also made possible through the broader aesthetics of performance. Across Australia ochre and other natural pigments, often understood to be the residue of ancestral substances, empower and transform the bodies of those who wear them. In Arnhem Land simple woven armbands, necklaces (fig. 92) and breast girdles are made resplendent with the addition of possum fur and feather string; sacred baskets and armbands are hung with composite tassels of feathers, string and beeswax. The decorations transform the bodies of the participants, who are celebrating the lives of the ancestral beings and re-creating their presence through the richness of their attire (figs 93–94).

In the Kimberley region, elaborate string *ilma* (dancing boards) are central to dance performances and the evocation of ancestral presence (fig. 95). A carved pearl shell in the British Museum's collection depicts two dancers, painted in ochre designs and themselves wearing pearl shell pendants, jointly holding an ilma during a performance (fig. 96).

Among the most dramatic expressions of these ancestral transformations occurs in the use of masks and headdresses. These appear across Australia in a number of forms, made with various materials and activating different meanings. The Museum has an exceptional collection of *krar* or *buk* – turtle-shell masks – from the Torres Strait Islands (figs 97–98).

These elaborate creations balance technical skill and sculptural innovation with the complex meanings to be conveyed in different contexts of funerary and increase rites, as well as other categories of sacred ceremony.[76] A.C. Haddon, who collected several such masks during the Cambridge Anthropological Expedition to Torres Straits in 1898, acquired the bonito fish dance mask (fig. 98) while on an earlier visit in 1888. This was used, in Haddon's records, as part of a 'death dance'. '[T]here is no doubt that certain masks at all events were regarded as sacred objects, probably they varied in this respect. On more than one occasion I have known natives to refuse through fear to put on a turtle-shell mask, as it was not the right occasion so to do.'[77]

The sacred and potentially transformative power of masks was obvious to Haddon. It must also have been evident to early missionaries, such as Reverend Samuel Macfarlane (1837–1911), and this may have played a part in the movement of these masks out of Island life and into museums.[78] The meanings that orbit these masks today are inflected with the contexts of their collection. These contexts – the active Christianisation of the Islands – were also those in which the creation of such masks was discouraged. Therefore, the moment of collection that preserved individual masks is tied to broader interventions in Torres Strait Islander culture, which sought to prevent the masks from being created in the future. Islanders were active in these

92.
Necklace of feathered string

North-east Arnhem Land, before 1896
Red, green, variegated red and blue, and red and green feathers, fibre; L. 310 mm (doubled)
British Museum, London
Oc1896,-.1052 Exh. BM

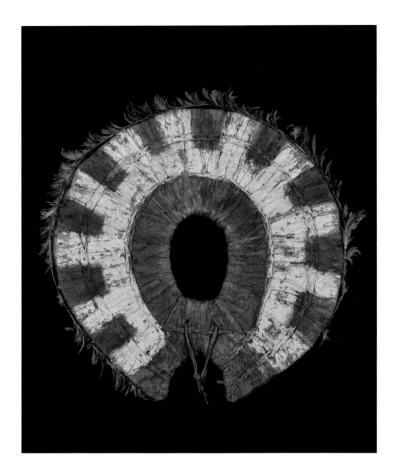

93.
Bark belt

Attributed to Western Arnhem Land, Northern Territory,
before 1896
Stringybark (*Eucalyptus tetrodonta*), natural pigment;
Diam. 254 mm
British Museum, London
Oc1896,-.126 Exh. BM
Donated by Sir Augustus Wollaston Franks

94.
Head ornament

The specific origin and function of this object have not been
recorded. Paperbark sheets are wrapped over a frame of
pindan wattle and secured with bark and mat rush stitching;
feathers are tied around the edge. At least five types of plants
have been used in its manufacture.

North-west Australia, before 1926
Pindan wattle (*Acacia tumida*) wood, broad-leaved paperbark (*Melaleuca
leucadendra*), mat rush (*Lomandra*) fibre, flax lily (*Dianella longifolia*) fibre,
pandanus (*Pandanus*) fibre, reed grass (*Phragmites vallatoria*) fibre, river red gum
(*Eucalyptus camaldulensis*) wood, cotton tree (*Hibiscus tiliaceus*) fibre;
L. 575 mm, W. 510 mm, D.18 mm
British Museum, London
Oc1944,02.2106 Exh. BM
Donated by Irene Marguerite Beasley

95.
Roy Wiggan with a completed *ilma*
The shape evokes the *ilma* held by the
dancing figures on the pearl shell pendant
in figure 96.

Broome, Western Australia, 2013
Photograph: John Carty

96.
Pearl shell pendant
The dancing men carry an *ilma* and wear
pearl shell pendants around their waists.

Kimberley region, Western Australia, before 1926
Pearl shell, charcoal; H. 156 mm, W. 120 mm, D. 5 mm
British Museum, London
Oc1954,06.378 Exh. BM
Donated by Wellcome Institute for the History of Medicine

exchanges, and Jude Philp reflects that 'cultural objects such as masks relating to non-Christian ceremonies and beliefs may also have been given to Macfarlane as an outward token of a conversion to the Christian faith' (fig. 97).[79] For other men, such as Maino, trading a mask and his father's things with Haddon to put in a museum may have been a visionary way of ensuring their continuity into the future (see pp. 237–9).

Such masks and headdresses endure, bridging time and space and history; their power continues to be explored and mobilised in Islander culture today. Alick Tipoti (b. 1975) is one artist who is exploring the use of fibreglass (in place of turtle shell) to create masks and headdresses (see pp. 248–9). Such innovation has a long tradition in the Torres Strait, through James Eseli (b. 1929) and Ken Thaiday (b. 1950) whose headdresses and 'dance machines' have long been appreciated as significant works of art. Indeed,

97.
Crocodile mask
The elaborate construction, from plates of turtle shell, demonstrate the skill of its maker, a young man named Nigi. Feathers, nuts, coloured cloth and designs in lime enhance the form to striking effect. In the 19th century, the people of Mabuiag were masters of the art of making masks of turtle shell. Such masks represent deep and spiritual knowledge of their ancestors and their lands and seas. It may have been given to the missionary Reverend Samuel Macfarlane.

Parts of this image have been digitally obscured at the request of the traditional owners of Mabuiag.

Attributed to Nigi, Mabuiag
Mabuiag, Torres Strait, Queensland, before 1885
Turtle shell, wood, metal, fibre, goa nut, wool, fabric (cotton), human bone, cassowary feather, lime?; L. 2130 mm
British Museum, London
Oc,+.2489 Exh. BM
Donated by Sir Augustus Wollaston Franks

innovation in the use of new materials is an integral part of Torres Strait Islander traditions. Cassowary feathers in such masks were often traded into the Torres Strait from Papua New Guinea. Likewise, the kind of *warup* (drum) that might have been played as these masks were worn would have been traded in from the north before being finished by Torres Strait Islanders (fig. 99). The human face in the bonito mask is made from tin, while the crocodile mask collected from Maino by Haddon uses metal saw blades for the teeth. The masks in the British Museum are themselves expressions of dynamic traditions and expansive relationships in an ever-changing world.

98.
**Mask in the form of a human face
and a bonito fish**

Attributed to Kuduma, Muralag
Collected Nagir, Torres Strait, Queensland, before 1888
Turtle shell, goa nut, cassowary feather, shell, paint;
H. 310 mm, L. 710 mm, W. 880 mm
British Museum, London
Oc,89+.74 Exh. BM
Donated by A.C. Haddon

Contemporary art

One of the major changes since the last exhibition of the Australian Aboriginal collections from the British Museum, nearly fifty years ago, is an increased recognition of Aboriginal art. The complexity of Indigenous Australian aesthetic traditions, always reflected in the Museum's collections, had been dimmed by the evolutionary light cast on Aboriginal society and obscured by a lack of familiarity with the diversity of forms produced across the continent. In recent years Aboriginal and Torres Strait Islander people have increasingly engaged with the world outside through art. The rich archive of images on rock surfaces attests to a long history of changing traditions and new materials have clearly been incorporated through trade within Australia. That dynamism continues today. Art has been one of the ways in which people have engaged with the colonisers of their country and responded to the immense changes that have been brought as a consequence. Indigenous aesthetic and ritual forms are being transformed into contemporary art and making a significant contribution to Australian culture, while at the same time maintaining their value as part of continuing traditions of belief and practice. This dynamic engagement across cultural boundaries is unfolding as one of the significant narratives of contemporary world art.

99.
Drum
Warup drums, with an hourglass form, are used to accompany dances. This example is exceptional for its flowing form and the designs of human figures and animals, including dog, crocodile, turtle, cassowary and fish. A cross on the skin suggests that Christian beliefs were incorporated into its making.

Saibai, Torres Strait, Queensland, *c.* 1874–86
Cordia subcordata wood, lizard skin, cassowary feather, goa nut, lime; L. 1100 mm, W. 560 mm, D. 500 mm
British Museum, London
Oc,+.3401 Exh. BM

The most visible expressions of this process for international audiences have undoubtedly been the acrylic paintings produced by desert artists (fig. 100). With their bright palette, optical dotting and booming geometries, these paintings resonated with twentieth-century tastes for minimalism and abstraction in Western art. But they are not Western art and nor are they simple translations of 'traditional' Aboriginal practices.

Desert paintings, which emerged in places like Papunya, Yuendumu and Balgo in the 1970s and 1980s, transferred the aesthetics of sand sculptures, rock art, body painting and performance into a fundamentally new medium. The iconic dots of paint used to compose these images are commonly traced to men's ground sculpture and ceremony, where balls of bush cotton are applied to the ground, to sacred objects or to the dancers' bodies to give colour and form to the *kuruwarri* (sacred designs). These 'dots' were also shaken off the dancer's bodies during the performance as traces of ancestral power. In ceremonies where ancestral energies are manifest in cotton 'dots' being shaken off, such power is also activated today by the expressive placing *on* of dots, and the ways in which they shimmer off the canvas.[80] This shimmer is also a defining feature of Yolngu bark paintings, where the finely cross-hatched lines animate the design and composition (figs 101–102).[81]

Whether through the mesmerising lines of Yolngu artists, or the luminous energy of desert dotting, all of these artists create optical effects that capture the eye, their audience, and refuse to let it rest. This is no accident of an increasingly globalised art world, but a deliberate and strategic manifestation of Aboriginal aesthetic principles. Painting, indeed art in all its forms, was a way of making visible to white people the authority of pre-existing religious and political systems. We see this in the case of the Yolngu bark petition and the Spinifex Native Title paintings (see figs 81–82, pp. 204–5). In each case art is a generous and diplomatic act of translation, of communication, between often vastly different cultures. So this is not ethnographic art, nor is it Western art. These are emergent forms: forms born of shared histories and addressed to a shared present. They make often uncomfortable conceptual and political claims on their audience, challenging the preconceived categories of art, culture and tradition that we bring to them. In this they are the most contemporary of art.

A piece of stone designed to function as a spearhead can, in its movement through space, become a ceremonial object in another community, or a work of art in a museum (see pp. 34–7). Over time, objects gain new significance and become valued in different ways. Pearl shell pendants, for example, although always appreciated for their aesthetic properties, begin to be made for sale as works of art (see p. 42). Aboriginal and Torres Strait Islander culture continues to move, to be redefined and renewed. This has always, necessarily, been the way of successful cultures. This, in turn, is the challenge that Indigenous artists offer the culture of their audiences.

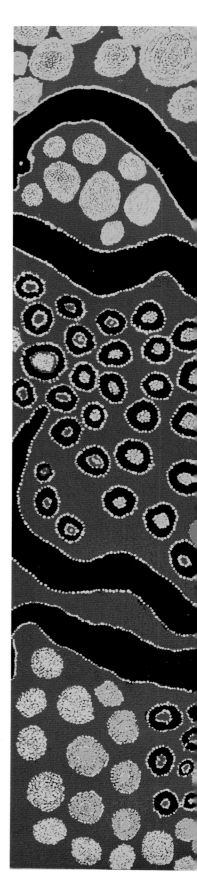

100.
Pukara
Pukara is an important men's *Tjukurpa* or 'Dreaming' site. It is associated with the Wanampi (water snake man), and here a father and son are depicted at the top of the canvas. They are travelling on the boy's initiatory journey, their actions and encounters creating the waters, geographic features and meanings of the land through which they pass. The three snakes at the bottom represent snake men also on their way to Mulaya. As much of the ritual knowledge is restricted to senior men, only a very general story can be shared with outsiders.

Roy Underwood (b. c. 1937), Lennard Walker (b. c. 1946), Simon Hogan (b. early 1930s) and Ian Rictor (b. c. 1960), Pitjantjatjara Tjuntjuntjara, Great Victoria Desert, Western Australia, 2013.
Acrylic on canvas; H. 1980 mm, W. 2180 mm
British Museum, London
2013,2035.1 Exh. BM

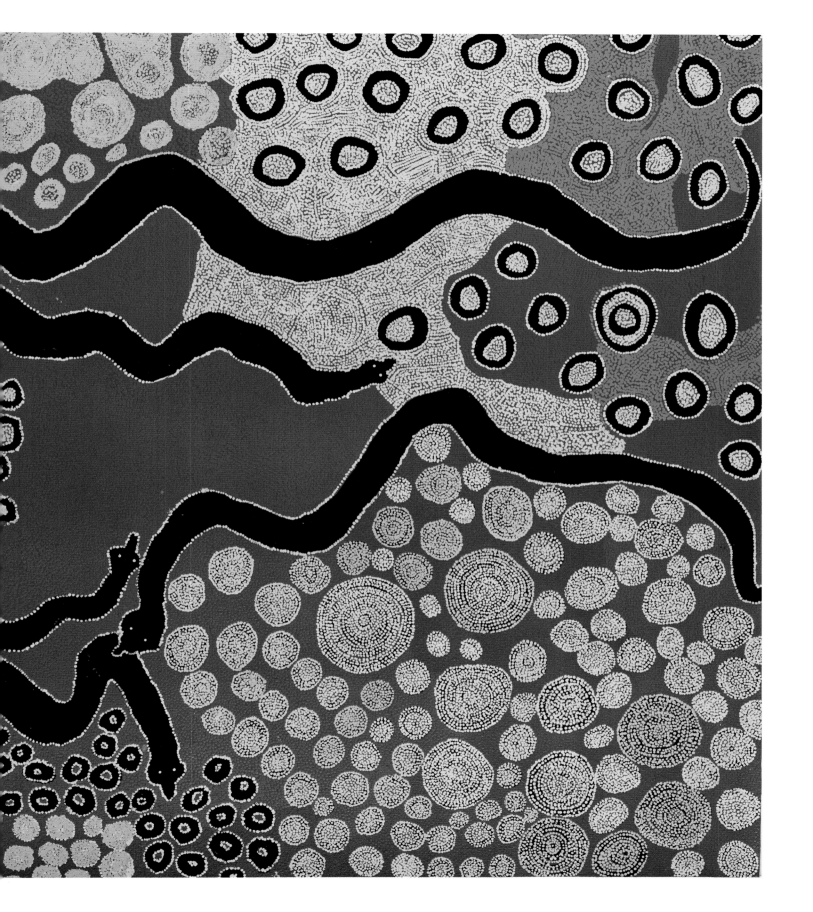

101.
Wawilak Sisters

Wandjuk Marika's painting includes objects associated with the Djungguwan fertility ceremony that re-enacts events in the journey of the Wawilak sisters. The two sisters travelled from inland to the Arnhem Land coast where in a dramatic final episode they were swallowed and then regurgitated by the great Rainbow Serpent. The painting includes images of the ceremonial *djuwany* posts that represent the sisters on their journey, the didgeridoo that accompanies the ceremonial performance, and the spears, spear throwers, baskets and boomerangs that they carried with them.

Wandjuk Marika (1927–1987), Rirratjingu clan, Dhuwa moiety, Yolngu
Northeastern Arnhem Land, *c.* 1960s?
Natural pigment on bark; H. 1700 mm, W. 720 mm
British Museum, London
2009,2014.1
Bequeathed by William Yuille

102.
Yathikpa ga Baraltja
This painting depicts two areas of the artist's clan country in Blue Mud Bay.

The top panel shows the Baraltja flood plains and the ancestral python Buruttji who dwells there; the bottom panel shows the Yathikpa area of coastal saltwater.

The imagery relates to a mythical episode concerning a dugong hunt. The hunter's harpoon struck the sacred rock Marrtjala (the oval shape in the middle section of the painting) causing the ancestral fire to flare and boil the waters. This fire had been carried to Marrtjala on the back of Bäru, the ancestral crocodile.

Bäru is depicted swimming in the sacred design that represents this area of water. The patterns on his back symbolise the ancestral fire, and also the lines of horny scales that crocodiles bear on their backs as scars from this ancestral event.

Bakulangay Marawili (1944–2002), Madarrpa clan,
Yirritja moiety, Yolngu
Yirrkala, northeastern Arnhem Land, Northern Territory,
c. 2002
Natural pigment on bark; L. 1520 mm, W. 195 mm
British Museum, London
Oc2003,01.5 Exh. BM
Sponsored by British Museum Friends
and Howard and Frances Morphy

Painting country
John Carty

Paintings of country in Aboriginal art are commonly understood to be representations of Dreamings or of places. But such paintings are at once far more intimate and layered with meaning than such terms convey. Uta Uta Tjangala's (c. 1926–1990) monumental *Yumari* (1981) is an artwork that encompasses the complexity of Aboriginal art, and the genre of desert painting in particular, in ways that allow and demand richer frameworks of understanding.

Yumari has featured in multiple exhibitions and publications in Australia,[82] which have enshrined its reputation as one of the iconic paintings in the emerging canon of Aboriginal art. Far from a simple translation of ritual forms into new media, *Yumari*'s epic conflations and inversions of the figure and ground, the human and the geometric, the representational and the abstract, continue to challenge and captivate audiences. Even without access to the restricted ritual knowledge that informs the painting, *Yumari* is a conceptually breathtaking composition (fig. 103).

What makes *Yumari* so challenging, and so important, are the relationships between the personal, historical and ancestral that it holds in tension as painted 'country'. On the surface, Yumari is a big 'Dreaming' painting, confidently asserting the sacred realm of Indigenous religion and knowledge. The artist seeks to resolve, within the grand scale of the canvas, the even grander scale of several major Dreamings for which he is custodian. The painting incorporates *Tjuntamurtu* (short legs), an ancestor associated with Tjangala's conception.[83] The lines of circles at the bottom of the painting are the *Kanaputa* (Digging Stick Women). The adjacent meander is *Lirru* (King Brown Snake) who encountered the *Kanaputa* as it travelled west to *Wilkinkarra* (Lake Mackay). The title of the painting 'Yumari', under which all these narratives are subsumed, references one of Tjangala's principal artistic themes: the story of an old man, Yina, who transgressed Aboriginal law by having sex with his mother-in-law (Yumari) at the site that now bears the name.[84]

Yina is embodied, following convention, as his own enlarged penis: the red rectangular form running horizontally beneath the figurative man. There are, however,

103.
Yumari

Uta Uta Tjangala (c. 1926–1990), Pintupi
Papunya, Northern Territory, 1981
Acrylic on canvas; L. 3672 mm, W. 2268 mm
National Museum of Australia, Canberra
1991.0024.3946 Exh. BM

104.
Directing the painting of Yumari

Uta Uta Tjangala (back, right), Anatjari Tjakamarra
(foreground) and John Tjakamarra (back, left).
Vincent Megaw (b. 1934), born Middlesex, England
Papunya, Northern Territory, July 1981
Gelatin silver print on paper; H. 203 mm, L. 253 mm
British Museum, London
Oc,B93.22

different interpretations as to the identity of this figure. Vincent Megaw, who photographed the process (fig. 104), identifies the figure as Yina, the old man; whereas anthropologist Fred Myers identifies him as Tjuntamurtu.[85] Either way, the painting can be appreciated for the singularity of its formal ambition. But analysis of Tjangala's oeuvre suggests that Myers's interpretation is correct.[86] Furthermore, how we interpret the identity of the giant man has significant implications for our understanding not only of what the artist is doing in this painting, but also what desert painters are doing more broadly with art.

Myers argues that, through his conception ancestor, Tjuntamurtu the central figure of *Yumari* is most appropriately understood as Tjangala himself.[87] This is both an anthropological insight, revealing the ontological relationship between a conception ancestor and a desert person, and a historical observation. Tjangala was one of the Pintupi people ushered onto government settlements such as Papunya in the 1950s and 1960s. Tjangala, along with the other Pintupi, was doubly exiled by history: not only was he a desert man stranded in a colonial settlement, but by virtue of being 'Pintupi' at Papunya he was also living on other people's country. Tjangala was thus a passionate advocate for the Pintupi returning to their own country, and it was in the ensuing context of debates about the Aboriginal homelands movement that Tjangala's 'man' briefly

became the dominating figure of his paintings. *Yumari* was painted after the artist returned from a visit to that very site in 1981, a period in which he became increasingly involved in the politics of both Pintupi and personal autonomy. It is in this context that Myers suggests the proper subject of this painting is 'the artist himself… surveying the Country to which he hopes soon to return'.[88] 'A clearer expression of a painter's identity is difficult to imagine.… In representing his identity in the land the artist crosses back and forth between the landscape, the figures who created it and which it manifests, and the human incarnations of it, including himself.'[89]

The towering figure of Tjuntamurtu in this painting is most appropriately conceived, therefore, not as a representation of a Dreaming ancestor by Tjangala, but as a self-representation of Tjangala through his Dreaming ancestor. In Australia, where ancestors either created the features of the earth or became those features, there is no coherent separation of the Dreaming ancestors and the land: they are country. Painted country, as the sedimentation of myth, history and personal experience into place, is perhaps better understood through an expanded idea of portraiture, of identity expressed through land, than it is through Western genres of abstraction or landscape. In this way *Yumari* can be appreciated as a different *kind* of self-portrait, for a differently composed self.[90]

Extraordinarily, *Yumari* is now the watermark on the Australian passport. It is fair to say the Australian Passport Office probably did not understand the scale or power of this painting when they chose it as the image that defines Australian identity. But it is testament to the persuasive power of Aboriginal artists to reclaim spaces in the Australian imaginary just as they continue to reclaim the land that was taken away. *Yumari* now sits, an open page at the world's borders, as the unsettled image that both verifies and challenges the identity of Australians.

Contemporary Aboriginal art addresses the great challenges, the silences and the emergent ceremony of Australian life. In 1988, as Australia prepared for a celebration of 200 years of European settlement, the artists of Ramingining carved 200 larrakitj, burial poles or hollow coffins, one for each year of occupation. The installation, conceived as a war memorial, was dedicated to the Aboriginal men and women who died over those two centuries defending their country.

The Aboriginal Memorial, which now takes pride of place in the collection of the National Gallery of Australia, is an elegant and powerful transformation of Aboriginal meaning and ritual into cross-cultural contexts (fig. 105). Larrakitj have been turned into art, but they are no less important and no less efficacious in that function.

Gawirrin 1 Gumana's larrakitj (fig. 106 and see fig. 82, p. 94) is among the most challenging of artworks in the British Museum's Australian collection. The memorial pole is emblazoned with the designs of Barama, a key creation ancestor who brought with him the laws of society, of the natural world, and the ritual song and dance that ensured the maintenance of such laws. The larrakitj, however, is Janus faced: two ancestral figures look out at us, one from either side of the pole. According to Gawirrin, one is Barama and the other is Captain Cook. He has never specified which is which.[91] How we are to interpret this is the gift, the challenge, of the artist. The pole is, unambiguously, a statement of the pre-existing law of the country into which

105.
The Aboriginal Memorial
An installation of 200 hollow log coffins, or memorial poles, from central Arnhem Land, marking the bicentenary of the arrival of British settlers in Australia. The Memorial commemorates the thousands of Indigenous Australians who lost their lives defending their land since 1788. Forty-three Yolngu artists contributed to the work.

Ramingining region, central Arnhem Land, 1987–8
National Gallery of Australia, Canberra
NGA 87.2240.1 – NGA 87.2240.200

106.
Barama/Captain Cook (detail)

Gawirrin 1 Gumana (b. 1935)
Dhalwangu clan, Yirritja moiety, Yolngu
Yirrkala, northeastern Arnhem Land, Northern Territory,
c. 2002
Pigment on wood; H. 3120 mm, Diam. 200 mm
British Museum, London
Oc2003,01.2 Exh. BM
Sponsored by British Museum Friends

the British planted their own flag pole. But in his inclusion of Cook within that law, as an ancestor capable of coexisting with Barama, this larrakitj is also a gesture of considerable political and historical generosity.

Sometimes art is a funerary rite, or an initiation into new ways of seeing. Some art presents legal and historical arguments. Where customary Aboriginal economies have been corroded by colonisation, art is also, among other things, an increase ceremony: an intervention in the ecological and economic status quo, a way of increasing the availability of resources in a radically transformed environment. Wandjinas are repainted today on Kimberley rock walls, and they are painted on canvas for sale to art collectors and tourists just as they were painted on plywood for early collectors. They also preside like questioning, silent gods, in noisy spectacles such as the opening of the Sydney Olympics in 2000 (fig. 107) watching how we navigate new ideas of Australia today.

The achievements and enduring qualities of Aboriginal civilisations have in the past been under-recognised in part because of their ephemeral nature and subtle long-term impacts on the continent. While Western travellers sought monuments carved in stone or wrought in iron and written testaments, in Australia they found none. Europeans saw, or rather failed to see, a continent forged by fire, mapped in song, by people who had created a deep and enduring spiritual and economic relationship with the land many thousands of years before bibles, before pyramids, before Captain Cook set foot on the continent's shores.

The achievements of Aboriginal Australians have been at once too big, and too understated, for outsiders to appreciate in their fullness. The wooden, fibre and stone objects that constitute much of the British Museum's collection of Australian material are deceptively humble. Properly understood they are the keys to a continent. They speak of how it was made home and the hands that made it so. Appreciated alongside the contemporary art of Indigenous Australians, they tell a story, unfolding still, of resilient and creative peoples who forged a distinctive and enduring way of being in the world. Australia is the monument, too vast to see in its entirety, to the diverse genius of the first peoples to call it home.

107.
An immense Wandjina, created by Donny Woolagoodja, at the opening ceremony of the Sydney Olympic Games, 2000

Photograph: Pool Jo Sydney

Encounters in country

Maria Nugent

Australia's human history spans at least sixty millennia. The history of British colonisation in the country covers less than a quarter of one millennium but that comparatively short period of time produced radical disruption and change. Hardly any aspect of the Indigenous people's world was untouched by the colonial encounter. This is an incredibly complex and diverse story to tell. It is complex because colonisation did not occur in a single moment or proceed in a straight line. Experiences of colonialism varied enormously across time and place. Contributing to these differences was the diversity that existed among Indigenous people when the colonisers arrived. At the time British occupation began in 1788 it is estimated that there were approximately 250 languages spread across the continent. If the Indigenous population was diverse, so too were the colonists. They came from different places, cultures and classes, bringing with them varied interests, expectations and attitudes. The result was (and is) a history characterised both by intimacy and violence, coercion and cooperation, continuity and discontinuity. While some aspects of culture and society were lost or destroyed under the weight of colonisation, much has lasted as well. It is possible to say, then, that Indigenous people have endured colonisation in both senses – and endure it still.

The aim of this chapter is to outline and survey broadly some of the main contours of the British colonial encounter in Australia. While space does not allow a comprehensive overview, it is possible to describe some key sites, moments and themes that help to illuminate and illustrate the nature of interactions and relations between Indigenous Australians and settlers over nearly 250 years. The British Museum's significant collection of Australian Indigenous material, much of which was acquired and assembled in the context of British colonisation, beginning with objects associated with late eighteenth-century maritime voyages and continuing with some very recent acquisitions, provides a rich resource for interpreting and presenting stories of – and from – Australia's colonial past and present. These objects, which also include important documents, photographs and artworks, were made and used under various conditions and contexts, and were collected and circulated as part of different kinds of relationships and exchanges and for assorted reasons (see Chapter 3). They provide, then, the material for a compelling history.

Australia's colonial history is not always easy to read and learn about. There are aspects to it that are confronting and unsettling for current generations. Like all colonial histories, harsh conflict was involved. The essential truth is that Aboriginal people were dispossessed from their land by force, their populations reduced by disease and violence, and their cultural beliefs and practices disrespected and sometimes destroyed. Some Aboriginal groups bore the brunt of the dispossession more acutely than others. Everywhere, however, Aboriginal people were forced to come to terms with the new colonial order. Some of the ways in which they sought to negotiate and to mitigate the impacts of colonisation, and to preserve as well as rebuild their societies, are examined in what follows.

Early European encounters

As noted in the previous chapter, Aboriginal people in the northern part of the continent had a long history of contact with people from archipelagos to the north. But it was not until 1606 that the first known encounter between Aboriginal people and Europeans occurred when a Dutch expedition under the command of Willem Janszoon (1570–1630) landed on Cape York. The ship had been sent by the United East India Company, or *Verenigde Oostindische Compagnie* (VOC), to investigate 'rumours of trade opportunities and gold in the uncharted waters lying to the east of the Spice Islands' (or Moluccas).[1] This encounter was violent, with one Dutch sailor speared to death. Other Dutch expeditions visited the region intermittently in the seventeenth century.[2] At the close of the century, the English buccaneer William Dampier (1651–1715) made contact with Aboriginal people when he twice visited the continent's north-west coast. On one occasion he tried to persuade some Aboriginal men to carry water for him but without success. In published accounts he reported that they 'have no houses', did not seem to 'worship anything', did not pasture livestock or till soil, and did not possess 'any… sort of metal'. He is responsible for the description 'the miserablest People in the World', which informed European impressions for some time to come.[3]

State-sponsored British maritime exploration in Australia did not begin until almost a century later with Lieutenant (later Captain) Cook who, rightly or wrongly, occupies a pivotal and contested place in the Australian historical imagination. Cook's encounters on the Australian east coast are, as Nicholas

Thomas puts it, 'much-celebrated and much-lamented'.[4] For settler Australians, they have long been celebrated as inaugurating the British history and heritage of Australia; they are lamented by Indigenous Australians as initiating the death and destruction that colonisation caused (see pp. 128–9).

The British Museum has in its collections an unadorned wooden shield (fig. 1) that is believed to have come from Cook's first face-to-face encounter with Aboriginal people in Australia.[5] The incident with which it is associated was a dramatic one, and is described in the *Endeavour* voyage's records. As Cook, Joseph Banks and others in the landing party rowed to shore, two Gweagal men stood on the beach, shouting loudly and waving spears. In response, the landing party fired at them, wounding one in the leg, which caused him to pick up a shield for protection. When the sailors went ashore, they 'went up to the houses' where they found some children taking cover. According to Banks, they decided not to disturb (i.e. kidnap) the youths, but for safe measure they did take away 'all the lances which we could find about the houses, amounting in number to forty or fifty', believing they might have been poison tipped.[6] Only four of these spears survive, and are now held by the Museum of Archaeology and Anthropology, University of Cambridge (fig. 2). Despite the voyagers' suspicions, they were not offensive weapons: 'We found that the very most of them had been usd in striking fish, at least we concluded so from sea weed which was found stuck in among the four prongs'. While the landing party had sought to disarm the local people, they succeeded instead it seems in depriving them of their food-gathering implements.

Before returning to his ship, Cook paused briefly to examine some canoes pulled up on the beach. His assessment was scathing: 'three Canoes lay upon the bea[c]h the worst I think I ever saw they were about ~~10~~ ¹² ᵒʳ ¹⁴ feet long made of one peice of the bark of a tree drawn or tied up at each end and the middle kept open by means of peices of sticks by way of Thwarts'. Other

1.
Shield
Likely to have been collected during James Cook's week-long visit to Botany Bay in 1770.

Attributed to Botany Bay (Sydney), New South Wales,
c. 1770
Red mangrove (*Rhizophora stylosa*) bark;
L. 90 mm, W. 29 mm
British Museum, London
Oc1978,Q.839 Exh. BM

descriptions of watercraft and fishing implements made during this encounter were not quite so damning. A remarkable drawing by Tupaia (*c.* 1725–1770), a Ra'iatean man who had joined the voyage in Tahiti after forming a friendship with Banks, which shows three Gweagal people fishing from two canoes, provides a more documentary, less judgemental, image (fig. 3).[7]

The shield, the spears and the drawing constitute a remarkable assemblage of objects connected with an encounter that later came to be seen as foundational in Australia's history. But because that foundational moment has become so weighted with contested historical and political significance, today these objects provoke mixed reactions among Aboriginal people. Some see the shield especially as little more than evidence of a violent assault by a British expedition against Aboriginal people as they sought to gain access to their country, a pattern that was repeated throughout

2.
Spears
The fishing spears, with three or four bone-tipped prongs, resemble the one shown in Tupaia's drawing of people at Botany Bay (fig. 3).

Botany Bay, New South Wales, 18th century
Wood, plant fibre, resin, bone;
L. 1384 mm, W. 20 mm; L. 1320 mm, W. 22 mm;
L. 1382 mm, W. 20 mm; L. 1530 mm, W. 20 mm
Museum of Archaeology and Anthropology,
University of Cambridge
D 1914.1; D 1914.2; D 1914.3; D 1914.4

3.
People in canoes at Botany Bay
Tupaia joined Cook's voyage in Tahiti. His arrival in Botany Bay marked one of the earliest encounters between Aboriginal and Polynesian people. This is among the first visual representations of Indigenous Australians to reach Europe.

Tupaia (c. 1725–1770), born Ra'iatea
Botany Bay, New South Wales, 1770
Pencil and watercolour on paper; H. 263 mm, W. 362 mm
British Library, London
Add. Ms.15508, f.10 Exh. BM

Australia's colonial history (see pp. 74–8). Others acknowledge its significance as a rare surviving example of their ancestors' material culture, preserved from a time just before British occupation began. This is especially true for Aboriginal people living around Botany Bay and Sydney, where British settlement commenced in 1788. For some of them, the shield and the spears provide a connection to their ancestors, while also having wider national significance. Shayne Williams from the La Perouse Aboriginal community at Botany Bay, for instance, has said of these objects collected in 1770, that 'they are a tangible part of our culture. They are the oldest Aboriginal artefacts taken from the mainland, so they also have national significance for people right across the country'.[8]

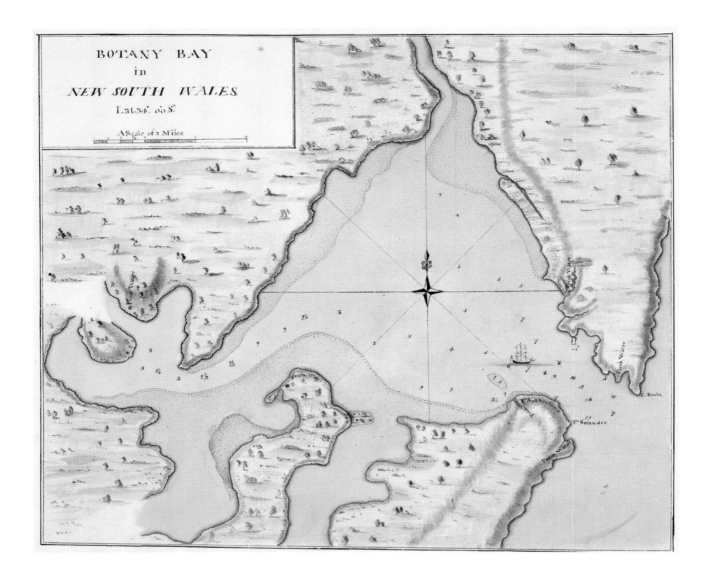

The encounters that occurred at Botany Bay in 1770 have been the subject of a great deal of discussion, and there is no need to describe them in detail here.[9] It seems clear, though, that the landing party's impatient advance did not help create conditions for close interactions. For the remainder of the *Endeavour*'s stay at Botany Bay – eight days in all – very little contact between the two groups occurred (fig. 4).[10] Early in the week, Cook recorded in his journal that 'all they seem'd to want was for us to be gone'. By the end of it, on the eve of the *Endeavour*'s departure, he wrote that: 'However we could know but very little of their customs as we never were

4.
Chart of Botany Bay
Cook and his wife Elizabeth owned
this chart. It would have been drawn, based
on originals, after Cook returned to England.
The vegetation, depth of the bay and sites of
fresh water are clearly marked.

Britain, after July 1771
Ink on paper; H. 310 mm, W. 430 mm
British Library, London
Add. 31360, No.32 Exh. BM

able to form any connections with them, they had not so much as touch'd the things we had left in their hutts on purpose for them to take away'. The local people's actions across that week, as recorded by the voyagers, suggest that they were mostly intent on containing the presence of these uninvited strangers, minimising their incursions into their country, and managing their potentially dangerous effects. It is impossible to know with any certainty how they conceived of the sailors, although one interpretation that became common in the context of later colonial encounters was that Aboriginal people sometimes saw strange white men as ghosts or dead kin returned.[11]

After leaving Botany Bay, the *Endeavour* spent the winter surveying the east coast, a sojourn that was extended by six weeks at a place now called Endeavour River in Queensland after the ship had been wrecked on a reef. Here closer contact with Aboriginal people was made. From the evidence Cook provides, it appears that he had learned a valuable lesson at Botany Bay. Rather than advance boldly, he instead ordered his men not to approach the Guugu Yimithirr people who came to look at the stranded ship. Slowly and carefully Tupaia brokered relations, and eventually some Guugu Yimithirr men went on board the *Endeavour*. Things were exchanged – Cook gave one man an old shirt, which he was later seen with tied around his head – and some words were recorded.

Cook's final act before leaving the east coast was to perform a 'ceremony of possession'.[12] Sailing north towards New Guinea, he paused briefly on the island of Bedanug (but which he named Possession Island), climbed with a small contingent to the top of its highest hill, hoisted the English Colours, and in the name of King George III (1738–1820) 'took possession of the whole Eastern Coast', calling it New South Wales. Some Torres Strait Islander people were present on the island that day and probably witnessed this strange scene. But it was performed less for their sake than for other European navigators who might in the future explore these parts. In making this act of possession, Cook was claiming for himself and his king the rights of 'first discoverer'.[13] A colonial claim to the territory would depend on subsequent occupation.

When Cook voyaged along the eastern coastline over four months in the middle of 1770, the prospect of British settlement in this far-flung land was remote. Yet, when the British government began to consider possible sites for establishing a penal colony, which it did in the wake of the loss of its North American territories, Botany Bay came into consideration because of Cook's explorations and reports.[14] Joseph Banks, no less, testified in its favour. In this respect, Cook's visit in 1770 became part of a sequence of developments leading to British colonisation of Australia that would ultimately have far-reaching ramifications for Indigenous people across the continent, the effects of which are ongoing today.

'Everything after Cook was between all of us'
Maria Nugent

Aboriginal people across Australia have long told stories about Captain Cook, the earliest of which were written down by colonists in the 1830s. These Aboriginal interpretations of Cook, which can be found in places Cook visited and places he did not, are expressed in art, story, song, text and performance. In most of them, Cook is portrayed as a land-hungry, immoral, colonial everyman, who fails to recognise in proper ways the people who are the custodians and owners of the land he entered uninvited. A few describe him in more positive light, as someone responsible for bringing valuable new goods and technologies. Whichever the case, such stories are at their core about the colonial structures of Aboriginal people's lives – about the relationships that exist between themselves and white people and about the dilemmas that colonisation posed for them, and poses for them still.

One contemporary Aboriginal artist fascinated by Cook is Vincent Namatjira (b. 1983). A descendant of the famous Arrernte watercolour artist Albert Namatjira (1902–1959), Vincent was born in Hermannsburg but after his mother died he lived for much of his childhood in Perth. His interest in Cook grew after seeing the replica of the *Endeavour* in Fremantle while on a school excursion. His painting (fig. 5) portrays Cook's written claim of possession of the east coast of New Holland in 1770 as an extension of his naval uniform. In this way, the painting suggests that Cook embodies the history of British possession of Aboriginal people's country, and with his declaration introduces his own law over it. As Hobbles Danayarri (1925–1988), another Aboriginal historian and storyteller, has said: 'Him [Cook] been bring lotta book [law] from Big England right here now. They got that book for Captain Cook from England. And that's his law'.[15]

For Vincent Namatjira, 'Everything after Cook was between all of us', expressing the idea that since 1770 the histories of Aboriginal people and British settlers became entangled and inseparable. There cannot be one without the other. But the implications of this remain unfinished business for all Australians.

The historical relationship between Aboriginal and non-Aboriginal people is also a theme that photographer Michael Cook (b. 1968) examines in his work. His art practice reminds us about the perspectives from which Australia's history has largely been told. By means of staging reversals, as he does in the photograph *Undiscovered #4* (fig. 6), Michael Cook provokes audiences not only to consider what history looks like from the other side of the beach, but also to reconsider the relationships and structures implied by themes like 'discovery' that have long shaped the Australian historical imagination.

5.
James Cook – with the Declaration

Vincent Namatjira (b. 1983), Pitjantjatjara
Indulkana, South Australia, 2014
Acrylic on canvas; H. 1010 mm, W. 760 mm
British Museum, London
2014,2007.1 Exh. BM

6.
Undiscovered #4

Michael Cook (b. 1968), Bidjara
Brisbane, Queensland, 2010
Inkjet on paper; H. 1357 mm, W. 1118 mm
National Museum of Australia, Canberra
IR6338.0004 Exh. BM

British occupation begins

The British occupation of Australia began in 1788 with the arrival of the 'first fleet' of eleven ships carrying 550 officers and marines, and 736 settler-convicts, of which about 188 were women and also included a smattering of children, to establish a penal colony at Botany Bay. In contrast to other parts of the British colonial world, such as North America and Canada – or in the northern regions of Australia (see p. 122) – British settlement around Sydney was not preceded by sustained contact between Aboriginal people and other outsiders, such as traders, missionaries or whalers. Here the interim between the fleeting visit of the *Endeavour* expedition and the arrival of hundreds of British marines, soldiers and settler-convicts intent on moving in was short. There can be no doubt that Aboriginal people experienced this as an invasion. Most immediately devastating was the outbreak of disease. Within a year of British settlement, a smallpox epidemic spread through the Aboriginal population in the Sydney region.

The British government's decision to establish a penal colony on Australia's east coast was built on a shallow bedrock of knowledge about Aboriginal people, their material culture and languages, their country and land use practices, and their religious life, social systems, political organisation and aesthetic practices. Cook's expedition had produced some observations and details, but they were in the main speculative given that only superficial contact had taken place. Not only did British settlers arrive with hardly any knowledge about the Aboriginal population but they also came with a very different way of understanding the world. They struggled to interpret what they saw. They did not realise, for instance, that the landscape they admired was 'human-made', the result of sophisticated and intricate land management regimes, including the controlled use of fire, over millennia. As historian Mark McKenna notes, the country's 'antiquity' was 'hidden from the settlers by their failure to know Aboriginal languages and cultures that might have afforded them understanding'.[16]

In the opening years of British settlement at Port Jackson (now Sydney) some effort was made to correct the depth of ignorance about the place where, and the people among whom, the British had taken up residence. Early accounts describe faltering efforts to learn the local people's languages, to decipher their social organisation, to understand their land use methods and to grasp their religious beliefs. A much admired instance of an attempt at serious knowledge exchange was Lieutenant William Dawes's (1762–1836) lessons with some young Eora, as the Sydney people were known, including a boy called Nanbarry, a girl named Boorang, her brother, Yirinibi, and Patyegarang, a young woman. They were his main informants for the vocabulary and phrases he recorded in a series of notebooks, which also document his struggling efforts to make sense of how the language worked.[17] Dawes's notebooks were discovered, belatedly, in 1972 in the collections of

7.

The notebooks of William Dawes
This page records a conversation with Patyegarang, a young Aboriginal woman. Dawes's work on the language of the Sydney region ended when he returned to Britain in 1791. He later became involved in William Wilberforce's campaign for the abolition of slavery.

William Dawes (1762–1836), born Portsmouth, England
Sydney region, New South Wales, 1790–1
Ink on paper; H. 160 mm, W. 80 mm
SOAS Library, University of London
MS 41645, Notebook B, p. 34 Exh. BM

the University of London's School of Oriental and African Studies (fig. 7). They are a testament to the young Eora people's willingness to show the newcomers something of their world.

Important, too, in early interactions was the exchange, trade and barter of material objects. Archaeologist Isabel McBryde notes that 'barter or exchange proved a constant feature of interaction between British and Aborigines at Port Jackson'.[18] In the absence of a shared language, this exchange of objects mediated relationships. Both sides brought to these transactions their own practices of trade and exchange. For their part, the British had come stocked with 'articles for traffick'. Aboriginal people were also practiced in exchange relations and networks, linked as they were by complex exchange networks extending over vast distances, which provided access to certain raw materials as well as highly valued objects (see pp. 31–3). Within the early Sydney settlement, certain objects became especially prized. Iron tomahawks, for instance, were much sought by the Eora and were regularly traded for various types of spears and fishing lines (figs 8–9).

Yet relations between the Berewalgal, as the British came to be known, and the many clans that occupied the Sydney region, including the Gweagal, Gadigal, Gameyegal, Wangal and Wallumedegal, were always fragile and often turned violent.[19] This was due to multiple triggers, but chief among them was that the convict settlement imposed on and threatened Aboriginal people's territory and resources. The British government had launched this colonial project without any clear policy regarding the recognition of Aboriginal people's rights in and to land and with no definite plan for acquiring territory on proper or agreeable terms from its owners. Governor Arthur Phillip's (1738–1814) instructions were only to 'endeavour by every possible means to open an Intercourse with the Natives and to conciliate their affections, enjoining all Our Subjects to live in amity and kindness with them'.[20] Despite these sentiments, the reality on the ground was that the British assumed occupation and possession of Indigenous people's country ultimately by force. Relationship to and management of land is central to Aboriginal society and identity (see pp. 45–9), and the colonial seizure of land was the source of sustained or intermittent resistance and violence, whenever and wherever settlers went.

8.
Hunting spear

Port Jackson, New South Wales, before 1844
Wood; L. 2502 mm, W. 25 mm, D. 25 mm
British Museum London
Oc.955 Exh. BM
Donated by Henry Christy

9.
Fishing spear

Port Jackson, New South Wales, before 1844
Wood; L. 2700 mm, W. 70 mm, D. 30 mm
British Museum, London
Oc.944 Exh. BM
Donated by Henry Christy

Other outposts: in the west and in the north

For about the first forty years after 1788, British occupation was confined mainly to the south-east of the continent, fanning westwards and northwards from Sydney, as well as covering most of Van Diemen's Land (now Tasmania) where another penal colony had been established in 1803. British settlement spread further afield during the 1820s when some small outposts were founded on the north and west coasts, huge distances from Sydney (fig. 10). These garrisons were motivated by a desire on the part of the British government to forestall territorial competition from other European nations, but they were also planted with a view to future settlement and economic development.

Histories of these outposts provide something of a contrast to the fast-moving and brutal frontiers that characterise the colonial encounter in other parts of the continent. Situated as they were on the edge of the Aboriginal

10.

Map of British colonial occupation in Australia, c. 1838
This map shows settlements clustered around the coast and river valleys. By the end of the decade this would begin to change rapidly as colonists expanded into the interior.

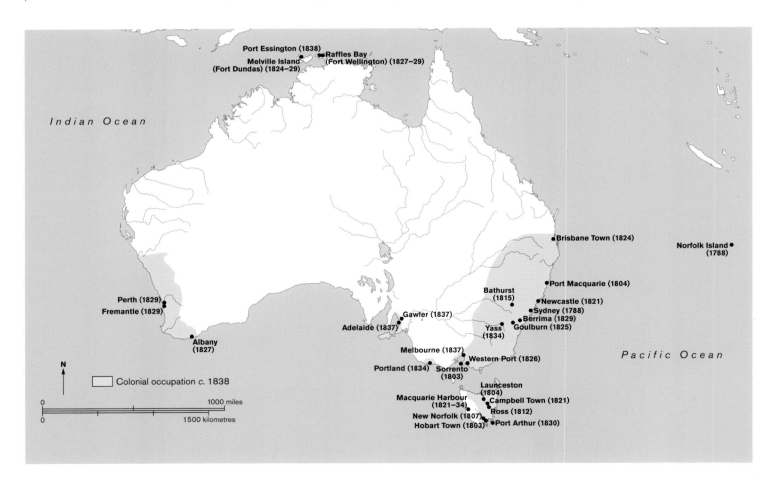

11.
Hafted axe

This type of axe, known as a *kodj*, was made only by Noongar people in the south-west of Western Australia. The rounded stone is shaped for pounding, while the sharp stone is for cutting. Its collection is attributed to naval surgeon Alexander Collie.

Albany, Western Australia, *c.* 1830s
Wood, stone, grass tree (*Xanthorrhoea*) resin; L. 385 mm,
W. 110 mm, D. 50 mm
British Museum, London
Oc.4768 Exh. BM
Donated by Henry Christy

12.
Knife

Its collection is attributed to naval surgeon Alexander Collie.

Albany, Western Australia, *c.* 1830s
Wood, quartz, resin; L. 385 mm, W. 27 mm, D. 50 mm
British Museum, London
Oc.4774 Exh. BM
Donated by Henry Christy

world and composed of quite stable and small populations, these garrisons tended to enjoy reasonably close cross-cultural relations. Absence of competition over land and resources (the garrisons were provisioned from Sydney) contributed to the equilibrium.

In 1826 a contingent of British soldiers was sent to King George's Sound (Albany) on the south-west coast of the continent. This bay and region had been visited repeatedly by European expeditions prior to this, including George Vancouver (1757–1798) in 1791, Matthew Flinders between December 1801 and January 1802, Nicolas Baudin's (1754–1803) French expedition in February 1803, and Phillip Parker King in 1821 (see p. 213). Friendly interactions had on the whole characterised these fleeting visits, and peaceable relations continued when the contingent of British soldiers and marines took up residence. At the heart of this settlement were some young Noongar men who engaged with the soldiers, including one known as Mokare (*c.* 1800–1831). Historian Tiffany Shellam has described him as 'informant, intermediary, guide and close friend of several of the newcomers, telling them stories about his people, their culture and history, describing some of their religious and cultural rituals, and illuminating personal relationships and family genealogies'.[21] Aboriginal men like Mokare and his compatriots are remembered today for their capacity to move between two worlds and for their ability to finesse relations with outsiders. Some developed close and abiding friendships with newcomers. Famously, Alexander Collie (1793–1835), the surgeon at the garrison, who became especially close to Mokare, wished to be buried beside him (figs 11–12).

Similarly friendly relations were not sustained at the 'free' colony that was established a few years later in 1829 on the Swan River (present day Perth), 260 miles north of King George's Sound. This colony for free British settlers was a joint venture between the British government and private capital. Prospective settlers were sold grants of land and dreams of future prosperity. But the colony had a fraught foundation, teetering on the edge of failure, both because the new settlers struggled to make productive use of the country and because it was not long before they were in conflict with the Noongar people. Indications that this would be so were there from the outset: a preliminary report had recorded that the Aboriginal people in the area 'seemed angry at our invasion of their Territory'.[22] Within a short time the situation had escalated, leading to a brutal incident known as the Pinjarra Massacre.

While some settlers were in conflict with Aboriginal people, others were open to learning from and about them. Among the early British settlers in the Swan River colony was a man named Samuel Neil Talbot (1799–1863). Born in England, he arrived in Western Australia in late 1829, when the settlement was in its infancy. Talbot accompanied a party that explored the Collie River, probably with the assistance of Aboriginal guides, in March 1830. Later that year, he left Western Australia for Tasmania, but returned in early 1838. It was at this time that he assembled a large collection of Aboriginal objects. In 1839 he donated seventy artefacts to the British Museum including a digging stick and a honey gathering stick or hook, evidence of the continuation of the local people's food gathering and harvesting practices (figs 13–14). In his descriptions of these and other objects, Talbot expressed admiration for their ingenuity, in ways that contrast with later nineteenth-century ethnographic descriptions more influenced by and freighted with scientific theories of race. Of the honey hook he collected at Swan River, Talbot wrote: 'a long rod, used for the purpose of gathering yellow flowers from the Banksia, it has a bow or piece of wood about 6 inches long, tied and set with gum, for the purpose of pulling, and hooking down the ripe flowers from the tops of the trees from which they suck honey'. Regarding the digging stick, he emphasised its

13.
Digging stick

Swan River, Western Australia,
c. 1838
Wood; L. 1100 mm, Diam. 30mm
British Museum, London
Oc1839,0620.32 Exh. BM
Donated by Samuel Neil Talbot

14.
Honey gathering hook

Swan River, Western Australia,
c. 1838
Wood, resin, fibre; L. 2080 mm,
W. 25mm
British Museum, London
Oc1839,0620.65 Exh. BM
Donated by Samuel Neil Talbot

15.
**Painting of a kangaroo and
human-like figures**
Specific meanings are not recorded for
this painting, but the figures are likely
to represent spirit ancestors. Bark paintings
from the 1800s are rare.

Attributed to Port Essington, Northern Territory,
likely before 1868
Pigment on bark; H. 555 mm, W. 615 mm, D. 65 mm
British Museum, London
Oc1967,+.1 Exh. BM

16.
Painting of a human-like figure

Attributed to Port Essington, Northern Territory,
likely before 1868
Pigment on bark, H. 935 mm, W. 310 mm
British Museum, London
Oc1973,Q.17 Exh. BM

multiple functions: 'used for all the purposes of a spade, it is with this they dig the native potato, ground nuts and dig their wells, strip the trees of long pieces of bark for making their huts, cooking and the women also use it as a weapon when they fall out with each other.'[23] Set against these favourable descriptions of the Noongar people's productive use of the environment, the settlers' widely reported struggle to yield crops from the same ground seems all the more stark.

On the continent's north coast the situation faced by British soldiers at another military outpost was bleaker still. After a series of failed attempts during the 1820s, an outpost was eventually established at Port Essington

17.
Fishing spear
Lieutenant Ince, a British naval officer, acquired this fishing spear at a time when there was a well-established system of trade between Aboriginal people and European settlers at Port Essington.

Port Essington, Northern Territory, early to mid-1840s
Wood; L. 1830 mm, Diam. 20 mm
British Museum, London
Oc1846,0809.5.a
Donated by J.M.R. Ince

18.
Basket

Port Essington, Northern Territory, before 1855
Fibre, natural pigment; H. 440 mm, W. 190 mm
British Museum, London
Oc1855,1220.175 Exh. BM
Donated by the the Lords of Admiralty/Haslar Hospital

19.
**Ruins of chimneys at the settlement
of Port Essington (Victoria Settlement),
established in 1838 and abandoned
in 1849**

Cobourg Peninsula, Arnhem Land, Northern Territory
Photograph by Auscape/UIG

in 1838.[24] Although Aboriginal people in the area had long been accustomed to interacting with outsiders, welcoming the Makassan fishermen who came each year to harvest trepang (figs 15–16 and pp. 26–8), relations with the British were at first violent. They gradually became closer, eventually giving rise to a lively bartering economy in which fish, crabs and oysters were exchanged for biscuits and clothing (figs 17–18). Other reports indicate that the settlement's blacksmith was making spearheads for the Aboriginal people from iron.[25] Yet the settlement was constantly blighted by outbreaks of disease, with terrible consequences for the Aboriginal population as well as the soldiers and their families. The young scientist Thomas Huxley (1825–1895) travelling on HMS *Rattlesnake* wrote in a letter in early 1849 that: 'to speak of this place as a settlement is a mere abuse of words – the country in the neighbourhood is the most wretched, the climate the most unhealthy, the human beings the most uncomfortable, and the houses in a condition the most decayed and rotten. I have no doubt of its shortly being abandoned by the Government.'[26] The British government abandoned the settlement later that year (fig. 19).

FIELD PLAN of
MOVEMENTS of the MILITARY.

OYSTER BAY
Called by the French
Baie Fleurieu or Baudins Bay
discovered by
Commodore Baudin in 1802.

REFERENCE.

A A A	Position from which the Detachments advanced on the 7th Octr
B B B	Captn Donaldson's position on the 12th Octr
C C C	Captn Wentworth's position on the 12th Octr
D D D	Major Douglas's position on the 12th Octr
E E E	Captn Wentworths position on the 16th Octr
F F F	Major Douglas's position on the 16th Octr
G G G	Position of the Forces on the 20th Octr
H H H	Do. on the 24th Octr
K K K	Do. on the 18th Novr
L L L	Position to be taken up on the 22nd Novr
M M M	Do. on the 25th Novr
N N	Captn Donaldson's Division arriving on the 1st Novr

Fast frontiers: Van Diemen's Land and the Port Phillip District

The situation that Aboriginal people were facing in the south-east of the continent in this same period was very different. By the 1820s and 1830s some of the fastest and most destructive frontiers in Britain's colonial history were underway. First in Van Diemen's Land (now Tasmania) and then in the Port Phillip District (now Victoria) Aboriginal people were rapidly and violently dispossessed of their country. They were brutal times and spaces, but from these ruins of colonialism come histories of survival together with clear articulations by Aboriginal people of their sovereignty, society and selves as they sought persistently to hold colonial authorities accountable for their actions, and as they pursued and hoped for just and proper treatment.

In Tasmania, Aboriginal people's country was alienated by the British colonial authorities as grants were issued to free settlers at a remarkably rapid rate. Historian James Boyce notes that 'over a million acres were granted in a frenzy of land handouts to free settlers between 1824 and 1831'.[27] In 1828 Governor George Arthur (1784–1854) had sufficient intelligence to report to the Colonial Office in London that Aboriginal people 'already complain that the white people have taken possession of their country, encroached upon their hunting grounds, and destroyed their natural food, the kangaroo'.[28] In response, Aboriginal people mounted guerrilla-style resistance. Conflict and fighting escalated between 1828 and 1830, which the colonial authorities sought to quell by martial means. On 1 November 1828, Governor Arthur imposed martial law in the settled regions against the 'Aboriginal natives', and encouraged 'roving parties' to round them up. As Lisa Ford and David A. Roberts note, 'martial law asserted that Aboriginal people were governed by British law at the same time as it authorised the use of military violence against them'.[29] In 1829, the colonial government had devised the infamous 'Black Line', which involved an attempt to corral Aboriginal people into a corner of the island (fig. 20). It was an expensive fiasco. The escalating conflict between Aboriginal people and settlers was described at the time as the 'Black War'.[30] The effects on Aboriginal people were devastating. Historian Lyndall Ryan notes that within a generation of white settlement the Aboriginal population had been reduced from around 6,000–8,000 people to near extinction. Her estimate of the Aboriginal to settler death ratio during the Black War was 4:1.[31] While other factors were involved, historians agree 'that violence played a significant role in the rapid collapse of the Aboriginal population'.[32]

Proclamation boards, as they are now known, are poignant objects through which to interpret aspects of the Tasmanian frontier (fig. 21). They were designed in the midst of the violence in an attempt to communicate the legal consequences of violent acts and the colonial government's wishes for the cessation of hostilities. These boards were the brainchild of the Surveyor General, George Frankland (1800–1838), who had observed that the

20.
Military Operations Against the Aboriginal Inhabitants of Van Diemen's Land, 1831
This map depicts the 'Black Line': a state-sanctioned military campaign to drive all of the Aboriginal people in Tasmania onto a peninsula in the south-east.

George Frankland (1800–1838), born England
Ink on paper; H. 595 mm, W. 463 mm
National Archives, London
MPG 1/519

21.
Proclamation board
Hung on trees, the boards were conceived as a way to communicate ideas of British justice to Tasmanian Aborigines.

Tasmania, c. 1829
Paint on board; H. 330 mm, W. 225 mm
Museum of Archaeology and Anthropology,
University of Cambridge
Z 15346 Exh. BM

'Aboriginal natives of Van Diemen's land are in the habit of representing events by drawings on the bark of trees'. He hoped that by using pictorial language the problem the government had of communicating with people 'whose language we are totally unacquainted' might be overcome. It was an experiment, but he believed that 'everything ought to be tried to accomplish a reconciliation'. Through strips of illustrations Frankland 'endeavoured to represent in a manner as simple and as well adapted to their supposed ideas as possible, the actual state of things (or rather the origins of the present state) and the desired termination of hostility'.[33] Depicted were idealised images of 'friendship, equality before the law, and mutual punishment for Aborigines and Europeans alike'.[34] They were not so much a visual narrative of actual relations and historical development as a pictorial declaration of the 'underlying principle of justice that the rule of law acknowledges and draws upon', argues legal scholar Desmond Manderson.[35] The proclamation visually made 'represents an idea of justice occasioned by the clash between colonial and Indigenous people'.[36] As such, the proclamation boards are a tangible and sobering reminder of the wide gap that lay between the principles, desires and ideals that the colonial government regularly expressed and the brutal realities on the ground as it continued to wage a war against Aboriginal people in pursuit of territory. The irony of these proclamation boards is that the colonial government and settlers did not adhere to the very principles they illustrated even though it was their law and 'idea of justice' that they sought to impose on Aboriginal people.

The government-appointed 'conciliator', George Augustus Robinson, carried some sketches and boards with him during his so-called 'friendly mission' to the Aborigines.[37] He had been commissioned in 1830 by the colonial authorities to attempt to enter into negotiations with Aboriginal groups, even as state-sanctioned violence against them continued, in a bid to

bring about a resolution and reconciliation. To this end he undertook a series of journeys throughout the island, in the company of some Aboriginal people, on a diplomatic quest. His 'mission' had only mixed success, and in the end he was largely responsible for hatching a plan to remove all Aboriginal people from mainland Tasmania and exile them on outer islands. By November 1830, he had sent thirty-four Aboriginal men and women to Swan Island. By the following September, the government's 'Aborigines Committee' was pursuing as policy Robinson's scheme of island-exile, and had decided on Flinders Island in Bass Strait as the location for an Aboriginal settlement.[38] The conditions under which Aboriginal people believed they were going to Flinders Island were deceptively unclear. Most thought it was only a temporary arrangement, but their exile commenced without an end date (figs 22–23).[39]

The Aboriginal establishment on Flinders Island, which eventually became known as Wybalenna, meaning 'black men's houses', was designed not only to realise a colonial desire for a Tasmania free of Aborigines. Like many colonial institutions of the time, its aims were also to transform its exiled Aboriginal residents into 'civilised', Christian subjects, and so it belongs to a longer history of the institutionalisation of Aboriginal people under colonial conditions. These coercions were often met with resistance as residents did what they could to retain their existing ways of life, even when so far removed from their own country and in the face of a terrible death toll. Superintendents' reports record the absence of residents from the settlement for days at a time, when they would go to other parts of the island to camp, hunt and fish, and congregate beyond the overseers' eyes.[40] They also had contact with other Aboriginal women who were living with sealers on nearby islands.[41] At the same time, some of the residents, the younger ones especially, acquired things such as literacy and bible knowledge, which they would ultimately use to good effect to challenge the very terms of their imprisonment. And they responded to their situation with courage and creativity and 'a high degree of sagacity and astuteness'.[42] This is most evident in a petition to Queen Victoria (1819–1901) penned in early 1846.

Between 1842 and 1845, the situation at Wybalenna had deteriorated badly, due in large part to the autocratic and tyrannical methods of a new superintendent. By early 1846 some of the residents had prepared a petition to be sent to Queen Victoria complaining of their treatment and requesting her personal intervention (fig. 24). Historian Henry Reynolds has described the petition as 'one of the most important… documents relating to the history of relations between indigenous and immigrant Australians', and its content as representing 'the most important Aboriginal historical interpretation available for the colonial period'.[43] This would not be the only time Aboriginal people would seek to circumvent colonial authorities and appeal directly to the British monarch or the Crown's representatives, or that they would use petitioning as a means to pursue their political goals.[44] Both methods would become key features of Aboriginal people's politics as they struggled against

22.
Club
The Quakers who collected this club visited Flinders Island to investigate reports that Aboriginal women were living with sealers in conditions akin to slavery.

Flinders Island, Tasmania, before 1832
Wood; L. 625 mm, Diam. 22 mm
British Museum, London
Oc1921,1014.81 Exh. BM

23.
Shell necklace
Women on Flinders Island made necklaces to wear and to sell at local markets, maintaining their traditions in exile.

Flinders Island, Tasmania, before 1846
Maireener shell (*Phasianotrochus irisodontes*), fibre;
L. 960 mm
British Museum, London
Oc1846,0729.2 Exh. BM
Donated by Lord Stanley

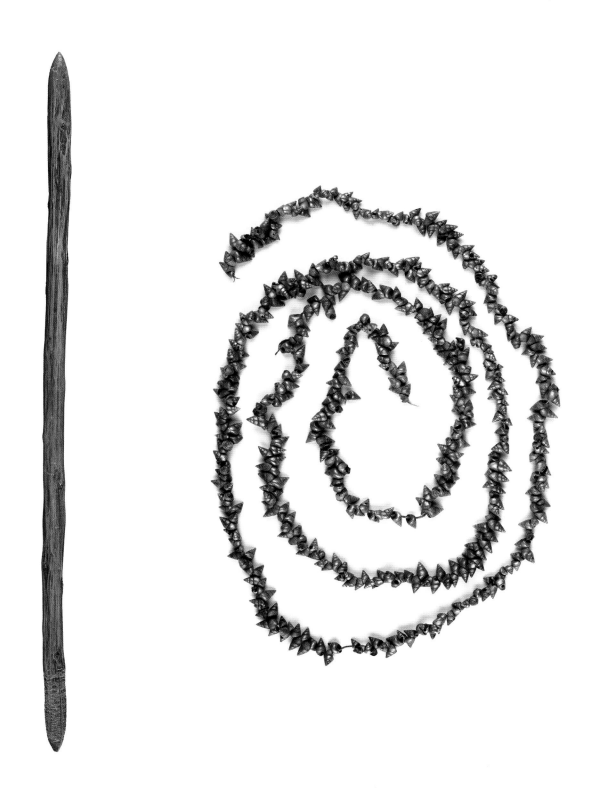

Encounters in country

Goose Island

To Her Majesty Queen Victoria, the Queen
of England and Van Diemans Land &c &c &c

The Humble Petition of the Free Aborigines
Inhabitants of Van Diemans Land now living
upon Flinders Island in Bases Straits &c &c

Most Humbly Sheweth

That we your Majestys
Petitioners are your Free Children, that we were
not taken Prisoners, but freely gave up our Country
to Colonel Arthur then the Governor, after defending ourselves.

Your Petitioners humbly state to your Majesty that Mr Robinson made for us and with
Colonel Arthur an agreement which we have not
lost from our Minds since and we have made
our part of it good.

Your Petitioners humbly tell your Majesty
that when we left our own place we were Plenty
of People, we are now but a little one.

Your Petitioners state they are a long time
at Flinders Island and had Plenty of Super
=intendants and were always a quiet and free
People, and not put into jail.

Your Majesty's Petitioners pray that you
will not allow Doctor Jeanneret to come again
among us as our Superintendent as we hear
he is to be sent another time, for when
Doctor Jeanneret was with us many Moons
He used to carry Pistols in his Pockets and
threatened very often to shoot us and make us
run away in a fright. Doctor Jeanneret
Kept Plenty of Pigs in our Village which
used to run into our houses and Eat up our
Bread from the Fires and take away our

Flour Bags in their Mouths, also to brake into our
Gardens and destroy our Potatos and Cabbages

Our Houses were let fall down and they were
never cleaned, but were covered with Vermin and
not white washed. We were often without clothes
except a very little one and Doctor Jeanneret did
not care to mind us when we were Sick until
we were very bad & Eleven of us died when
he was here He put many of us into jail for
talking to Him because we would not be his
Slaves, He Kept from us our Rations when
He pleased and some times gave us Bad
Rations of Tea and Tobacco. He shot some
of our Dogs before our Eyes and Sent all
the other Dogs of ours to an Island and
when we told them that they would Starve
He told us they might Eat each other. He
put Arms into our hands and made
us to assist his Prisoners to go to Fight
the Soldiers, we did not want to Fight
the Soldiers but He made us go to Fight.
We never were taught to Read or Write
or to Sing to God by the Doctor, He taught
us a little upon the Sundays and His
Prisoner Servant also taught us, and His
Prisoner Servant also took us plenty of
times to jail by His Orders.

The Lord Bishop seen us in this bad
way and we told His Lordship plenty
how Doctor Jeanneret used us

We Humbly pray Your Majesty the Queen
will hear our prayer and not let Doctor
Jeanneret any more to come to Flinders Island
and we your Majestys Servants and Children
will Ever pray as in Duty bound &c &c &c

Walter G. Arthur
Chief of the Ben Lomond Tribe

John Allen

Davy Bruney

Neptune

King Alexander

Augustus

Tom Thumb

Washington

the increasing power of colonial governments and authorities over their lives and affairs, and as they sought repeatedly to have their rights as sovereign people recognised. Whenever necessary, Aboriginal people would address their complaints to higher authorities in Britain, such as the reigning monarch, in the hope that the system of humane government and justice that the colonists were supposed to uphold would eventually, if only occasionally, turn out to be more than just a lie.

The Flinders Island petition catalogued a litany of grievances, including the withholding of rations, the shooting of their dogs and various everyday humiliations. Just as significantly it articulated how its Aboriginal authors saw themselves and understood the contract they had with the colonial government. They described themselves as 'the free Aborigines Inhabitants of V.D.L.', and they told the Queen that 'Mr Robinson made for us and with Colonel Arthur an agreement which we have not lost from our minds since and which we have made our part of it good'.[45] Their complaint was that while they had remained resident on Flinders Island, they had not been treated in the ways promised or expected. Disappointment and disillusionment over broken promises is a thread that runs through relations between Aboriginal people and settler society. As the Flinders Island petition demonstrates, Aboriginal people often responded to their situation by reminding settlers and their governments of past agreements and calling on them to acknowledge and fulfil their responsibilities towards the people they had dispossessed.

Among the other signatories to the Flinders Island petition was Calamarowenye, who signed as King Tippoo (c. 1803–1860), the European name that had been bestowed on him. A year earlier he had had his portrait painted by the colonial artist John Skinner Prout (1805–1876). In early 1845, Prout spent eight days on the island during which he created a portfolio of sketches of many of the residents, each of which conveys something of the sitter's individual personality (figs 25–26).[46] They are surprisingly sympathetic portrayals given they were produced when images of Aboriginal people were becoming increasingly caricatured and derogatory.[47] 'He was obviously sensitive to their predicament', perhaps because during those eight days he heard them describe their situation, listened to their grievances and observed the conditions under which they lived.[48] Prout also made a portrait of Tanganutara (Sarah; c. 1806–1858), who in the wake of the petition and along with other residents had her complaints put on the public record. She resented the treatment of her children, Fanny Cochrane Smith (1834–1905) and Adam (1838–1857), complaining they were 'flogged too much' by the teacher. Fanny herself, then aged about thirteen, testified to ill treatment.[49] Prout and his family remained closely involved in the lives of the Flinders Island people, including after their return to the main island where the forty-seven remaining residents were resettled at Oyster Cove south of Hobart.[50] The petition had, at one level, worked because it triggered the closure of the

25.
Sarah from Cape Portland V.D.L.
Tanganutara (Sarah) gave evidence to an enquiry about the ill treatment of her daughter Fanny Cochrane Smith and other children at Flinders Island. Cochrane Smith later made the only recordings of Tasmanian Aboriginal songs.

John Skinner Prout (1805–1876), born Plymouth, England
Tasmania, 1845
Watercolour on paper; H. 215 mm, W. 150 mm
British Museum, London
Oc2006,Drg.12 Exh. BM

26.
King Tippoo from Hobart Town V.D.L
Calamarowenye (King Tippoo) was one of the signatories to a petition to Queen Victoria for improvement to the conditions of Aboriginal people on Flinders Island (fig. 24).

John Skinner Prout (1805–1876), born, Plymouth, England
Tasmania, 1845
Watercolour on paper; H. 230 mm, W. 158 mm
British Museum, London
Oc2006,Drg.18 Exh. BM

island institution. But this fell far short of its appeal to the Queen to ensure that her government's promises were made good.

By the early 1830s most of the land in Tasmania had been alienated, and so land-hungry men began to look across Bass Strait to the mainland for new frontiers for their sheep and cattle. Without colonial government authority, by 1835 they were moving in waves into the area that became known as the Port Phillip District (now Victoria). Many of these squatters were ex-convicts who had honed their bush skills, as well as their attitudes about Aborigines, on the Tasmanian frontier.[51] The land to the north and west of Melbourne, which had begun in 1835 as a makeshift 'tent city', was especially attractive to running huge flocks of sheep. Here were to be found extensive 'grasslands', the result of Aboriginal people's practices of 'fire-stick farming' carried out over millennia. As in Tasmania, pastoral expansion into the Port Phillip District was fast – 'as fast as any expansion in the history of European colonisation', according to historian Richard Broome. The ramifications for Aboriginal people were shocking: 'the intensity of the struggle over land in Port Phillip meant that the Aboriginal to European loss of life ratio, through violence on the Port Phillip frontier, was high at about 12 Aboriginal deaths to every European death'.[52]

The opening up of the Port Phillip frontier in the 1830s and 1840s coincided with a high point of British humanitarianism. In 1833 Britain had abolished slavery and by 1836 the British Parliament had established a Select Committee on Aborigines in British colonies led by Thomas Fowell Buxton (1786–1845). It reported on the treatment of Aboriginal people across the British empire, including the Australian colonies. These humanitarian currents, which raised questions about 'the nature of Britishness, the morality of colonisation and the status of indigenous people', contributed to some efforts being made in the Port Phillip district to ameliorate the effects on Aboriginal people of pastoral expansion and colonial settlement.[53]

This context, along with raw memories of the Black War in Tasmania, is believed to have contributed to a group of colonists seeking to enter a treaty with the Kulin people for access to their country.[54] The treaty, now popularly known as Batman's Deed or Batman's Treaty because of the involvement of John Batman (1801–1839), was initiated and drafted by a group of Tasmanian land speculators, who formed themselves into a corporation that became known as the Port Phillip Association (fig. 27). Although the activities of these men and their treaty have been much discussed, many of the details surrounding how they entered into treaty negotiations with some Aboriginal 'chiefs' and what actually transpired on the day of the treaty-signing are confused and contradictory, and loaded by legend-making over many decades. Opinions are now divided on how the text and the event ought to be interpreted.

Encounters in country

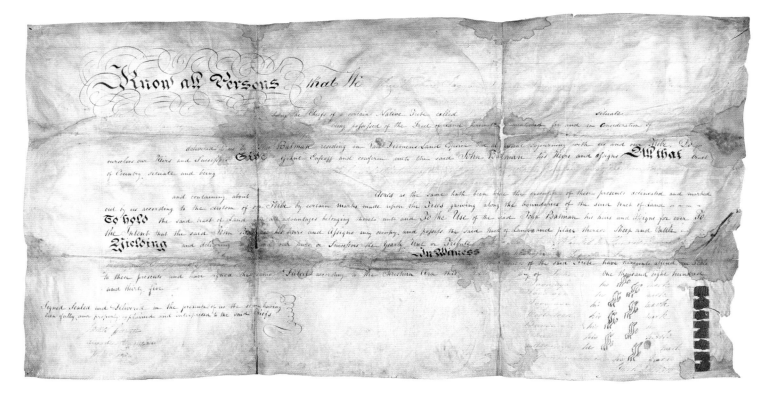

Some historians consider it little more than a cynical move by land-hungry men to trick Aboriginal people into giving up their country in exchange for 'mere trifles'. The goods listed in the treaty included blankets, knives, scissors, tomahawks, looking glasses, handkerchiefs, shirts and flour.[55] Others argue that the treaty-signing event represented a 'coincidence of ritual'.[56] On the settler side, it followed a form of conveyance known as *enfoeffment* in which, through a series of acts such as walking the boundaries of the property and handing over some soil or the twig of a tree from it, 'a ritual of possession' is performed. On the Kulin side these same acts, anthropologist Diane Barwick has suggested, were akin to *tanderrum*. This was a ceremony that Aboriginal people performed to grant others access to country and its resources on a temporary and non-exclusive basis. While Aboriginal people have a sense of ownership of land, they conceive of it as 'a right to *use* the *resources* on particular parts of the landscape for a particular purpose'.[57] The implication is that the agreement the Kulin entered into with the Association was for limited access not absolute title. The treaty is, in that sense, a clear statement of their rights to negotiate about land and access to it, and evidence of their willingness to do so in the face of colonial incursion. That willingness was perhaps influenced, as historian Robert Kenny has recently argued, by what the Kulin knew about the situation that other

27.

The 'Batman Land Deed' (counterpart)

The deed was a contract for an exchange of land around the region of Melbourne between Aboriginal 'chiefs' and John Batman. It was signed by Jagajaga, Jagajaga, and Jagajaga ('three brothers'), Cooloolock, Bungarie, Yanyan, Moowhip, and Mommarmarmalar. The circumstances in which the deed was made are debated.

Victoria, 1835
Ink on vellum with wax seal; H. 340 mm, W. 660 mm
British Library, London
Add Ch 37766 Exh. BM

Aboriginal groups, around Sydney and in New South Wales, had faced earlier as settlers had encroached into their country.[58] Yet, whatever the Kulin believed they were agreeing to, in the end the treaty was not upheld. The Colonial Office in London refused to recognise it. The British government was opposed to private individuals entering into contracts over land with Aboriginal people in its Australian colonies, preferring instead to claim the entire territory for the Crown and assuming complete sovereignty or radical title over it.[59]

Within this period, 'protection' became the dominant method used by colonial authorities and missionaries towards Aboriginal people as they sought to spare them from the worst excesses of colonisation. To this end, a protectorate for Aborigines, known as the Port Phillip Protectorate, was established in 1839. It involved the appointment of a Chief Protector – in this case, G.A. Robinson, fresh from his experience as 'conciliator' in Tasmania – and a handful of assistant protectors, who were to encourage Aboriginal people to settle down on small reserves, where they could by tuition and example become 'civilised' and 'Christianised'. Protectors were also 'charged… with the task of shielding Aboriginal [people] in the district from "cruelty, oppression and injustice" and "from encroachments on their property"'.[60] Aboriginal people did not fully embrace the system, remaining resentful and resistant to the alienation of their country although, as historian Tracey Banivanua Mar argues, in some instances Aboriginal people in the Port Phillip district 'made good use of the protectorate system and humanitarian networks not just to seek refuge from raging frontier violence, but also to articulate longer-term demands'.[61] From the outset, though, the Protectorate was poorly resourced for the monumental task involved and met with intense settler resistance and obstruction. Within a decade, it had been disbanded.

High on the list of Aboriginal people's longer-term demands was good and sufficient country – country of their own choosing – on which to rebuild their shattered societies and to mend their ruptured worlds. Throughout the 1840s and 1850s some groups lobbied the authorities to recognise their rights in land and to compensate them for having been dispossessed of it, including by granting them reserves on which they might become farmers and engage in the colonial economy, and by these means enjoy some degree of independence and autonomy. One such settlement was Coranderrk near Healesville outside Melbourne, which had been established in the early 1860s. In time it became a successful and prosperous farming community, as well as a site of savvy and sophisticated politics. Like the Flinders Island people before them, the Coranderrk people pursued a politics of diplomacy, engaging governors, premiers and monarchs in their political struggles, and through various means, including petitioning and gift-giving, incorporating them into relationships of obligation and reciprocity.[62]

William Barak, Coranderrk and the arts of diplomacy
Maria Nugent

William Barak (fig. 28) was born on the Yarra River around 1824, not long before the influx of white people into his father's country. He had reputedly witnessed as a young boy the signing of Batman's Treaty (see pp. 147–8). As an adult, he became a leader (or *ngurungaeta*) of the Kulin people. Barak came from a long line of ngurungaeta, and his ancestors were the custodians of the Mount William stone axe quarry, which supplied highly valued greenstone axe heads over vast trade routes (see p. 33).

In the late 1850s and early 1860s, along with other Kulin people, Barak was involved in negotiations with the colonial authorities for suitable and sufficient land on which to establish an independent Aboriginal farming community. They had first selected land at Acheron but were swindled out of it. They chose another run in the hills outside Melbourne on the Yarra River, which they called Coranderrk after a flowering bush.

The Coranderrk people engaged in a politics of diplomacy, which drew on their traditional practices, to secure some rights to the land and to shore up their future. In 1863 a deputation of Coranderrk men walked to Melbourne to attend the Governor's levee in honour of Queen Victoria's birthday, which that year was also a celebration of the recent marriage of her eldest son, Albert (1841–1910), Prince of Wales. They gave an address, which assured the monarch of their loyalty, and presented gifts to the royal family. They sent spears, clubs, hatchets, boomerangs, shields and throwing sticks to the Prince of Wales and his brother Prince Alfred (1844–1900); grass nets, a basket and a possum-skin rug (*coogra*) for Queen Victoria; and a 'dress of emu feathers' for the Prince of Wales's new wife, Alexandra (1844–1925) (fig. 29).[63] Soon after sending these gifts, the colonial government in Melbourne formally reserved the land at Coranderrk for an Aboriginal settlement. This gave rise to a belief that Queen Victoria had given the land in recognition of the Kulin as original owners and in compensation of their dispossession.[64] They continued to engage in the arts of diplomacy in the decades to come, including in 1886

presenting the outgoing Victorian Premier, Graham Berry (1822–1904), who was about to return to England, an illuminated address, in which they implored him to 'keep remembering the Natives for the Natives will remember you for your doing good to Coranderrk'.[65]

In his old age, William Barak spent time drawing and painting (fig. 30). He is one among a small group of Aboriginal people in the nineteenth century to create drawings on paper or cardboard that documented, and communicated to Europeans, important aspects of their history and culture. He made use of traditional materials, like charcoal and ochre, supplemented with new ones, such as Reckitt's Blue and manufactured paints. Unlike some other nineteenth-century Aboriginal artists such as Tommy McRae (*c.* 1835–1901) and Mickey of Ulladulla (*c.* 1820–1891), whose work made searing and astute observations of the colonists, Barak's output was almost exclusively concerned with his own people. Art historian Judith Ryan says that 'the central preoccupation of Barak's work is ceremony, a powerful cultural memory for the artist and something of immense fascination for Europeans'.[66] By the time he began to draw, the Kulin were no longer performing ceremonies as their social and cultural practices had been ruptured by colonisation. Barak's drawings of ceremonies that he had witnessed, been told about, or participated in, represent a remarkable feat of memory. They are 'narratives that eloquently recount many of the important features of Kulin society, which he genuinely wanted "others" to understand'.[67] Many of Barak's drawings ended up in private collections and public museums in Europe as well as Australia. The watercolour shown in figure 30 was produced in 1895 and depicts a ceremony with men dancing holding boomerangs while women, dressed in possum-skin cloaks, sit in the foreground beating time.

28.
William Barak with lyrebird feathers

Arthur Baessler (1857–1907), born Glauchau, Germany
Coranderrk, Healesville, Victoria, 1892
Photographic print on paper; H. 319 mm, W. 237 mm
Staatliche Museen zu Berlin, Preußischer Kulturbesitz,
Ethnologisches Museum

29.
Emu feather skirt
Aboriginal women in Victoria sent an emu
feather skirt, like this one, to the Princess
of Wales upon her marriage in 1863.

Victoria, 1840s
Emu feather, fibre; L. 1290 mm (without ties), W. 400 mm
British Museum, London
Oc1981,Q.1757 Exh. BM
Donated by Joseph Barnard Davis

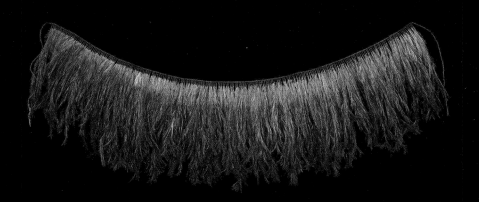

30.
Ceremony
In the foreground, figures, probably women,
sit wrapped in cloaks. A central figure holds
two boomerangs, often used as clap sticks
in ceremonies. Their dynamic poses suggest
that the dancing men who face the viewer are
being accompanied by music and song.

William Barak (1824–1903), Wurundjeri/ Woiwurung
Victoria, 1895
Watercolour, graphite and ochre on paper;
H. 555 mm, W. 571 mm
National Museum of Australia, Canberra
2004.0071.0001 Exb. BM

Exploring histories

Territories are not only claimed and colonised by means of occupation and settlement. Colonial possession is also enacted and imagined through processes of naming, charting, drawing and myriad other forms by which knowledge about places and people is codified and circulated. Exploration was a key site through which knowledge was accrued, providing reams of raw data that fuelled scientific study and speculation as well as colonial expansion. There is growing interest in and acknowledgment of the depth of Aboriginal knowledge upon which the activity or enterprise of exploration relied. Exploration archives and records are being reappraised and drawn on as sources for histories of cross-cultural encounters, including exchanges between European and Aboriginal epistemologies.[68] This work begins to unsettle the status of expedition leaders as singularly responsible for the so-called 'discoveries' made in their names.[69]

In Australia Aboriginal people contributed to and participated in exploration in many ways, including in some cases by being employed on expeditions as 'professional' guides, go-betweens and interpreters. Even though today some of these 'intermediaries' provoke ambivalence because they are seen as having contributed to opening up Aboriginal country to colonial expansion and thus collaborating with colonists, there is also a certain admiration for the ways in which they applied their knowledge, skills and agency to new conditions.[70]

Professional Aboriginal guides were particularly valued for brokering relations between exploration parties and the Aboriginal people encountered in the course of expeditions. When the British navigator Captain Matthew Flinders undertook a short maritime expedition along the north-east coast in 1799, he was accompanied 'by Bongaree, a native, whose good disposition and manly conduct had attracted my esteem' (figs 31–32).[71] Bongaree (or Bungaree; c. 1775–1830) later volunteered to join Flinders's circumnavigation voyage. Flinders recorded in his journal that he had previously 'experienced much advantage from the presence of a native of Port Jackson, in bringing about a friendly intercourse with the inhabitants of other parts of the coast'.[72] According to historian Bronwen Douglas, 'the content and wording of [Flinders's] own journal suggest that the most potent element in local [Indigenous] responses to the strangers and repeated expressions of eagerness to communicate with them was Bungaree'.[73] In those encounters with 'stranger-Aborigines', Bungaree's body was often a focus for attention. He had been ritually scarified on his upper body, later described as being 'a vertical set of three parallel straight bars on his shoulders and upper chest and two sets of five, one above the other on his right breast, those on the breast being slightly diagonal'.[74] Captain Phillip Parker King recorded on a later survey that during one particular encounter with Aboriginal people some distance from Sydney Bungaree's scarifications were 'the subject of particular

31.
Portrait of Bungaree, a Native of New South Wales
Bungaree accompanied Matthew Flinders on the first circumnavigation of Australia and played an important role in brokering relations with Indigenous people encountered. He was also a well-known figure who navigated the politics of early colonial Sydney.

Augustus Earle (1793–1838), born London, England
Sydney, New South Wales
Oil on canvas; H. 685 mm, W. 505 mm
National Gallery of Australia, Canberra

32.
Club belonging to Bungaree
An inscription suggests he gave this club to a British settler.

Sydney region, New South Wales, before 1830
Wood; L. 755 mm, Diam. 87 mm
Pitt Rivers Museum, University of Oxford
1900.55.57 Exh. BM
Donated by Robert Francis Wilkins

33.
Piper
John Piper was engaged as a guide by explorer and government surveyor Major Thomas Mitchell.

William Henry Fernyhough (1809–1849), born Staffordshire, England
Sydney, New South Wales, 1836
Ink on paper; H. 200 mm, W. 118 mm
National Library of Australia, Canberra
nla.pic-vn3789425

PIPER.
THE NATIVE WHO ACCOMPANIED MAJOR MITCHELL
IN HIS EXPEDITION TO THE INTERIOR.
Printed by JGAustin&Cº Nº 19 Bridge Street Sydney

remarks; and when he pointed to the sea, to shew them whence he came, they set up a shout of admiration and surprise'.[75]

Similarly, when the surveyor-explorer Major Thomas Mitchell set out on his third expedition in New South Wales in 1836, in which he traced the rivers Darling and Murray, he was accompanied by an Aboriginal man 'who called himself John Piper and spoke English tolerably well' (fig. 33). Mitchell invariably described Piper as an interpreter. Piper had offered his services to the expedition while it was preparing for departure from Sydney; had agreed

to accompany it as far as it went (which is to say that he gave an undertaking not to leave part way through); and set the price for his services as a horse, clothing and food. The expedition's records provide many details of Piper's work in brokering relations with Aboriginal people through whose country the expedition travelled. 'I sent Piper forward', Mitchell notes at one point, 'to tell them who we were, and thus, if possible, prevent any alarm at our appearance'.[76]

There is also ample evidence testifying to just how much exploring parties depended on the hospitality and knowledge of the Aboriginal people whose country they traversed. A celebrated example in the history of Australian exploration is the assistance that the surviving members of the Robert O'Hara Burke (1821–1861) and William John Wills (1834–1861) expedition received from the Yandruwandha people of Cooper Creek on their desperate return from a failed expedition to the Gulf of Carpentaria in 1861 (figs 34–36). During expeditions, exploration parties would regularly find themselves either shadowed – 'at length I perceived them peeping at us from behind trees'[77] – or actually accompanied by Aboriginal people for a certain distance before being passed onto another group at a boundary invisible to the explorers but well known among neighbours. Mitchell much admired Aboriginal people's intimate knowledge of their country, writing in his journal that to them 'the surface of the earth is, in fact, as legible as a newspaper, so accustomed are they to read in any traces left thereon the events of the day'.[78] And invariably explorers depended on Aboriginal people's hospitality for sustenance. Again Mitchell described an incident in which some local Aboriginal people guiding his party supplied them with honey sourced from a tree, causing the explorer to admire their 'ingenuity and skill in supplying wants which we, with all our science, could not hope to attain'.[79] It was not surprising then that Mitchell was keen to keep relations friendly and open, noting at one point that 'as I felt we were rather unceremonious invaders of their country it was certainly my duty to conciliate them by every possible means'.[80]

A common means for conciliation was the distribution of gifts. Both maritime and inland explorers usually went prepared with presents to give to Aboriginal people in exchange for assistance and information. Matthew Flinders, for instance, lists among the supplies he took on his circumnavigation voyage 'also various articles for presents to, and barter with, the native inhabitants of the countries to be visited'.[81] Mitchell was fond of presenting tomahawks to Aboriginal men he encountered, although by his third expedition he was expressing frustration at the bad effect he believed these presents were having. 'It was evident now', he wrote in his journal, 'how injudicious we had been in giving these savages presents; had we not done so we should not have been so much importuned by them'.[82] His complaint was that Aboriginal people's desire for certain things meant that they demanded objects rather than earned them. This echoed a common claim

34. (previous page)
Channel country
Usually extremely arid, this area floods after heavy rains and comes alive with plants and animals. Some permanent waterholes and periodic flows of water supported many Aboriginal groups to live across this vast region. The explorers Robert O'Hara Burke (1821–1861) and William John Wills (1834–1861) traversed Channel country on their expedition in 1860–1.

Channel country, south-west Queensland
Photograph: Ian Rolfe

35.
Breastplate
The Yandruwandha people of Cooper Creek, were presented with this breastplate, after giving aid to the explorers Burke, Wills and John King (1841–1872) when they were exhausted and starving on their return from an expedition from Melbourne to the Gulf of Carpentaria (1860–1). Only King survived.

Xavier Arnoldi (Engraver; c. 1823–1876), Melbourne, Victoria, c. 1862
Brass; H. 93 mm, W. 207 mm, D. 1 mm
National Museum of Australia, Canberra
IR4974.0001 Exh. BM

36.
Hand axe
Collected during the 1860–1 Victorian exploring expedition led by Burke and Wills.

Stone, L. 162 mm, W. 60 mm, D. 37 mm
British Museum, London
Oc.9127 Exh. BM
Donated by Sir Augustus Wollaston Franks

37.
Bark receptacle with contents
Collected by David Carnegie

Western Australia, c. 1896
British Museum, London
Donated by David Wynford Carnegie
Container
Bark; L. 467 mm, Diam. 55 mm
Oc1898,-.56

Bone nose ornament
Bone, gum, red cockatoo feather; L. 190 mm
Oc1898,-.57

Wooden pins
Wood, bandicoot (*Peragale lagotis*) fur; L. 161 mm (a), L. 140 mm (b)
Oc1898,-.58.a-b

Wooden pins, tied together
Wood, feather, fibre; L. 257 mm, W. 39 mm
Oc1898,-.59.a-b

Girdle
Fibre, feather; L.106 mm, W. 9 mm
Oc1898,-.61

Thirteen flint flakes
Oc1898,-.62.a-m

made by settlers that Aboriginal people did not understand the proper relations between things and their value, and they were moreover seen as being easily corrupted by outside influences. Mitchell had definite ideas about the function that objects ought to have performed in these cross-cultural encounters, when he noted that 'still less were we inclined to give tomahawks on demand, since our presents had not been received with that sense of obligation which might have been shown by any class of human beings, however savage'.[83]

Other explorers eschewed gift-giving or other conciliatory methods, preferring instead to use force and coercion. Among the large company of explorers traipsing through nineteenth-century Australia was the young and brash British adventurer and prospector David Carnegie. Born in London in 1871, he arrived in Western Australia, via India, in company with his friend Lord Percy Douglas (1868–1920) in 1892. Learning that gold had been found at Coolgardie, they immediately set out to join the rush. Carnegie engaged in a series of prospecting expeditions with some success, and subsequently led an exploration party in 1896 through the colony's far

northern regions. He is remembered in the annals of Australian exploration for his practice of kidnapping or capturing Aboriginal people and forcing them to reveal their water sources. In regard to some of his collecting practices during his explorations (fig. 37), he wrote:

> Quaintest of all these articles were the native 'portmanteaus', that is to say, bundles of treasures rolled up in bark, wound round and round with string – string made from human hair or from that of dingoes and opossums. In these 'portmanteaus' are found carved sticks, pieces of quartz, red ochre, feathers, and a number of odds and ends. Of several that were in this camp I took two – my curiosity and desire to further knowledge of human beings, so unknown and so interesting, overcame my honesty, and since the owners had retired so rudely I could not barter with them. Without doubt the meat-tins and odds and ends that we left behind us have more than repaid them. One of these portmanteaus may be seen in the British Museum, the other I have still, unopened.[84]

Not all knowledge exchanges in the context of exploration were so violently extractive. Some early explorations, especially those involving botanists, naturalists and other scientists, produced enduringly important records of Aboriginal practices and languages. Exploration contributed to dawning awareness about the linguistic diversity that existed among the Aboriginal population in Australia. Midshipman John Septimus Roe (1797–1878), for example, noted in his journal in 1818 that Aboriginal 'languages can change within 50 or 60 miles' along the coast.[85] It also enabled valued word lists and vocabularies to be made. Naturalists on exploration expeditions were responsible for some of the earliest and most detailed descriptions of Aboriginal people's environmental knowledge and land use practices. This knowledge, which now has considerable value in the context of efforts to rectify and ameliorate contemporary environmental damage, depended greatly on the Aboriginal people who accompanied these expeditions.[86] Historian Tiffany Shellam describes, for instance, the contribution of a young man known as Manyat, who accompanied the surgeon Alexander Collie on natural history expeditions in south-west Australia in the 1830s, in which he would apply knowledge he had learnt as a boy through stories and songs about plants and geographical features in regions he had never before visited. In the process he acquired new knowledge, assembling his own collection of specimens of trees to take back home with him.[87]

The acquisition and assemblage of material objects and natural specimens were part of the knowledge economy of exploration. Explorers were by definition collectors. Conditions for collecting were various. Already mentioned was the exchange of European goods for Aboriginal ones. On

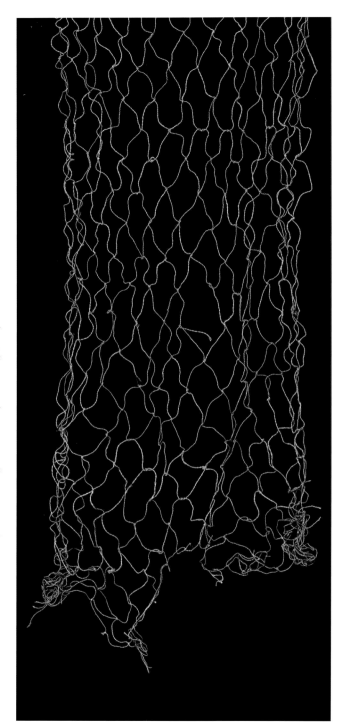

other occasions, Aboriginal people appear to have presented things to explorers without expectation of return. Mitchell, for instance, describes a situation in which some Aboriginal men 'insisted on presenting their clubs and woomeras to our men', and another when 'A small tribe came forward and laid down a number of newly-made nets at my feet. I declined accepting anything however save a beautifully wrought bag'.[88] He must have accepted at least one net, however, because there is an example in the British Museum's collection that carries a small paper label which reads: Net presented by the natives to Thomas Mitchell on his first passage of the river Murray (figs 38–39).[89] Aboriginal guides were also regularly involved in these object exchanges, and in the work of collecting and connoisseurship more generally. Bungaree's assessment of other Aboriginal groups' belongings was sometimes recorded. According to one account: 'Bong-ree readily admitted that [their huts] were much superior to any huts of the natives which he had before seen'. And like Manyat, Bungaree, it seems, was assembling his own collection: 'He brought away a small hand basket, made of some kind of leaf, capable of containing five or six pints of water'.[90]

While objects were bartered and traded, just as comonly things were confiscated or stolen. Within the British Museum's collection are a spearhead and a spearthrower that were acquired during Lieutenant Phillip Parker King's survey on the north-west coast during 1821 (figs 40–42). These objects were included in a large stash of material that was taken by the expedition at Hanover Bay. King recorded that:

> Upon the beach we found two catamarans, or floats, on each of
> which a large bundle of spears was tied with ligatures of bark;
> and on searching about the grass we soon found and secured
> all their riches, consisting of water-baskets, tomahawks, spears,
> throwing-sticks, fire-sticks, fishing-lines, and thirty-six spears;
> some of the latter were of large size, and very roughly made, and
> one was headed with a piece of stone curiously pointed and
> worked. This last spear is propelled by a throwing-stick, which
> was also found lying by it.[91]

'All their riches' were seized as retaliation for the spearing of the expedition's surgeon the day before. In their journals and other writings, the sailors rationalised their actions by blaming the Aboriginal men for the violence, representing them as 'treacherous' and so in their eyes deserving of retribution and punishment. In a letter to his family, one of the expedition, the young naval surveyor John Septimus Roe, concluded his account of the violent altercations at Hanover Bay by saying that 'we do not think they will be in any great hurry to communicate with strangers'.[92] This not only reinforces the ways in which Roe believed – or needed to believe – that the expedition had gained the upper hand in this encounter but also suggests how conscious

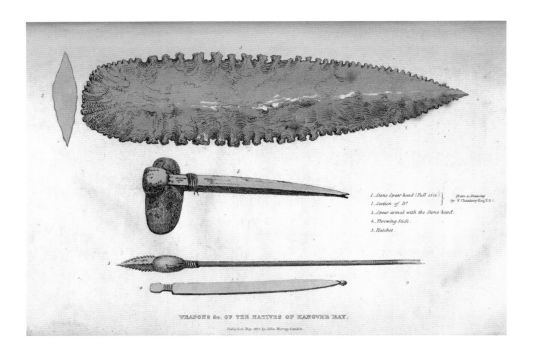

early explorers were that their actions could have ripple effects for other explorers. The navigator Matthew Flinders was alert to this. After taking captive a young man at Caledon Bay in the north as punishment for theft, Flinders reluctantly decided to release him after a couple of days, even though he thought he might be a valuable source of knowledge, because he did not want other explorers 'to suffer a hostile or violent reception from the Caledon Bay Aborigines as a "consequence" of his [own] actions'.[93]

Whether privately or publically funded, exploration in Australia was undertaken in service of colonial expansion. Overland exploration parties proceeded just ahead of – or behind or in tandem with – the movement of settlers, pastoralists and speculators into new regions. Yet it is clear that many of the Aboriginal people explorers encountered were already well aware that 'white men' were occupying the country. Some whom Mitchell met had smallpox marks on their bodies; others had already learnt a name for the strangers. He wrote in his journal that he 'heard calls in various directions, and whitefellow pronounced very loudly and distinctly'.[94] Intelligence about white people travelled through Aboriginal people's extensive communication networks; soon they would arrive in person, with their cattle and their sheep, to stay.

40.
Spearhead
After the ship's surgeon was speared by an Aboriginal man at Hanover Bay, Phillip Parker King took this spearhead, canoes and other items in retaliation.

Hanover Bay, Western Australia, before 1821
Stone; L. 140 mm, W. 38 mm, D. 7 mm
British Museum, London
Oc.8767 Exh. BM
Donated by Sir Augustus Wollaston Franks

41.
Weapons of the Natives of Hanover Bay
The weapons were collected by Phillip Parker King's crew at Hanover Bay. The group includes a spearhead like the one now in the British Museum collection. John Septimus Roe, an officer on board the ship, wrote 'our surgeon Dr. Montgomery was severely wounded by a spear in the back, and we were obliged to shoot one of them as a punishment for their base and treacherous conduct.'

Engraving after a drawing by F. Chantrey Esq. FRS

Expanding frontiers

In 1872 and 1877, John Ewen Davidson (1841–1923) donated to the British Museum objects he had obtained in the colony of Queensland in the 1860s. After visits to the West Indies and British Guiana, London-born and Oxford-educated Davidson had arrived in Queensland in 1865 where he set about establishing sugar plantations and mills.[95] He moved into an especially violent frontier, one that 'bristled with weaponry' on both sides. Queensland's frontiers were at this time, as historian Raymond Evans notes, 'suffused with acts of violence and terror, a consequence of both a single-minded determination to dispossess [Aborigines] and a spirited indigenous defence'.[96]

Davidson's donations derive from and are testaments to this terrible history (fig. 43). His personal journal charts his gradual desensitisation to the violence he witnessed and later participated in, as well as recording the contexts in which his collecting was carried out. Of an incident in the Mackay area in September 1865, he wrote that 'the blacks ran off a short way on seeing us but were not frightened when we fired (in the air)… and I went up to the camp and took some boat shaped pieces of wood [possibly *coolamons*] and a nullah nullah as trophies!'[97] Concluding a violent encounter by collecting Aboriginal people's possessions was, it appears, Davidson's usual practice. About a year later he recorded another instance when he and his business partner shot at some Aboriginal people, killing one and wounding others, noting that: 'There was plenty of blood on one or two shields, which we picked up'.[98] Aboriginal people used shields and other weapons in 'spirited defence' against the incursions of armed colonists (see pp. 74–8). Spears, which could be loaded quickly on spearthrowers, were a match for guns until the invention and issue to colonial and native police forces of a 'repeating rifle capable of considerable destruction'. Snider carbines and Martini-Henrys arrived on the Queensland frontier from the early 1870s and early 1880s respectively.[99]

Pastoralism had expanded quickly into Queensland from the 1840s. By the late 1850s mining frontiers opened up, attracting large immigrant populations. Soon fledgling maritime and plantation industries, such as the sugar industry in which Davidson was involved, were being developed, setting Queensland apart as the only colony where pastoral, mining, shipping and

42.
Spearthrower
It is likely that this spearthrower was collected by the crew of Phillip Parker King's ship, *Mermaid*.

Hanover Bay, Western Australia, *c.* 1821
Wood, gum, grass; L. 845 mm, W. 50 mm
British Museum, London
Oc.982
Donated by Henry Christy

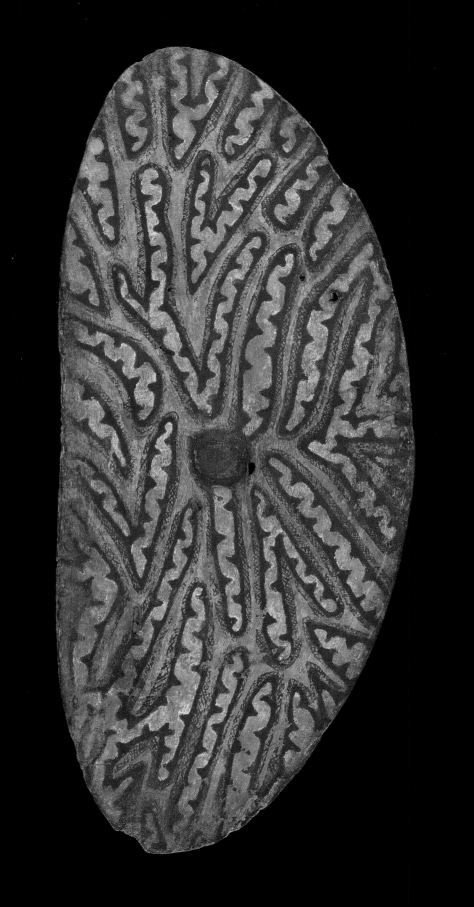

43.
Shield
Collected by John Ewen Davidson, who participated in expeditions during which Aboriginal people were killed on the Queensland frontier.

Rockingham Bay, Queensland, before 1872
Fig tree (*ficus albipila*) wood, natural pigment;
H. 998 mm, W. 425 mm
British Museum, London
Oc.7696 Exh. BM
Donated by John Ewen Davidson

44.
Message stick
The design depicts geographical features and a ship. The inscription reads 'Extreme N.W. of W. Australia. F.N. Broome. 27.??.85'. Broome (1842–1896) was the Governor of Western Australia, 1883–9.

Western Australia, before 1885
Wood; L. 254 mm, W. 23 mm, D. 5 mm
Oc,+.2424 Exh. BM
Donated by Frederick Napier Broome

45. (following page)
Windjana Gorge
In this gorge on 16 November 1894, Jandamarra and other Bunuba people entered into battle with armed police (see pp. 168–9).

Windjana Gorge, Kimberley region, Western Australia
Photograph: Dan Proud

agricultural industries advanced in concert.[100] In Western Australia pastoral frontiers expanded into the north from the 1860s, followed by mining from the 1880s. Ports gradually opened up on the far north-west coast, including Broome in the 1880s, linking these frontier industries to global markets (fig. 44).

Australia's northern frontiers expanded during a period when racial attitudes were hardening. The popularisation of racial theories that placed Aboriginal people at the bottom of the scale of human evolution provided a readily available justification used by some sections of settler society for the atrocities committed. There were other ways to deny the horrible reality of the situation. A colonial vernacular peppered with euphemisms developed. As historian Tom Griffiths notes, 'Aborigines were "civilised" or "dispersed" or "pacified", white settlers went on a "spree" and boasted of the "black crows" they had shot'.[101] This language not only served to secrete the violence to avoid possible legal consequences, but also worked to ease disquieted consciences. It was a language that disguised the true nature of what was actually happening.

In some respects, pastoralists and other settlers had the tacit support of colonial governments and authorities for the violent dispossession of Aboriginal people from their lands. Little was done on these northern frontiers to prevent the violence or to protect Aboriginal people from it. Indeed, some historians have argued that colonial governments, such as Queensland's, 'entertained a general, implicit policy to aid and encourage the destruction'.[102] In some places much of the explicit violence was committed by native police corps, which sometimes operated as though they were above the law, functioning as roving 'death squads' intent on exterminating Aborigines.[103] Along with non-Aboriginal police, these travelling bands comprised Aboriginal men recruited from other regions, who considered themselves enemies to the Aboriginal people they pursued. It is clear from Davidson's journal that he travelled with the native police in Queensland, and that they were engaged in killing local Aboriginal people encountered on the way. In one entry he wrote: 'some [Aborigines] were seen ahead and shot down; it is a strange and painful sight to see a human being running for this life and see the black police galloping after him and hear the crack of the carbines'.[104]

In addition to shootings, massacres and murders, poisoning, sexual assaults on women, kidnapping and enforced labour were all features of these frontier worlds. As one official in the Colonial Office in London wrote in 1866: 'I believe it to be no means easy to exaggerate the recklessness with which blacks have been destroyed (in some cases by strychnine like foxes) in Queensland'.[105] As on earlier frontiers, the impacts on Aboriginal populations were unimaginable. It is estimated that in Queensland, for instance, by the 1890s there had been 'a demographic slump of some 90 per cent, owing to a combination of disease, starvation, a rapidly falling birth rate and overt violence'.[106] Violent frontier conflict, including recorded massacres, continued

'Let us hear no more of Pigeon': violence in the Kimberley
Ian Coates

By the 1890s the Kimberley region in north-west Australia was a violent place. Aboriginal people had seen settlers, with their sheep and cattle, encroach further onto their land. They responded by taking stock, burning the grasslands and occasionally attacking settlers, before retreating to the ranges.

In response, the settlers called on the police for greater protection. They undertook regular patrols, dispersing Aboriginal people and confiscating objects from 'native camps' they came across; those that were suspected of attacks on settlers were fired upon – some were killed.

Police Sub-Inspector C.H. Ord (fig. 46) donated some of the material taken from camps to the British Museum in 1899, and in an accompanying letter wrote:

> I had been stationed in the far Nor West on the arduous & unpleasant duty of arresting or dispersing the blacks out back from Derby who were responsible for a number of murders of whites who were opening out new country. I had managed to accumulate a quantity of native weapons & thought they might be of value or interest to the museum… the weapons are genuine native weapons of the type taken by the police from native camps.[107] (fig. 47, and see fig. 13, p. 37)

In 1895 Ord was responsible for the police hunt for the most infamous of the Kimberley 'outlaws' – Jandamarra, aka Pigeon (1873–1897). Jandamarra was a young Bunuba man who, after a brief period in jail for stock stealing, worked as a police tracker. However, in October 1894, after he had helped capture a group of Bunuba people near Lillimooloora station, Jandamarra made a choice to fight with his people, not against them. He shot and killed his colleague Constable Richardson (d. 1894), released the prisoners and fled to the ranges. From this point on Jandamarra waged a two-and-a-half-year-long campaign against settlers and the police.[108]

Opinions differ about whether Jandamarra's actions were an organised rebellion or series of opportunistic attacks. However, it is clear that Jandamarra struck fear into the hearts of the settlers and the police. He was able to use his knowledge of the rocky escarpments to evade capture. At one point the Commissioner of Police wrote to Ord: 'Pigeon and party must be got rid of forthwith. The fact of his being at large is a disgrace to the police. Head the party and let us hear no more of Pigeon.'[109]

Following an attack on the Oscar Range homestead, in which a settler was killed, the police finally cornered Jandamarra near Tunnel Creek. After a long battle, Jandamarra was shot and killed on 1 April 1897. His death was widely reported in the Australian press (fig. 48).

Since his death Jandamarra has become an important part of Australian history – for both Indigenous and non-Indigenous people. His story has inspired music, opera and theatre performances. An old label on a boomerang (fig. 49) reputedly belonging to Jandamarra refers to him as a 'black bushranger'. Duncan Ord, C.H. Ord's grandson has said: 'I think my grandfather would be, if he were around today, delighted that his foresight in gathering some of these things up and sending them to the Museum for interpretation in the future, that it would bring that history back and maybe some of the things that maybe he found uncomfortable would be revisited in another era.'[110]

For Bunuba people today, such as June Oscar a Bunuba elder, Jandamarra has become the focus around which they view the conflict of the past and inspiration for the future: 'As far as we're concerned, Jandamarra lives on. His spirit lives on, his people still live on. His spirit is carried in this country by people who speak the same languages as he did. For as long as we're alive, the children will know the story of Jandamarra.'[111]

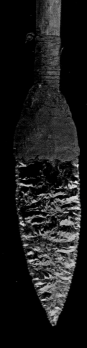

46.
C.H. Ord on his horse Isodore

Western Australia, *c.* 1896
State Library of Western Australia, Perth
026295PD 1896

47.
Spear with a point of green glass

Acquired by C.H. Ord
Kimberley region, Western Australia, *c.* 1890s
Wood, sinew?, gum, glass;
L. 1520 mm, W. 31 mm, D. 15 mm
British Museum, London
Oc1899,-.461 Exh. BM
Donated by C.H. Ord

48.
Telegram to Sub-Inspector Ord, from George Phillips, 29 February 1896

State Library of Western Australia
WA SRO ACC 430 653 1896

49.
Boomerang
An inscription attributes the boomerang to resistance leader Jandamarra. It has been suggested that he abandoned it after a battle with police.

Kimberley region, Western Australia, *c.* 1890s
Wood, pigment; L. 525 mm, W. 74 mm
Museum Victoria, Melbourne
X 49848 Exh. BM

in some northern regions up to the 1910s and 1920s. One of the latest known massacres took place in 1928 around Coniston in central Australia, when a series of reprisals for the murder of a white man resulted in the deaths of more than sixty Aboriginal men, women and children. This is violence that until recently was still within living memory.

Aboriginal histories and memories of frontier violence

Memories and stories of massacres and other frontier violence have been passed down and preserved within Aboriginal people's oral histories and traditions.[112] Some contemporary Aboriginal artists have produced paintings of killings and other aspects of frontier history. Gija artist Queenie McKenzie's (c. 1930–1998) painting *Mistake Creek Massacre*, produced in 1997, is one example (fig. 50). It depicts an event that is believed to have occurred in about 1915 in the east Kimberley region when eight Aboriginal people were killed. This is an event about which there is a rich store of Aboriginal stories and memories.

Some of these artworks have also been drawn into debates in Australia concerning contested interpretations of colonial frontiers. During the late 1990s and early 2000s academic historians' accounts of frontier violence came in for sustained criticism by some conservative commentators and this became known as the 'history wars'.[113] When the National Museum of Australia bought *Mistake Creek Massacre* in 2005 the painting was caught in the crossfire. It was publicly attacked as an inaccurate portrayal because it depicts a scene that shows two Aboriginal men and one white man as responsible for killing eight Aboriginal people. Some conservative historians, Keith Windschuttle most prominently, believed that no white man had been involved in the massacre and that the violence had been between Aboriginal people only.[114] In the process, Aboriginal people's memories were condemned as faulty. Yet, like many violent incidents on the Australian frontier, this is a matter on which the archival record provides no absolute certainty. Police records of the time show that the white man originally suspected as being involved was eventually released without charge, but questions about his involvement lingered.[115] Indeed, the historians who have most thoroughly researched the episode are adamant there is accord between Gija people's oral histories and the evidence contained within the archival record.

The controversy continued when the painting was considered for inclusion within the National Museum of Australia's National Historical Collection. Conservative members of the Museum's Board blocked its listing on the quite narrow basis that it was not historically, or factually, accurate. Six years later, by which time the history wars had all but petered out, McKenzie's painting was once again recommended for inclusion. The document arguing the case stated: '*Mistake Creek Massacre* records well-established Indigenous

50.
Mistake Creek Massacre

Queenie McKenzie (*c.* 1930–1998), Gija
Kimberley region, Western Australia, 1997
Pigment on canvas; H. 910 mm, W. 1210 mm
National Museum of Australia, Canberra
AR00196.001 Exh. BM

beliefs about the history of settler violence on the Australian frontier and illuminates ongoing processes of historical debate and understanding that relate to a core theme in Australian society'.[116] A more expansive and reasonable interpretation of what constitutes a contribution to historical understanding was, it appears, applied to its assessment this time around. The histories and experiences of Australia's colonial frontiers will never be fully known or completely comprehended by reference to the colonial archival

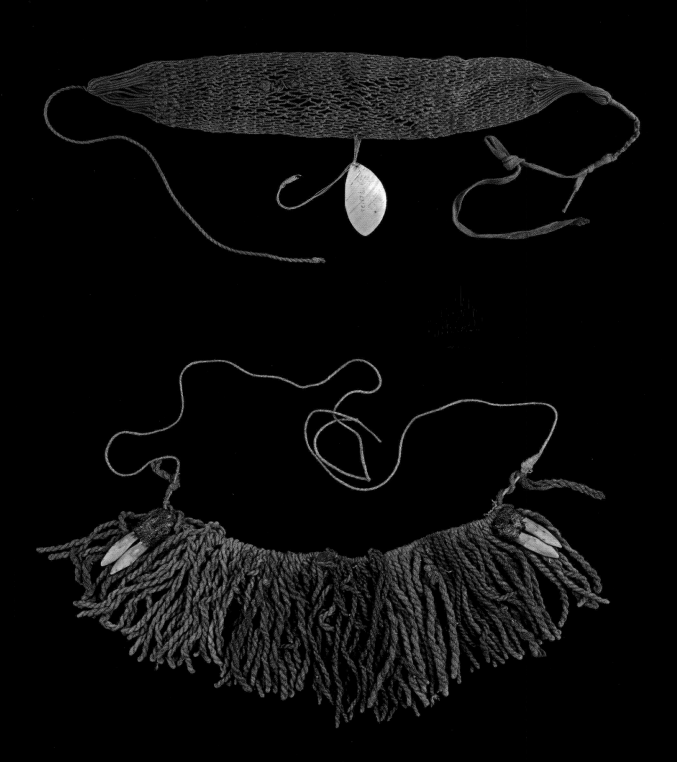

51.

Woman's head-band

The maker has used locally available plant fibres.

Nowunjunger (Mary), Yirandali, Lammermoor, Queensland, before 1901 Sandstone, desert bloodwood gum, clay, flax lily (*Dianella*) fibre, bark fibre, fresh water mussel (*Velesunio ambiguous*) shell; L. 330 mm (excluding ties). British Museum. London Oc1901,1221.14 Exh. BM Donated by Robert Christison

52.

Women's skirt

The maker has substituted plant fibre for wool.

Lammermoor, Queensland, before 1904 Wool, animal teeth; H. 100 mm, L. 330 mm, D. 30 mm British Museum, London Oc1904,1002.5.a Exh. BM Donated by Robert Christison

53.

Pituri bag

The brightly dyed wool used in making this bag could have been reused from a government-issued blanket.

Gregory River region, Queensland, before 1897 Pituri (*Duboisia hopwoodi*) leaf, fibre, wool, human hair; H. 170 mm, W. 380 mm, D. 120 mm British Museum, London Oc1897,-.636 Exh. BM

record alone, which in any case is incomplete and was often made intentionally to obfuscate truths. Aboriginal interpretations of the frontier – in visual, oral, memorial, material and other forms – illuminate these colonial spaces of terror and death in important ways, adding much to contemporary understandings of this troubling aspect of Australia's colonial history.

Other frontier histories: coexistence and cooperation

Amid the violence, in certain places or over time, some pastoralists and Aboriginal groups developed a 'delicate balance of interdependence'.[117] This was especially so when Aboriginal people's labour was required to ensure the economic viability of pastoral runs. Aboriginal men and women as well as children participated, sometimes voluntarily, sometimes not, in the pastoral economy as stock-workers and shepherds, as labourers for land clearing and fencing, and as domestic workers. They were usually paid for their labour in rations of food, clothing, blankets or tobacco.[118] Such things were incorporated into existing practices, often becoming items for barter and exchange, or being used as substitutes for other materials, such as the use of blankets for carrying babies or for making bags, or sheep's wool for garments like skirts (figs 51–53). To some extent pastoralism could be accommodated by Aboriginal cultures, since it allowed people to remain on their own country and maintain their connections with it. Shepherding and other stock-work, for instance, provided scope for Aboriginal people to be on country, and the seasonal nature of some of the work could be articulated with existing cultural responsibilities and practices.[119]

Lammermoor station in western Queensland was a large nineteenth-century pastoral property with a history more marked by coexistence with

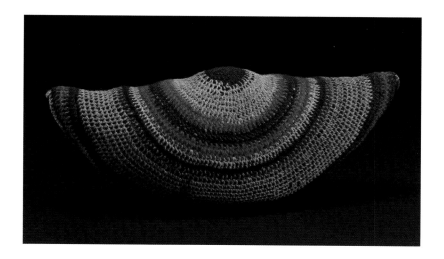

Aboriginal people than conflict towards them (fig. 54). Scotsman Robert Christison (1837–1915) established the station in the early 1860s and from the outset was intent on pursuing a policy of peaceable relations with the Yirandali people. Christison donated material to the British Museum in the opening years of the twentieth century, and his daughter Mary Montgomerie Bennett (1881–1961) contributed more material in the 1920s (see pp. 240–1). Included in these collections is a set of message sticks, which shed some light on the nature of relations between Christison and his Yirandali workers (figs 55–58). Roughly notched and carved, one stick from 'Mickey' conveys a request for a coat, hat and shirt. Another announces a man's intention to leave the station for a while to go 'walkabout', but promising to return. Mundane these messages might seem, but the latter in particular suggests something far-reaching. To go 'walkabout along a bush' is to exercise and enact rights of possession and continuing connection to one's own country. Access to Aboriginal labour depended on the station owner accommodating his workers' enduring responsibilities and relationships to people and place. That Aboriginal people's native title rights could coexist

54.
Yirandali men and women at Lammermoor pastoral property
By working on the property, Aboriginal people could maintain traditions and retain links with important places in their country.

Mary 'Ann' Christison (1843–1879), born London(?), England
Lammermoor, Queensland, late 19th century
Albumen print on paper; H. 74 mm, W. 102 mm
British Museum, London
Oc,B78.1

55–57
Message sticks
These message sticks were used by Yirandali people on Lammermoor pastoral property. They record mundane communications, such as requests to send spare clothes. Donated by the property owner, Robert Christison.
Lammermoor, Queensland, late 19th century

Nowunjunger (Mary), Yirandali
Wood; L. 88 mm, W. 10 mm, D. 8 mm
British Museum, London
Oc1901,1221.18 Exh. BM
Donated by Robert Christison

Mickey, Yirandali
Pine wood, charcoal, emu fat;
W. 10 mm, L. 120 mm, D. 8 mm
British Museum, London
Oc1901,1221.17 Exh. BM
Donated by Robert Christison

Unknown maker
Pine wood; L. 132 mm
British Museum, London
Oc1901,1221.20 Exh. BM
Donated by Robert Christison

58.
Message stick

Cairns, Queensland, before 1900
Wood; L. 119 mm
British Museum, London
Oc1900,0723.59 Exh. BM

with the interests of pastoral leaseholders was belatedly recognised when the High Court of Australia handed down its decision in *Wik Peoples* v. *State of Queensland and Others* in 1996. In this case, the High Court held that the pastoral leases in question did not automatically extinguish any surviving native title rights and interests because such leases did not grant exclusive possession.[120] A century earlier this unprepossessing message stick had given expression to this arrangement in practice.

Exclusion: incarceration and institutions

In the British Museum's collection are some nineteenth-century objects that were made by Aboriginal men incarcerated in colonial prisons. A small stick punctured with feint dots in opposed triangular shapes was made at the 'native prison' on Rottnest Island (fig. 59). Situated about eleven miles off the south-west Australian coast from Fremantle, and now a popular tourist destination, the aptly named Rottnest Island was for much of the nineteenth century used to house and isolate Aboriginal prisoners. Around 3,700 Aboriginal men and boys from all over the colony of Western Australia were incarcerated there between 1838 and 1904. Many had been found guilty by the colonial justice system for such deeds as cattle spearing, stealing and assault, committed as new settlers encroached on their country.[121] Punishment included exile from their country and their kin. Some imprisoned on the island were a very long way from home, including men convicted on the Kimberley frontier in the far north-west. Other prison-made objects in the Museum's collection are a spearthrower and a shield made respectively by Douga Willin from Gippsland (fig. 60) and 'Lallan Yering, son of Mum-Jet, from Boolook Ba Boollook' (now Bacchus Marsh; fig. 61), who were both serving sentences in Pentridge Prison in Melbourne in the 1860s.[122]

Beyond the biographical, these objects are pointers to a pervasive history of the policing and incarceration, the institutionalisation and governance, the management and control, of Aboriginal and Torres Strait Islander people under colonial conditions.[123] Isolation and incarceration were rationalised by colonial authorities as providing conditions for the 'improvement', 'progress' and 'civilisation' of Aboriginal people. The statute

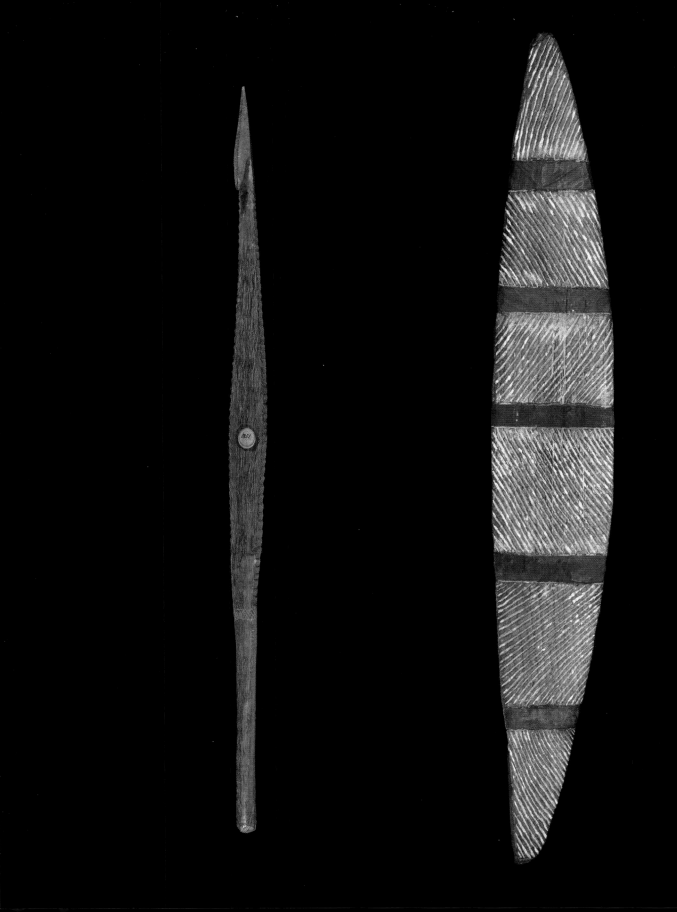

establishing Rottnest Island prison, for instance, included the clause: 'That such of the Aboriginal race as are sentenced to transportation or imprisonment may be conveniently kept in order that they may be instructed in useful knowledge and gradually trained in the habits of civilised life'.[124]

The objects from Pentridge Prison are suggestive of this theme as well. From the available evidence it is likely that they were produced, probably even commissioned, for the Melbourne International Exhibition in 1866 and 1867, and were possibly also included in the 1867 Paris Exposition Universelle. Those responsible for organising Aboriginal exhibits understood the undertaking not only in terms of the preservation of history and traditions, but also as aimed at Aboriginal people's 'improvement' through 'industry'. Materials made in prisons or on Aboriginal settlements were displayed in these exhibitions, as historian Penelope Edmonds points out, in ways in which discourses of 'improvement, transformation and state correction are apparent'.[125]

'Institutions provided the dominant technology for governing Aboriginal and Torres Strait Islander populations', historians Anna Haebich and Steve Kinnane note.[126] In all Australian colonies (later states), reserves and settlements, missions, hospitals and asylums, prisons and other places of punishment, training centres, schools and children's homes were established as spaces where Aboriginal people were isolated from the wider Australian population and where 'practices of "punishment, protection and prevention" typical of other custodial institutions' were imposed.[127] These institutions were designed variously to segregate, protect, punish, control, isolate, improve, educate, train, convert, civilise, assimilate and so on. Some colonial and later state governments favoured large institutions that sought to control every aspect of Aboriginal people's lives. This was the practice followed in Queensland, where 'whole communities were forced into large settlements'.[128] When Lammermoor station was sold by the Christisons in the early twentieth century, some of the Aboriginal people living there were moved to Cherbourg, one of the largest Aboriginal settlements in Queensland.

Elsewhere in Australia, smaller Aboriginal settlements were established, sometimes the direct result of opposition from white Australians to the presence of Aboriginal people living in and around rural towns. Carrolup in south-west Western Australia is an example of such a settlement (see pp. 184–5). It was established around 1910 after a sustained campaign from white townsfolk to have Aboriginal people removed out of sight. These isolated settlements and institutions, dotted throughout the densely settled landscape but largely invisible to the wider white society, created a quite particular geography of Australian race relations. Settler Australian attitudes towards Aboriginal people were often expressed in spatial ways, including through the formal and informal imposition of curfews, segregation within public spaces, such as hospitals and cinemas, and exclusion from other establishments, like schools and hotels.[129]

State-imposed interventions into almost every aspect of Indigenous people's lives were made possible by the 'inordinate powers invested in senior administrators', such as the so-called Chief Protector of Aborigines, within the government bureaucracies that oversaw Aboriginal and Torres Strait Islander affairs. (The Torres Strait Islands came under Queensland's jurisdiction in 1879.) Their considerable powers were underwritten by restrictive and discriminatory legislation introduced in most Australian states between 1897 and 1911, and repeatedly amended and tightened in decades following, which included provisions regarding the legal guardianship of children, freedom of movement and choice of marriage partner, among other things. From this time on, Australian governments at all levels used legislative means to exclude and restrict Indigenous people from gaining rights and privileges that are typically identified with citizenship.

Attitudes towards Indigenous people were informed and influenced by various discourses about them and their place within colonial society. On the one hand, there was a notion that Aboriginal people, especially of full descent, were dying out or 'doomed to extinction'. It was common, for instance, for the death of an elderly Aboriginal person in intensely settled regions to be reported as the passing of the 'last of their tribe'. These ideas were influenced by the popularisation of social Darwinism. On the other hand, there was increased concern about what was perceived as the growing 'mixed race' population, which fuelled governmental and charitable attention on the Indigenous family as a site for intervention. During the opening decades of the twentieth century, as state control over Aboriginal people's lives

62.
Members of the Stolen Generations react to 'The Apology to the Australian Indigenous Peoples' given by Prime Minister Kevin Rudd in 2008
From left, Netta Cahill, Lorna Cubillo and Valerie Day.

'For the pain, suffering and hurt of these stolen generations, their descendants and for their families left behind, we say sorry.'
Kevin Rudd, Australian Prime Minister, 2007–10 and 2013

Parliament House, Canberra, 13 February 2008
Photograph: Juno Gemes

strengthened, increasing numbers of fair-complexioned Aboriginal children were removed from their families and placed in institutions with a view to their eventual 'absorption' or 'assimilation' into white society (see pp. 184–5).

The children removed (the precise numbers are unknown) from their families later became known collectively as the Stolen Generations, and in 2008 the then Prime Minister of Australia issued an apology for the practice (fig. 62). Such an apology had been a recommendation of an inquiry undertaken in 1996 by the Human Rights and Equal Opportunity Commission. Extensive testimony from members of the Stolen Generations from across the country was heard during the inquiry, and published in the *Bringing Them Home* report.[130] Growing public knowledge of this practice had far-reaching effects on Australian society, as it sought to come to terms with this traumatic history. Some sections of the Indigenous community, however, remain dissatisfied that compensation has not been forthcoming.

Postcards produced in the early twentieth century, which was the height of their popularity, provide an especially rich trove for teasing out various aspects of Aboriginal people's situation and experiences at this juncture in Australia's colonial history (figs 63–67). Designed to appeal to buyers, to preserve memories of experiences, to communicate ideas, to generate income or pledge support, they are dense with meanings. While some images were taken in studios, many of those of Aboriginal people and children were taken at Aboriginal settlements and missions, especially ones that were known tourist locations in this period. Settler Australians sought to satisfy their curiosity about Aboriginal people and a culture they believed was becoming a thing of the past by taking day trips or excursions to Aboriginal settlements. Lake Tyers in Victoria, La Perouse in New South Wales and Palm Island in Queensland were among some of the Aboriginal settlements that doubled as tourist sites.[131] Small-scale tourism provided Aboriginal residents with access to an informal cash economy through the making and selling of objects, such as boomerangs like those held by the young man in figure 63, and performing for tourists. This allowed for a degree of economic independence as well as the continuation of object-making and aesthetic practices. Some resident missionaries also sought to capitalise on visitors to help fund their activities, including through the currency of postcards.

Images used on early twentieth-century postcards drew on and responded to broader discourses about Aboriginal people. For instance, the postcard captioned 'Youth and Age' (fig. 63) suggests simultaneously a 'nostalgic desire' for the old man as representative of a 'dying race', while provoking questions about the future of the young man, who is portrayed as though caught somewhere between the past and the future. Figures 64–66 engage with a different discourse. Each portrays Aboriginal women with babies or young children, but in the absence of any father figure for the offspring. (This is true even for the studio portrait postcard captioned 'Four generations' (fig. 64).) This imagery reflects and reproduces turn-of-the-century attitudes and anxieties about Aboriginal women and children, about the future of Aboriginal families, and about the growing 'mixed race' population. Caught within a postcard's frame, Aboriginal women and children were portrayed as subjects for – or already of – institutional intervention.[132] It is no coincidence that these images were circulating at a time when the state was removing increasing numbers of children from their mothers and placing them in institutions.

For the Aboriginal people photographed, of course, the meanings encapsulated were very different from those intended by the photographer or assumed by the buyer. Aboriginal people were not merely passive subjects for photographers' visions. As historian Jane Lydon and others have shown, Aboriginal people engaged with photography from its very inception, and actively made use of it for their own cultural, political and aesthetic purposes.[133] Rather than provide unequivocal evidence for their anticipated demise, the colonial photographic archive is as much a testament to Aboriginal people's resilience in the face of colonial incursions and institutional interventions. Not for nothing are Aboriginal people reclaiming colonial images and postcards as part of their rich visual heritage and as treasured sources for family and community histories.

Opposing exclusion

When the Australian colonies federated in 1901, the founders of the new nation were united by a commitment to the development of a white Australia. Within that vision of the Australian community, little space was given to Indigenous people. Through legislative and other means and bolstered by general indifference, Indigenous Australians were denied many of the privileges of citizenship and other human rights enjoyed by non-Indigenous Australians. Exclusion and discrimination fuelled Aboriginal politics throughout the twentieth century. From the 1920s, Aboriginal political organisations emerged, including the Native Union of Western Australia, the Australian Aboriginal Progressive Association in New South Wales, and the Australian Aborigines Association in South Australia.[134] Others were founded during the following decade, such as the Victorian-based Australian Aborigines' League and the New South Wales-based Aborigines Progressive Association. They were influential in organising protests against celebrations held in Sydney on 26 January 1938 on the 150th anniversary of British settlement, declaring it 'A Day of Mourning'. The organisers issued notice to the Australian public that: 'We ask – and we have every right to *demand* – that you should include us, fully and equally with yourselves, in the body of the Australian nation'.[135]

As had been the case in the nineteenth century, Aboriginal activists appealed repeatedly to notions of British justice and fairness as well as referring to examples of British policy in other colonial contexts, such

63.
Postcard of two men at Lake Tyers
Posted to London with the message: 'Wishing you a happy Xmas'.

Lake Tyers. Gippsland, Victoria, early 20th century
Ink on card; H. 88 mm, W. 140 mm
British Museum, London
Oc,B141.21 Exh. BM
Donated by Jonathan C.H. King

64.
Postcard of an Aboriginal family ('four generations')
Posted to London.

South-east Australia, early 20th century
Ink on card; H. 140mm, W. 88 mm
British Museum, London
Oc,B141.12 Exh. BM
Donated by Jonathan C.H. King

65.
Postcard of women and girls at Albany
The crown motifs on the blankets worn by the two older women indicate that they are 'native' blankets issued by the government.
Posted to London with the message: 'Western Australia Landed here + stayed 2 days.'

Albany, Western Australia, early 20th century
Ink on card; H. 88 mm, W. 140 mm
British Museum, London
Oc,B141.11 Exh. BM
Donated by Jonathan C.H. King

66.
Postcard of a woman carrying a baby
Posted to London with the message: 'had our annual Social. I had a good bit to do with it… didn't do too good as the evening was wet… So with all good wishes from yours Sincerely Mary R.'

Location unknown, early 20th century
Ink on card; H. 140mm, W. 88 mm
British Museum, London
Oc,B141.27
Donated by Jonathan C.H. King

Youth and Age, Lake Tyers, Gippsland

Four Generations Aust. Aboriginals.

Native
Women,
Albany.

67.
**Postcard of a man
at Coranderrk**
Posted with the message
'My Dear Brother, I have seen
a lot of these blacks. This place
called Healesville is 39 miles
from Melbourne.'

Coranderrk, Healesville, Victoria,
early 20th century
Ink on card; H. 140 mm, W. 88 mm
British Museum, London
Oc,B141.15 Exh. BM
Donated by Jonathan C.H. King

Australian Black Gin
and Piccaninny.

CORANDERRK
NATIVE
HEALESVILLE

Encounters in country

The Carrolup children's drawings
Ian Coates

After an earlier history as a reserve (see p. 178), in 1940 the Carrolup Native Settlement in south-west Western Australia opened as a government institution for Aboriginal children removed from their families by the state. Carrolup was part of the government policy that sought to 'assimilate' Aboriginal children into white society. Children were removed from the influence of their parents and family, which was often deemed undesirable by government authorities, and educated in 'useful' skills to allow them to fit into white society. Removed from their families, boys were 'trained' in farm skills and girls in domestic duties. Such places were miserable for the children housed in them. However, for a brief moment in the late 1940s, the art of the children from Carrolup was prominent on the international stage. The arrival in 1945 of teacher Noel White and his wife Lily to the school brought a dramatic change to Carrolup; they encouraged music and art among the children, and it was art in particular that captured the children's imaginations. By 1947 they were producing dramatic works on paper that encapsulated the distinctive landscape and incorporated elements of the children's Noongar culture (fig. 68).

The children's artwork was first shown publicly at the local Katanning Show in 1946 and at the Lord Forrest Centennial Exhibition in Perth in 1947. Later that year 450 works on display at a Perth department store attracted great public interest. The children's work was exhibited in Albany, Sydney and New Delhi, and was used to demonstrate the success of Carrolup and the potential of its students. It also caught the eye of philanthropist Florence Rutter (1878–?). Rutter visited Carolup in 1949 and 1950 and with vigour undertook the task of raising money for art materials and promoting the children's art in Australia and overseas. On her return to London in 1950 she organised a series of displays of it in London and Holland. The seven drawings in the British Museum are likely to have been purchased at one of the exhibitions held in London: 'The drawings were amazing for untrained children. I was determined to do something for them. I am hoping a drawing may be put into the British Museum.'[136]

Some works were sold to raise money for art materials. However, back at Carrolup, this public success contributed to tension between training the children in 'useful' and vocational skills and the fostering of art.

In 1951 Carrolup closed, reopening as a farm school for teenage Aboriginal boys. The children from Carrolup were dispersed to the Catholic Mission at Wandering and Roelands Children's Home. Some of the children, such as Revel Cooper (c. 1934–1983) and Reynold Hart (1938–1981), went on to produce works as adults. Their work continues to influence Noongar artists today.

Ezzard Flowers, a contemporary Noongar artist says 'these drawings mean hope'.[137]

'We practised on brown paper, night after night for about two years, and our drawings started to win the respect of white people'
Reynold Hart, aged 12, 1950

68.
Dancing figure

Unknown artist, Noongar
Carrolup Native Settlement, Western Australia, 1945–53
Ink on paper, H. 277mm, W. 327 mm
British Museum, London
Oc2006,Drg.686 Exh. BM

as parliamentary representation of Maori in New Zealand, when articulating their political agendas. As before, they sometimes appealed directly to the reigning British monarch in pursuit of their aims. In 1933, for instance, William Cooper (c. 1860–1941) of the Australian Aborigines' League initiated a petition to King George V (1865–1936) appealing for intervention to 'prevent the extinction of the Aboriginal race and give better conditions for all, granting us the power to propose a Member of Parliament, of our own blood or white men known to have studied our needs and to be in sympathy with our race, to represent us in the Federal Parliament'.[138] The petition was presented to King George VI in 1937, but the Commonwealth government rejected its demand for parliamentary representation and refused to forward it to the monarch in England.[139] (When Prince William (b. 1982) visited the Aboriginal community in Redfern in Sydney in 2010, he was handed a copy of the original petition and told that 'as the future king he could help restore the rights and dignity of indigenous people'. In 2014, a copy of the petition was entrusted to the Australian Governor-General to give to Queen Elizabeth II (b. 1926).[140]) Although the federal government had obstructed the passage of the petition, by 1939 it had issued a new policy statement on Aborigines dubbed the New Deal for Aborigines, in which 'for the first time, an Australian government specified "citizenship" as the "final objective" of Aboriginal policy'.[141] The veteran campaigner Cooper referred to it as the 'Aboriginal Magna Carta' and urged its immediate implementation.[142] But war intervened, and Indigenous issues again took a back seat in Australian public and political life.

After the Second World War the push for equality and recognition gained strength. Momentum for change was spurred by increasing international criticism of Australia's race relations record. The gradual repeal and dismantling of discriminatory legislation began almost immediately, and was accompanied by efforts to formally include Indigenous Australians as citizens in the national community. At the same time, the wider Australian community 'made faltering steps to come to grips with the endurance of the Indigenous people', pushed along by Indigenous and non-Indigenous activists and campaigners.[143] While the quest to achieve legal equality was crucial, the changes they sought went well beyond that. For many Indigenous Australians, inclusion was understood as being 'treated with respect and dignity… welcomed as full participants in the life of the community', something that Aboriginal and Torres Strait Islander people had long been denied. While activists and their supporters were up against 'the sheer indifference of settler Australians' to the tiny Indigenous minority, nonetheless change did occur, slowly, and public attitudes did shift, gradually.[144] As the Carrolup children's drawings indicate, art was one sphere in which Aboriginal people in the mid-twentieth century gained some notice and respect (sport was another).

Yet the life story of the most famous and celebrated Aboriginal artist at the time, Albert Namatjira (1902–1959; fig. 69), also encapsulates the inconsistencies of laws, policies and practices, as well as the contradictory attitudes of white Australians. Although widely feted in Australia and overseas for his landscape paintings, and often held up as an example of a model Aboriginal citizen, in 1957 Namatjira was charged under the 1953 Northern Territory Welfare Ordinance Act for supplying alcohol to another Aboriginal person and was sentenced to six months' imprisonment. While he had been granted citizenship rights when the 1953 Ordinance Act was introduced, the majority of Aboriginal people in the Northern Territory, his immediate and extended family included, were wards of the state, and so denied the right to drink. These terrible events 'showed that the state and federal governments were wrong to set up "Aboriginal" and "citizen" as mutually exclusive categories'.[145] After a public outcry and a series of appeals, Namatjira's sentence was reduced, but the case affected him badly. The writer Douglas Lockwood (1918–1980) remarked: 'in my 20 years experience as a journalist and reporter, I have never witnessed a more deeply moving drama. Albert was a heartbroken old man, bewildered by events, for which, so it was implied, he was to blame'.[146] He died soon afterwards.

For Aboriginal people living in Australia's Central and Western Deserts, including some who had had little or no contact with whites, the 1950s and

69.
River Gum and Mount Gillen

Albert Namatjira (1902–1959), Arrernte
Northern Territory, Alice Springs region, c. 1951
Watercolour over pencil on paper; H. 290 mm, W. 394 mm
British Museum, London.
2011,7082.1 Exh. BM
Presented by Gordon and Marilyn Darling

1960s were a time of disruption and danger as the British and Australian governments commenced a programme of nuclear weapons testing. Immediately after the Second World War, a rocket-testing range in north-west South Australia, insensitively named Woomera (a word for spearthrower), was established. It was repeatedly claimed by governments that this area was 'uninhabited', but this was not so. It was home to the Yankunytjatjara and Pitjantjatjara (Anangu) people. As the anthropologist Donald Thomson explained at the time, the range was 'the violation of one of [the] last great strongholds of the Indigenous people of central Australia'. In response to a public outcry, the authorities appointed a 'native patrol officer' who was 'entrusted with ensuring the safety and welfare of Indigenous people' within the testing area.[147]

The first atomic tests were conducted around Maralinga in South Australia. When Totem 1 (also cruelly named) was detonated on 15 October 1953, 'the Yankunytjatjara people of Wallatina, Mintabie and Welbourne Hill became the first mainland Aboriginal people to face contamination from nuclear weapons' (fig. 70).[148] Further tests were carried out later that year and the next. As Kunmanara Cooper (1918/22–2010) recalled:

> While we were travelling there we heard a big noise. Maybe thunder, we thought. We didn't know about that bomb. So we turned away and travelled north. But we did get to Ernabella. And we felt the smoke, funny smell: it made us sick. It was smoke from the bomb – that big noise. Some were dying… everything came from that smell. So we didn't want to stop…[149]

The Aboriginal people affected never forgot the 'low drifting black mist stretching as far as they could see, passing over their camps, leaving deposits on the ground and resulting in both immediate and long term illness',[150] but they did not get to place their memories and experiences on the public record until 1984, when finally the Royal Commission into British Nuclear Tests was held.

The nuclear testing programme did not end at Maralinga. By 1958 work was underway to extend the range in a north-west direction all the way to the west Australian coast, cutting a huge 320-kilometre-wide swathe across the Gibson, Great Sandy and Little Sandy Deserts. Rockets would, for the first time, be 'shot across the desert' and 'life [there] would never be the same'.[151] This was a mammoth cold war enterprise that included the establishment of research facilities, such as the Giles Weather Station, and an extensive network of roads, which allowed access into previously remote country still occupied by Aboriginal people living a traditional life and largely unaffected by white society. Opponents continued to voice their concerns about the dangerous effects of nuclear fallout from the testing on Aboriginal people in these desert regions and the contact with whites that would result from the

70.
The cloud from the Totem I atomic bomb test in the Great Victoria Desert is silhouetted against the sun

Emu Field, South Australia
United Press Photo, 15 October 1953
National Library of Australia, Canberra
5095363 PIC 14623

intrusion of military and other personnel employed on the Weapons Research Establishment (WRE).

Regardless, the programme proceeded apace. Responsibility for mitigating effects on Aboriginal people continued to fall on the shoulders of native patrol officers. There were just two appointed to cover a huge area 'larger than France', and whose job it was to warn nomadic desert people of upcoming tests and to attempt to clear areas in time. To this end, they conducted patrols, making contact with small groups of people still living on and travelling through their country. Some Aboriginal people agreed to move,

or made their way, to settlements, but others chose not to. The patrol officers were not always able to communicate with people in time in the affected areas. Among the last groups in the region reached by a patrol officer when testing was still underway in 1964 was a group of Martu women and children, including a young woman, Yuwali (b. *c*. 1947), whose story has recently been recorded in a book *Cleared Out: First Contact in the Western Desert* and a film based on it (fig. 71).[152]

Negative publicity about the effects of the WRE on Aboriginal people in remote desert regions influenced Aboriginal activists in the south, providing impetus for renewed political activity, including the development of a national body, known initially as the Federal Council for Aboriginal Affairs (and later renamed as the Federal Council for Aboriginal and Torres Strait Islander Affairs). This organisation was instrumental in a campaign calling for a national referendum to delete two discriminatory references to Aboriginal people in the Australian Constitution, which had been introduced at the time of Australian Federation in 1901. Section 51 singled out the 'aboriginal race' as not included among the 'races' for which the Commonwealth government could make special laws. Section 27 stated: 'In reckoning the numbers of the Commonwealth, or of a State or other part of the Commonwealth, aboriginal

71.
Basket
'We couldn't go back to the old ways … [But] we left our hearts back in our country.' Yuwali

Yuwali, also known as Janice Nixon (b. *c*. 1947), Manyjilyjarra/Mangala
Parnngurr, Western Australia, *c*. 2010
Plant fibre, wool; H. 160 mm, Diam. 28 mm
British Museum, London
2011,2011.1 Exh. BM

natives should not be counted'. As historians Bain Attwood and Andrew Markus claim, Section 27 in particular indicated 'a racial assumption on the part of the makers of the Australian Constitution. Aborigines did not count, hence they did not need to be counted'.[153] After a long campaign, a national referendum was eventually held in May 1967 and Australians voted overwhelmingly in favour of the proposed changes. While these changes to the Constitution did not immediately grant Aboriginal people any greater rights, and many legislative restrictions had already been removed from the statute books prior to this, the 1967 referendum was and is still seen as a hugely symbolic achievement that expressed a new relationship between Aboriginal people and settler Australians. Currently, there are further moves to alter the Australian Constitution by referendum, but this time to include some form of acknowledgement of Indigenous Australians as the original people of Australia and as a continuing living culture.

Rights and recognition

From the 1960s and 1970s, the recognition of Indigenous people's rights in and to land emerged as the leading political issue. While Aboriginal people in densely settled regions had long campaigned for tracts of land to be granted to them both in recompense for their dispossession and as a base for economic independence and autonomy, the movement for land rights during this period developed into a national campaign linking the interests of Indigenous people across the country. Especially influential were the protests of the Yirrkala people in Arnhem Land against mining on their land, and their decision in 1962 to send a bark petition to the Commonwealth government. The petition was one of many drawn up by Indigenous Australians from the early years of European colonisation to the present (see fig. 24, p. 144 and p. 186), and like the others it demonstrated their desire to engage settler Australians and their governments in acts of diplomacy even though their sovereignty over their own country remained unrecognised.

Yirrkala Mission had been established by the Methodist Church in 1935. Yolngu people at the time understood that they had made peace with the outsiders and in many respects viewed the mission as their own creation. They lived relatively autonomous lives and the missionaries were both interested in their way of life and concerned with their rights. In the late 1950s Yolngu and the missionaries were made painfully aware of the fragility of their situation when mining exploration began and leases were taken out on the bauxite that formed the bedrock of the country. In 1962 the mission superintendent, the Reverend Edgar Wells (1908–1995), oversaw the building of a new church at Yirrkala. Yolngu, concerned that Europeans failed to recognise either their spiritual relationship with the land or their existing title to it, suggested that two large painted panels be produced to be placed on either side of the altar. The panels would comprise sacred paintings that represented each clan's spiritual relationship to the land. Wells readily agreed with this suggestion and the church panels were soon in place.

The following year two Members of Parliament, Gordon Bryant (1914–1991) and Kim Beazley Senior (1917–2007), visited Yirrkala to listen to people's concerns. They were deeply impressed by the panels in the church and immediately saw their connection to land rights. As a result of the visit Yolngu produced a petition expressing their concern over the incursions into their land by mining companies and asking that their rights in land from time immemorial be recognised. In order to foreground their system of ownership Yolngu sent two petitions, rather than one, reflecting the division of the land-owning clans into two moieties – Dhuwa and Yirritja. And rather than sending the petitions on a plain ground, they attached them to sheets of bark with borders painted with designs belonging to the respective moieties.

The petitions were not successful immediately, but they had considerable impact, perhaps because they were drawn up at a moment when Australians were becoming increasingly aware of the injustices of the past and were oriented to move towards a process of recognition of Indigenous rights (fig. 72). In 1971 the people from Yirrkala took the Commonwealth government and the mining company to court in what became known as the Gove Land Rights case. Although the applicants lost the case the moral climate had been changed in their favour. In 1976 the Commonwealth government passed the Aboriginal Land Rights (Northern Territory) Act, which enabled many Aboriginal people to claim title to what had hitherto been un-alienated Crown Land. The people of Yirrkala gained full title to their land under Australian law with the exception of those areas for which a mining lease had already been granted.

During this same period, the Gurindji people at Wave Hill, also in the Northern Territory, were embroiled in a dispute over deplorable wages and conditions with the large British pastoral company, Vesteys, for which many worked as stockmen. They resented being badly treated, 'like a dog alla time'.[154] They went on strike, as did other Aboriginal workers on other pastoral stations in the Northern Territory, but they made it clear the issue went beyond a demand for equal wages and better working conditions. What they wanted was a return of their lands. As lead stockmen Vincent Lingiari (1908–1988) explained: 'We want Bestey [Vestey] mob all go 'way from here. We Wave Hill Aborigine native people bin called Gurindji. We bin here longa time before them Bestey mob. They put up building, think 'em own this country. This is our country, all this country bin Gurindji country. Wave Hill bin our country'.[155]

These events in the north had a strong influence on Aboriginal politics in the south, especially in the articulation of land rights as a major issue. Already, though, a new style of politics was emerging there, led by a generation of young Aboriginal activists. In 1965, Aboriginal university student Charles Perkins (1936–2000), recently returned from England where he had been a

72.

Bark petition sent to the Australian Parliament in August 1963
Yolngu people sent the petition as a response to a government decision to grant leases to mine bauxite on their land without their consent.

Yirrkala artists, Dhuwa moiety (left) and Yirritja moiety (right), Yolngu
Yirrkala, Arnhem Land, Northern Territory, 1963
Pipe clay, charcoal and ochre on bark, ink on paper;
H. 469 mm, W. 210 mm
Parliament House Art Collection, Canberra
REPS02/0020.001, REPS02/0020.002

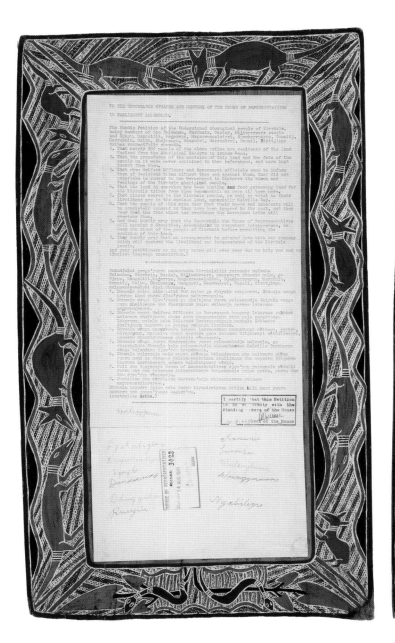
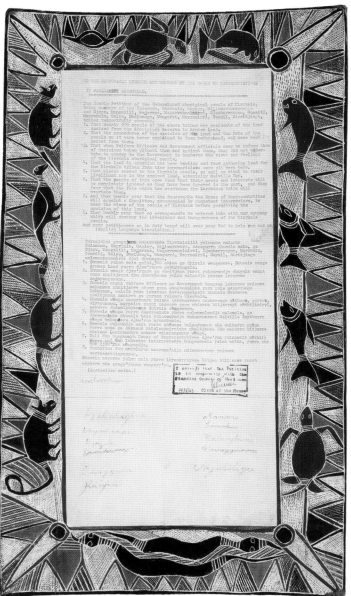

Encounters in country

WE · WANT LA

RIGHT

'RICHT

professional football player, instigated a 'freedom ride' around New South Wales, modelled on the freedom rides undertaken by civil rights activists across the southern states of North America, to expose the living conditions and racial discrimination experienced by Aboriginal people in rural areas. Receiving widespread media coverage and making extremely effective use of visual imagery, the NSW freedom ride succeeded in drawing public attention to Aboriginal issues in powerful new ways.[156] Throughout this period, politics became increasingly inseparable from art and other forms of creative expression and performance. In 1971, for instance, Bob Maza (1939–2000) and others founded the National Black Theatre, and it quickly became a focus for Aboriginal political and creative activity. Recently reflecting on the period, Aboriginal academic Marcia Langton commented that what was being created was 'a literary and artistic record that said: "we exist"'.[157]

Probably the most powerful and persuasive political performance of the era was the Aboriginal Tent Embassy set up on the lawns of Parliament House in Canberra on Australia Day in 1972 (figs 73–74). The impetus was a statement issued by the then Prime Minister Billy McMahon (1908–1988) on the Commonwealth government's policy on Aboriginal affairs that included the rejection of land rights. This was met with dismay and outrage. McMahon's statement prompted immediate action designed to express, in no uncertain terms, a refusal to accept the federal government's position. That night four young Aboriginal men drove from Sydney to Canberra where they planted a beach umbrella in the grass opposite Parliament House and founded the Aboriginal Tent Embassy. The embassy was confronting because it 'implied that aboriginal people comprised a distinct nation within Australia'.[158] Within

73.
'We want land rights. When. Right now'
Land rights placard from the Aboriginal Tent Embassy erected, as a site of protest, in 1972 at Old Parliament House.

Old Parliament House, Canberra, 1972
Paint on Masonite board; H. 485 mm, W. 815 mm
National Museum of Australia, Canberra
1987.0090.0001 Exh. BM
Donated by Charles Perkins

74.

The Tent Embassy before the tent

From left, Billy Craigie, Bert Williams, Michael
Anderson and Tony Coorey take a stance by
a beach umbrella in front of Parliament House,
Canberra, 27 January 1972. This was the first
day of the Aboriginal Embassy.

75.
Aboriginal flag
Black represents the Aboriginal people
of Australia; red, the red earth, red ochre and
a spiritual relation to land; and yellow, the sun,
the giver of life.

Designed by Harold Thomas (b. *c.* 1947), Luritja, 1971

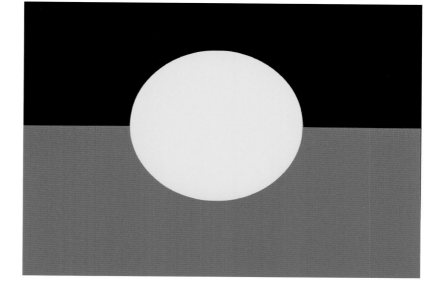

76. (overleaf)
Mer, Torres Strait
The island of Mer in the far eastern Torres
Strait is famous in Australian legal history due
to the court action initiated by Eddie Mabo
and others in support of rights to land and
the High Court of Australia's *Mabo* decision
handed down in 1992 (see p. 200).

Mer, Torres Strait, Queensland
Photograph: George Serras

a short time, the four embassy founders had been joined by scores of others, the single beach umbrella gradually gave way to a small tent city, and the original cardboard sign announcing 'Aboriginal Embassy' replaced with a fancier wooden one. Before long, the black, yellow and red Aboriginal flag was also flying (fig. 75). Designed the previous year by Harold Thomas (b. *c.* 1947), it came to represent Aboriginal unity, with the black symbolising people, the red the earth, and the yellow the sun.[159]

In December that year, McMahon's Conservative government lost office and was replaced by the first Labor government in twenty-three years. Under Gough Whitlam's (1916–2014) leadership it pursued a policy of recognising Aboriginal land rights. As already noted, the Commonwealth government introduced the Aboriginal Land Rights (Northern Territory) Act in 1976 (passed by the new Liberal government led by Malcolm Fraser (b. 1930)). Over the next decade most Australian states followed suit and introduced land rights legislation. Although many activists argued that land rights was 'an essential foundation for Aboriginal material and cultural well-being',[160] it was only ever going to be a partial basis upon which Indigenous people's futures could be built, and of greater benefit to some groups than others. What was important though is that the passing of land rights legislation was an instance of recognising that what had happened in the past in terms of the non-recognition and denial of Aboriginal sovereign rights to land was wrong.

This recognition registered a broader cultural shift, in which Australians began to acknowledge their colonial past. Indigenous politics increasingly focused on the legacies of the past on the present and the misrepresentation

of their historical experience, encapsulated in the slogan 'white Australia has a black history'. These politics reached a crescendo around the 1988 bicentennial celebrations of the British occupation, when large protests were staged. Drawing on earlier traditions of political action, some activists implicated Britain in Australia's colonial legacy, such as when, in a well-publicised event, Aboriginal man Burnum Burnum (1936–1997) stood on the cliffs of Dover, stuck a flag in the ground and claimed possession of Britain.

By the late 1970s in north Queensland another revolution in the recognition of Indigenous rights in land was slowly taking shape, but which would not come to fruition until the early 1990s. Historian Henry Reynolds recalls conversations he had with Eddie Mabo (1936–1992) from the island of Mer in Torres Strait about exploring legal avenues for the recognition of his and other Murray Islanders' title to land, including canvassing the possibility that 'legally the Murray Islanders would have a stronger case in the courts than [Aboriginal people] because they used the land for gardening' (fig. 77).[161] By 1981, the decision was made to mount a legal case, but it would take eleven years for it to work its way through the legal system.

On 3 June 1992, the High Court of Australia delivered its judgment in the case of *Mabo and Others* v. *Queensland (No. 2)*. (Six months earlier the lead plaintiff, Eddie Mabo, had died.) In what became widely known as the

77.
Hoe
The ownership and cultivation of gardens was important evidence during the *Mabo* case, for recognition of native title rights to land.

Torres Strait, Queensland, before 1889
Wood, shell; L. 115 mm, W. 450 mm, D. 36 mm
British Museum, London
Oc,89+.214 Exh. BM
Donated by A.C. Haddon

78.
Mask
Ceremonies involving wearing masks of turtle shell were an important part of traditional life on Mer.

Mer, Torres Strait, Queensland, before 1855
Turtle shell, shell, fibre, L. 400 mm
British Museum, London
Oc1855,1220.169 Exh. BM
Donated by the Lords of Admiralty

79.
Dhari
The *dhari* is a headdress made and worn by men in dance and ceremonies across the Torres Strait. This example uses cockatoo and cassowary feathers, but contemporary dhari are made from various materials, from chicken feathers to cardboard. The distinctive form has become a symbol of the Torres Strait and features on the Torres Strait Islander flag.

Tudu, Torres Strait, Queensland, before 1889
Cane, cockatoo feather, cassowary feather, pigeon feather?,
coix seed, cotton; L. 570 mm, W. 460 mm,
British Museum, London
Oc,89+.93 Exh. BM
Donated by A.C. Haddon

80.
Torres Strait Islander flag
Bernard Namok Jnr describes his father's design in this way: Blue represents the water; green, the land; black, Indigenous people; the dhari (headdress) the Torres Strait Islander people of Australia; white, peace or the coming of Christianity to the Torres Strait; the five pointed star, the five main island groups – the star also represents navigation as a seafaring culture. The Australian government recognised it as an official flag of Australia in 1995.

Designed by Bernard Namok Snr (1961–1993)
Waiben, Torres Strait, Queensland, 1992

Mabo decision, the High Court 'determined that the Murray Islanders had a form of land ownership in 1879', when the Islands had come under Queensland's jurisdiction, and which were 'governed by their own customs and rules' (figs 78–80).[162] The most far-reaching element in the decision was the rejection of the legal concept of *terra nullius* as a foundation for the Australian legal system. This overturned a long-standing and convenient myth about the basis upon which British claims to the territory had been originally made. Although the case applied to the Murray Islands, the implications of the High Court decision were much wider in that it 'upheld the view that English law recognised native title'. As Reynolds explains: 'While the Crown gained what was known as the radical title to all the lands in the colony the common law protected the property rights of the indigenous inhabitants'.[163] This meant that where native title rights had not been explicitly extinguished such as through the granting of freehold title, the way was open for Indigenous people's enduring and continuing rights in land to be recognised. As a result of the Native Title Act (Cwth) 1993, Indigenous people have lodged claims for recognition of their native title rights and interests all over the country. As at 1 January 2015, there were 302 registered native title determinations of which 243 recognised native title in all or part of the area and there were 959 Indigenous Land Use Agreements registered.

The native title process has brought to the fore Indigenous groups' particular ways of expressing connections to their country, of explaining their philosophies and of telling their histories. This has at times confounded the courts and legal processes, as they found themselves dealing with ways of conceptualising the world that are in many respects incommensurate with Western legal principles, traditions and thought. The native title process has had to adjust to accommodate and acknowledge Indigenous people's understandings, just as Aboriginal and Torres Strait Islander people have worked hard to translate their world views and connections to country in terms that are understandable to Western law traditions.

Art has had a vital part to play in processes of translation. One notable example is the *Ngurrara Canvas*, produced by senior traditional owners of the central Kimberley in 1997 during their native title claim. Ngarralja Tommy May (b. *c.* 1935), an artist and claimant on the case,[164] explains:

> I believe that [Native Title] is about Blackfella Law. The painting is only for proof. When I go to court to tell my story, I must listen very carefully before I open my mouth. Maybe the kartiya [white people] will say, 'We don't believe you'… That's why we made this painting, for evidence. We have painted our story for Native Title people, as proof. We want them to understand, so that they know about our painting, our country, our ngurrara. They are all the same thing.[165]

81.
Kungkarangkalpa (Seven Sisters) in production

Clockwise from far left: Myrtle Pennington (b. c. 1939), Pitjantjatjara; Ngalpingka Simms (b. c. 1945), Ngaanyatjarra; Kunmanara Hogan (c. 1945–2014), Pitjantjatjara; Yarangka Thomas (b. 1939), Pitjantjatjara; Tjaruwa Woods (b. 1954), Pitjantjatjara
Tjuntjuntjara, Great Victoria Desert, Western Australia
Photograph: Amanda Dent

Such paintings emerge out of the kinds of cross-cultural negotiations, translations and transactions that native title processes demand. Accepting paintings like these as evidence entails more than a tokenistic acknowledgment of Indigenous modes of representation. They demand, rather, the recognition of Indigenous ways of being.

One significant example of the value of art as evidence is the Spinifex Arts Project (fig. 81), which emerged in 1996 out of the documentation process for a native title claim. The Spinifex people speak the desert language of Pitjantjatjara, but they do not identify themselves primarily as Pitjantjatjara people.[166] Rather, their unique geographic, historic and political experience has lead them to identify themselves in relation to the environment they call home as *Anangu tjuta pila nguru* (people from the spinifex).[167] These are some of the groups who were forced to leave their country because of the British and Australian governments' atomic testing programme in the late 1950s and early 1960s (see pp. 188–9). They ended up hundreds of kilometres away in settlements and missions such as Cundeelee, but returned to their homelands in the 1980s, wanting to reclaim their lives, autonomy and land. Encouraged by the High Court's findings in the *Mabo* decision, they

82.
Men's Native Title Painting

Kunmanara Anderson (1938–2011), Kunmanara Anderson
(1933–2014), Byron Brooks (b. 1955), Kunmanara Brown
(1931–2009), Fred Grant (b. 1941), Ned Grant (b. 1942),
Lawrence Pennington (b. c. 1934), Ian Rictor (b. 1962),
Lennard Walker (b. 1946), Pitjantjatjara
Spinifex country, Great Victoria Desert, 1998
Acrylic on canvas; H. 1960 mm, W. 1280 mm
Spinifex Arts Project Community Collection, Tjuntjuntjara

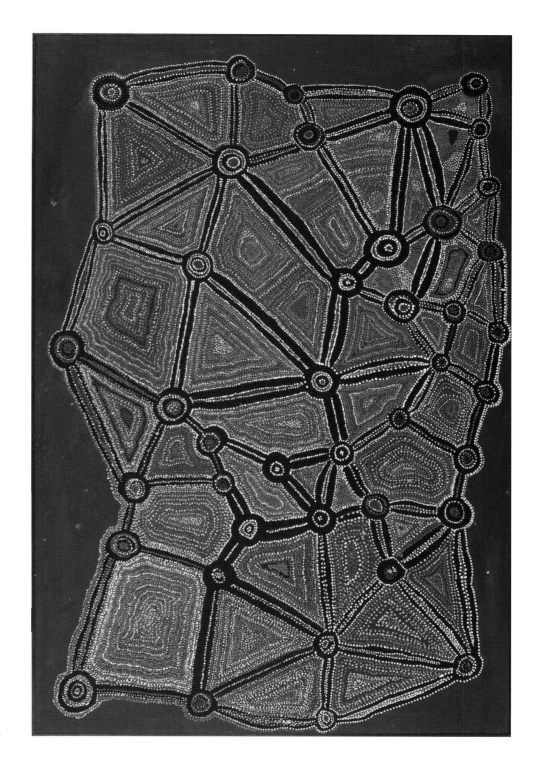

83.
Women's Native Title Painting

Kunmanara Anderson (*c.* 1940–2002), Kunmanara
Donaldson (1936–2008), Kathleen Donegan (b. 1944),
Estelle Hogan (b. *c.* 1937), Carleen West (b. 1945),
Pitjantjatjara
Spinifex country, Great Victoria Desert, 1998
Acrylic on canvas; H. 1870 mm, W. 1230 mm
Spinifex Arts Project Community Collection, Tjuntjuntjara

sought in the mid-1990s to reclaim title to their territory. As part of the native title documentation process, Spinifex people mapped their country in exhaustive and compelling detail, translating their concepts and custodianship – their law – into terms that would be legible to another system of law. Painting was how they could directly *show* their own forms of ownership.

No one person can speak for (or paint) Spinifex country in its entirety; individuals have rights to only certain sites or areas. It is, however, the relationship between these estates that constitutes the collective claim over the country. For this reason the Spinifex people produced two collaborative paintings – *Men's Native Title Painting* (1998; fig. 82) and *Women's Native Title Painting* (1998; fig. 83) – which encompass the entire 55,000-square-kilometre claim area by harmonising the contributions of many artists with rights to particular places. These two paintings encapsulate the complex legal arguments developed over hundreds of pages of evidence, asserting Spinifex rights with Spinifex authority. The paintings preface the agreement reached between Spinifex people and the Western Australian government.

However, not all Indigenous groups making native title claims have succeeded in having their enduring connection to land recognised through the formal legal processes. The situation has been particularly fraught for groups in south-east Australia whose lands were among the first to be colonised by the British. In one infamous case involving the Yorta Yorta people in Victoria the presiding judge declared that the 'tide of history' had 'washed away' any real acknowledgment of traditional laws and any real observance of traditional customs by the applicants. This was a judgment experienced by Yorta Yorta as yet another denial of their status and rights as the original owners of the country and as another form of dispossession.[168] As with earlier land rights legislation, the native title legislation and process promised more to Aboriginal people and Torres Strait Islanders in places where continuity of occupation of country and maintenance of traditional cultural practices have been possible. In contexts where this has not been the case, and where native title legislation has had limited application, some state governments have entered into land management arrangements and agreements with traditional owners who also seek recognition of rights such as to reclaim human remains from museums (see p. 227–9) and other kinds of cultural property.

A recent and relevant instance of this concerns the situation that emerged when the Dja Dja Wurrung people in Victoria took legal action in 2004 in a bid to prevent two objects on loan from the British Museum to Museum Victoria in Melbourne from returning to the United Kingdom. The objects were a bark etching and a bark figure of an emu (figs 84–85). (A third object in the case was a bark etching from the Royal Botanic Gardens, Kew.) They are extremely rare surviving examples of the ceremonial art of Aboriginal people of south-east Australia. They originate from a property named Fernyhurst in central Victoria, which was situated on the traditional

84.
Bark etching
At the top a man points a long spear towards a kangaroo.

Fernyhurst, Victoria, *c.* 1854
Bark, natural pigment; H. 670 mm, W. 310 mm
British Museum, London
Oc.1827 Exh. BM
Donated by Royal Botanic Gardens, Kew

85.
Figure of an emu
Bark figures and effigies were used in ceremonies in south-east Australia. Few have survived.

Fernyhurst, Victoria, *c.* 1854
Bark, natural pigment; H. 690 mm, W. 300 mm, D. 27 mm
British Museum, London
Oc,+.1281 Exh. BM
Donated by Royal Botanic Gardens, Kew

207

lands of the Dja Dja Wurrung people. John Hunter Kerr (1821–1874), a Scotsman who had migrated to Australia in 1839, purchased the property in 1849 (see pp. 147–9 for discussion of the Port Phillip frontier). Kerr was interested in the customs of the Aborigines on his property and they were, in turn, it seems, willing to share some knowledge about their ceremonies and practices with him. They acceded, for instance, to his request to perform a ceremony in daylight.[169] A photograph of the occasion taken by Kerr is among the first photographs of Aboriginal people in Victoria (fig. 86). In 1854 Kerr contributed the two Dja Dja Wurrung barks, an etching and other artefacts to a local exhibition;[170] the following year they were sent to Paris for the Exposition Universelle, after which they were acquired by the British Museum and Kew Gardens.

One hundred and fifty years later, the objects were borrowed for an exhibition titled *Etched on bark 1854: Kulin barks from northern Victoria* held at Museum Victoria in Melbourne from March to June 2004. Museum Victoria had obtained the necessary permits under Australian Commonwealth legislation to import and re-export the articles. Near the end of the exhibition, some Dja Dja Wurrung inspectors sought an emergency declaration under section 21c of the Aboriginal and Torres Strait Islander Heritage Protection Act (Cwth) 1984. A succession of emergency declarations to prevent their re-export was granted. To fulfil its contractual obligation under the loan agreement with the British Museum, Museum Victoria took legal action to challenge the validity of the emergency declarations and, in May 2005, the Federal Court of Australia ruled the declarations invalid.[171] The Minister responsible for the Aboriginal and Torres Strait Islander Heritage Protection Act (Cwth) 1984 decided not to use other powers under the legislation to prevent their return.

86.
Dja Dja Wurrung men performing a ceremony
The men negotiated terms and reimbursement when landholder John Hunter Kerr asked them to stage this ceremony during the day. Kerr's early photographic equipment was not sophisticated enough to capture the scene at night when it was normally performed.

Fernyhurst, Victoria, c. 1854
John Hunter Kerr (1821–1874), born Edinburgh, Scotland
Albumen print; H. 52 mm, W. 192 mm
British Museum, London
Oc,B80.19

87.
Gary Murray, Dja Dja Wurrung spokesperson, with a bark etching lent by Royal Botanic Gardens, Kew, on display at Museum Victoria, Melbourne

Museum Victoria, Melbourne, 2004
Photograph: Craig Abraham

Gary Murray (b. 1951), a Dja Dja Wurrung spokesperson, argued at the time of the court case that the objects were stolen and that: 'If the barks go back to England, we will be dispossessed a second time' (fig. 87).[172] Although we do not know what the Dja Dja Warrung thought when their objects were collected by Kerr, today they regard such collecting as a form of plunder and seek to re-gain control of their cultural objects.[173] In contrast, Dawn Casey (b. 1950), then Director of the National Museum of Australia, advised that 'by preventing the return of the artefacts to the British Museum, the government would put at risk the prospect of accessing the 40,000 other Aboriginal artefacts held in overseas institutions'.[174] The Australian government subsequently amended the Aboriginal and Torres Strait Islander Heritage Protection Act 1984 in 2006, providing for the issue of a Certificate of Exemption from Export Control under section 12 of the Protection of Moveable Cultural Heritage Act 1986 as protection from claims under the Aboriginal and Torres Strait Islander Heritage Protection Act 1984, where the certificate is given prior to the arrival of the objects in Australia. Subsequently, the Protection of Cultural Objects on Loan Act 2013 was introduced to ensure authorised institutions could import objects on loan for temporary public exhibition without fear of legal action.

This particular case, and others like it, touches on a number of the fraught and challenging issues with which the *Indigenous Australia: enduring civilisation* exhibition engages. Objects such as the Dja Dja Wurrung barks come to us from the colonial encounter between Indigenous people and British settlers on the nineteenth-century Australian frontier. This was a frontier in which few settlers were seriously interested in learning from Aboriginal people about their civilisation. Nevertheless, Aboriginal people often strove to engage Europeans in the meaning of their ceremonial life and to share knowledge about their own society with a settler society that seemed at times so determined to destroy it. Much of the collecting carried out around this period was done in a spirit of salvaging what remained from a society that almost all settlers believed would eventually become a thing of the past.[175]

Yet Indigenous Australians did survive the colonial encounter. They have endured. The objects that come to us from these pasts belong in a very deep sense to them – the living Indigenous cultures and people of Australia. But these objects are held (for) now, a long way from home, in the British Museum and other museums around the world. Museums, governments and Indigenous people, in Australia, in Britain and elsewhere, are continuing to grapple with and work through the issues involved in ensuring that connections between people and collections are maintained, and that these significant objects are drawn on in imaginative and appropriate ways to tell histories that enhance contemporary understandings of Indigenous Australian people and their cultures. This exhibition is just one small part of this very complex and ongoing process.

Out of country

Gaye Sculthorpe

Objects end up in museum collections as a result of particular circumstances, rarely systematic. Their histories reflect both specific local exchanges and the motivations of the maker, the collector and often various intermediaries. As with early collections in other museums, the circumstances of acquisition in the field range from willing exchanges, through fortuitous collecting, to sometimes knowingly taking items without consent.[1] From the establishment of the British Museum in 1753 until about 1860, the Australian artefacts acquired were rarely collected with the Museum in mind. Examining the ways in which objects, and some Indigenous people, ended up in Britain and in the British Museum in particular, reveals local cross-cultural histories as well as the transformation of British and Australian attitudes to Indigenous Australians and museums, a transformation that is ongoing through ever-increasing engagements today.

It is difficult to identify the first objects from Australia and how they entered the collection. Early Museum records often only generally describe donations without listing individual pieces. As the organisation of curatorial departments changed over the years and some items were donated with natural history specimens that later went to the Natural History Museum, when a new building opened at South Kensington in 1881, records were often dispersed. Although objects collected by Captain James Cook were acquired in 1771, 1775 and 1776, and 'artificial curiosities from the South Sea Islands' from Sir Joseph Banks in 1778, the first specific Australian artefact registered was in February 1798, when John Birch of Dean Street, Soho, donated 'a long bundle of arrows' from the Endeavour Strait.[2] Some clues as to the ages of objects exist on old Museum labels and by the names of places. For example, the name 'Terra Australis' on a label suggests a collection date prior to 1824, when the Admiralty officially adopted the name 'Australia' (fig. 1). Similarly, a

general location such as 'North West' or 'North East' Australia suggests an early voyage before Australian places were given English names.

Objects, ideas and people circulated widely in learned London society in the late eighteenth and early nineteenth centuries and key individuals often had links with a number of institutions. For example, Banks, the botanist on Cook's first voyage in 1768–71, became President of the Royal Society and in that position was an ex officio trustee of the British Museum from 1788 until his death in 1820. He was also the unofficial director of the Royal Botanic Gardens in Kew. Banks made a number of donations to the British Museum. It is not clear how or when the shield understood to have been collected at Botany Bay in 1770 came to the Museum (see fig. 1, p. 123) as it was found unregistered in the collection in 1978, but it is possible that it came via the Lords of the Admiralty, Cook or Banks.[3]

The earliest objects were collected by British people who were themselves 'out of country', such as Royal Navy personnel, temporary

residents, officials or missionaries who moved between various colonies and often back to the United Kingdom. In the mid-nineteenth century, items were also sent by Australian colonies to the UK and Europe for international exhibitions. Individuals both in Australia and Britain sold or donated pieces to the British Museum as a way of either making money or memorialising their ancestors' history or themselves. As well as objects, many human remains of Aborigines were collected in the nineteenth and early twentieth centuries and, along with some living Aboriginal people, brought to the UK. Although British anthropologists W. Baldwin Spencer and A.C. Haddon undertook significant collecting in Australia from around 1888 to 1923, the only British museum collecting expedition to Australia was that undertaken by the Natural History Museum in 1923–5 and this was arranged at the request of Australian museums (see pp. 234–5).

Royal Navy and colonial collecting

After Cook's first visit in 1770, the Royal Navy made numerous voyages to Australia with the prime purposes of pre-empting territorial claims from rival countries and mapping coastlines. These voyages continued into the late nineteenth century by agreement with Australian colonies, even after they began to establish their own naval forces.[4] Unsurprisingly, coastal and island locations feature prominently in collecting by naval personnel. Some strategic locations such as King George's Sound, the Torres Strait and Port Essington were visited several times providing opportunities for developing relationships and understandings across the cultural divide.

Temporary forays were made from ships onto land and objects were collected or exchanged for different reasons, both directly and indirectly. The collecting of the shield by Cook or one of his crew when it was dropped on the beach at Botany Bay in 1770 has been described (see p. 123). The men also confiscated about forty to fifty 'lances' (spears), which Banks noted were mostly not offensive weapons but used to catch fish.[5] It was as an act of punishment that Lieutenant Phillip Parker King took away a canoe and other objects at Hanover Bay in 1821, after his surgeon was speared (see p. 161).

Aboriginal people and Islanders quickly seized the value of metal that they did not possess and were eager to trade objects to obtain it. During his circumnavigation of the continent in 1802, then Commander Matthew Flinders and crew, wishing to 'secure the friendship and confidence of these Islanders', traded a saw, hammer, nails and 'other trifles' for pearl shells, cowrie necklaces, and bows and arrows (fig. 2).[6] King, during his surveying voyage of 1818–21, collected over 200 objects including spears, canoes and spear points. At King George's Sound (Albany) in 1821, he observed a lively trade in artefacts so hastily and somewhat imperfectly crafted that the ship's botanist Allan Cunningham thought they were made 'simply for sale'.[7] The

2.
***View of Murray's Islands (With Natives
Offering to Barter)***
Westall was an artist on HMS *Investigator*,
under Commander Matthew Flinders. On
arriving at Mer (Murray Island) in 1802, about
fifty Islanders came out in canoes to trade.

William Westall (1781–1850), born Hertford, England
Torres Strait, Queensland, 1802
Watercolour on paper; H. 257 mm, W. 383 mm
National Library of Australia, Canberra
Nla.pic-an4565639

3.

Turtle shell blade

Collected at Mer in 1836 by Lieutenant G.B. Kempthorne. He believed the turtle shell was 'depreciated by the wretched carvings which almost destroy the beauty of the shell'.

Mer, Torres Strait, Queensland, before 1836
Turtle shell, lime; L. 200 mm, W. 167 mm
British Museum, London
Oc1986,02.72

Aboriginal people they encountered kept their valued war spears and traded the more easily produced hunting and fishing spears for which they received one-eighth of a biscuit for each.[8] King was impressed by aspects of Aboriginal technology, discussing and illustrating items in his account of the voyage published in 1827.[9] Some objects collected by King (such as the spear point discussed on p. 161) entered the Museum's collection many years later in 1873 by transfer from the United Services Museum, whereas others, including a spear from Western Australia, were donated directly by him in 1831 after he returned from a voyage to the Pacific and South America. The whereabouts of the other items he collected, such as the canoes, have not yet been traced.

The Torres Strait between Australia and the island of New Guinea was strategically important as a shipping route used by many naval and passenger ships on their way to Sydney. Without local knowledge of the many reefs, the chance of shipwreck was very likely. In August 1834, the ship *Charles Eaton* sank and, after a year without news, rumours spread that survivors were alive and the ships *Isabella* and *Tigris* were sent out to search. The *Isabella* took articles for exchange and barter with the Islanders, a region in which trade and exchange played an important role in traditional life and where by then a lively trade with Europeans had been established.[10] The Bombay-based *Tigris* stopped at Mer (Murray Island) for two days in July 1836 and on arrival was surrounded by many Islanders in canoes who were eager to obtain European materials. Lieutenant G.B. Kempthorne (*c.* 1810–1870) described this trade in detail:

> An amicable feeling having been established, a brisk traffic soon commenced, the Natives holding up in their hands the articles they wished to dispose of, consisting of cocoanuts [*sic*], yams, plantains, tortoise-shells, and their implements of war – viz., bows, arrows, and spears. In exchange they received small looking-glasses, empty bottles, beads, clasp-knives, axes, and old clothes: but iron was of all commodities most sought for, and appeared to be most prized: they were constantly calling for 'tooree' 'tooree' (iron, iron) in the most eager and vociferous manner and we could hardly appease their wants. I firmly believe had we remained at Murray's Island another day, the vessel would have been stripped of all that metal – not a bolt, nail or hoop, would have been left.[11]

Kempthorne also noted the abundance of turtle among the reefs and the potential of turtle shell for trade in Europe but failed to appreciate the Islanders' sense of aesthetics:

> the natives destroying immense numbers for the sake of the shell, which they form into rude ornaments, and dispose of,

Out of country

4.
Mask
Collected by J.B. Jukes, a geologist on board
HMS *Fly* in 1844.

Erub, Torres Strait, Queensland, before 1844
Turtle shell, wood, human hair, fibre; L. 400 mm
British Museum, London
Oc1846,0731.3
Donated by J.B. Jukes

5.
Wig
J.B. Jukes persuaded an Islander named
Koiyop to sell him a wig in exchange for
a knife. According to Jukes, Koiyop asked
for a mirror to see how he looked as he was
worried that without his wig he would be
laughed at.

Erub, Torres Strait, Queensland, before 1844
Human hair, fibre; L. 370 mm, W. 220 mm
British Museum, London
Oc1846,0731.4
Donated by J.B. Jukes

whenever they have an opportunity, for old iron or axes, or other trifling articles. A trade of some value might be carried on in this single item alone, and I am only astonished vessels do not visit this spot oftener for the sake of this traffic. I feel convinced that, if the natives only knew of its importance, large quantities might soon be collected and kept in store, and it would not, moreover, be – as it is now – depreciated by the wretched carvings which almost destroy the beauty of the shell: the quality is excellent, the plates being large, thick, and splendidly marked, and, in its natural state, would no doubt realize a high price'.[12] (fig. 3)

Other naval crew such as geologists and surgeons were also interested in the new objects they saw. Joseph Beete Jukes (1811–1869) was a geologist on board HMS *Fly*, which visited Erub on a surveying voyage in 1844. Using metal knives as currency, he purchased a mask, wig and drum, which he donated to the British Museum in 1846 soon after his return. In a letter to Charles Darwin (1809–1882), he noted that: 'all my spiritual exercises procured on the Australian coast are now buried in the deep, deep, sea of the vaults of the British Museum' (figs 4–5).[13]

The visits of some of the ships live on in various Islander traditions. HMS *Rattlesnake* undertook a long surveying voyage in waters of northern Australia and New Guinea in 1846–50. Under the command of Captain Owen Stanley (1811–1850), its passengers included the naturalist John MacGillivray (1821–1867) and surgeon Thomas Huxley (1825–1895). The ship became well known for finding Barbara Thompson (1831–1916), a shipwreck survivor who lived with the Kaurareg people for five years.[14] In one of the Torres Strait Islander families today, the use of 'Rattler' as a surname may be drawn from this ship. Mr Tamat Rattler is a descendant of Tom Muri (1864–?), who is the man named as Tamari in a drawing made by the Australian artist Tom Roberts (1856–1931) in 1892. Mr Rattler suggests that the model ship forming part of the headdress drawn in the image is the *Rattlesnake* (figs 6–7).[15]

In the second half of the nineteenth century Royal Navy voyages were less frequent, often focusing on New Guinea, but some Indigenous Australian objects continued to be collected. Acquisitions from this time include several masks donated in 1870 by Lieutenant Robert H. Armit (1844–1891), who spent five years on a surveying voyage, and a rare human figure from Erub in the Torres Strait acquired from Julius Brenchley (1816–1873), who travelled on HMS *Curacoa* in 1865 (fig. 8).

Although many objects were exchanged directly by Aboriginal people and Torres Strait Islanders for goods they desired, European visitors sometimes knowingly took items without consent. The surgeon, R.W. Coppinger (1847–1910), on HMS *Alert* in 1881, removed 'some portable specimens of native art' from Clack Island in Queensland 'without many

6.
HMS Rattlesnake, *Leaving Port Essington, 17 November 1848*

The *Rattlesnake* made an extensive surveying voyage in northern Australia between 1846 and 1850. Naval officer and artist Stanley made sketches of what he saw and other officers traded objects with Aboriginal people and Torres Strait Islanders on these voyages.

Owen Stanley (1811–1850), born Alderley, England
Painted on board HMS *Rattlesnake*, before 1849
Watercolour on paper; H. 108 mm, W. 197 mm
Mitchell Library, State Library of New South Wales, Sydney
SAFE / PXC 281

7.
Tamari

Tom Muri, or Tamari, (1864–?) from Mori, wears a headdress in the form of a ship, perhaps HMS *Rattlesnake*. The artist, Tom Roberts, was a pioneer of Australian landscape painting.

Tom Roberts (1856–1931), born Dorchester, England
Torres Strait, Queensland,1892
Watercolour and graphite on paper; H. 273 mm, W. 177 mm
British Museum, London
Oc2006,Drg.407
Donated by Tom Roberts

8.
Human figures

Collected by Julius Brenchley, a collector and traveller on board HMS *Curacoa*.

Erub Torres Strait, Queensland, before 1865
Wood, hair (presumed human), cotton, vegetable fibre, coix seeds, pearl shell, cone shell; H. 750 mm, W. 160 mm, D. 185 mm
British Museum, London
Oc.6537 Exh. BM
Donated by Julius Lucius Brenchley

9. (overleaf)
Larapuna, Binalong Bay
This region on Tasmania's east coast was a rich hunting ground for Tasmanian Aborigines and contains many sites of significance. English navigator Tobias Furneaux (1735–1781) gave the area the name Bay of Fires in 1773 when he saw numerous fires lit by Aboriginal people on the shore. Larapuna was made part of the official name for this region in 2013.

Larapuna, Binalong Bay, south of Bay of Fires, Tasmania
Photograph: Sonia Massarova

conscientious scruples as to the sacred rights of ownership', which he 'carried off in triumph and deposited on board'.[16]

Many artefacts collected by Royal Navy personnel ended up in Haslar Royal Navy Hospital Museum in Portsmouth from the late 1820s. In 1855, significant collections from that museum were transferred to the British Museum, but unfortunately with little or no documentation.

For the benefit of the mother country

In 1837, the Trustees of the British Museum sought the help of colonial authorities to acquire 'such rare and curious objects as shall appear to be of sufficient importance to deserve a place in the National Museum'.[17] A letter was sent to governors of British colonies from Downing Street on 16 October 1837, which was reproduced in various colonial newspapers.[18] The request was supported in Van Diemen's Land (Tasmania; fig. 9) at least, with the local paper noting:

> still more happy should we feel, could we exercise with our contemporaries in this colony, a sufficient influence to prevent them hereafter from assailing each other in a manner which must forfeit for the colonists the esteem of other countries. Far better would it be for us, by simultaneous exertions, to assist the views of the British Government, and the trustees of the British Museum, in dedicating our attention to such objects as might further our best interests. Surely, in an infant colony like this, and only partially explored, there must be a great variety of objects which have escaped as yet the observance of scientific research, and when once known, would greatly add to our native resources and the benefit of the Mother Country.[19]

Perhaps it was this that inspired S. Neil Talbot (1799–1863) to donate a collection of seventy objects from the Swan River region in 1839 (see fig. 15, p. 38 and figs 13–14, p. 134).[20] Similarly, in 1847, George Whitcomb (1803–1881), an 'old colonist' of Tasmania who returned to live for some time in the UK, donated two Tasmanian spears.[21] Surveyor General of New South Wales, Thomas Mitchell, donated objects in 1839 and 1848, including a boomerang that he used as inspiration to design and patent a boomerang-shaped propeller for ships (figs. 10–11).[22]

The Great Exhibition at the Crystal Palace in London in 1851 and subsequent international exhibitions were important opportunities for the Australian colonies to promote their products, exhibit their progress, and encourage immigration and investment.[23] The colonies of New South Wales, Tasmania and Victoria often sent objects to such exhibitions.[24] The exhibitions

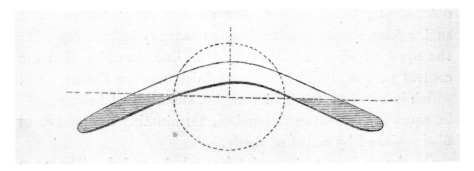

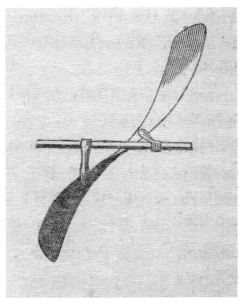

10.
Boomerang
Collected by Surveyor General of New South Wales, Thomas Mitchell.

Murray River, border of Victoria and New South Wales, before 1839
Wood; L 694 mm, W 440 mm, D. 11 mm
British Museum, London
Oc1839,1012.2 Exh. BM
Donated by Thomas Mitchell

11.
Diagram of the boomerang propeller
A boomerang from the Murray River was used as the model.

Designed by Thomas Mitchell, *c.* 1850
British Library, London
8805.c.74.(6.)

12.
Tasmanian Aborigines at Oyster Cove, c. 1851

Standing left to right: Meethecaratheeanna, Goneannah, Drunameliyar.
Seated left to right: Wobberrertee, Plowneme, Mary Ann Arthur, Calamarowenye, Drayduric, Truganini.
(Names attributed on the basis of comparison with people in other photographs.)

John Watt Beattie (1859–1930), born Aberdeen, Scotland
Oyster Cove, Tasmania, original photograph c. 1851
Photographic print, H. 162 mm, W. 210 mm
National Library of Australia, Canberra
nla.pic-an23182428

13.
Basket

It is likely this basket was collected by Joseph Milligan who sent items from Tasmania to the Great Exhibition in London, 1851.

Probably Oyster Cove, Tasmania, before 1868
Iris (*Diplarrena latifolia*) leaf fibre; H. 226 mm, W. 145 mm, D. 105 mm
British Museum, London
Oc.9895 Exh. BM
Donated by Royal Botanic Gardens, Kew

in London in 1851 and 1861 as well as the Expositions Universelles in Paris in 1855 and 1867 were the source of important Aboriginal objects that subsequently came to the British Museum through the bequest of the avid collector and philanthropist Henry Christy (1810–1865).[25] These include the bark etching and figure from central Victoria (see figs 84–85, p. 207) and weapons most likely collected from prisoners in Pentridge Prison, Melbourne (see figs 60–61, p. 177).

The secretary of the Tasmanian organising committee for the Great Exhibition of 1851 was Joseph Milligan (1807–1884), a Scottish surgeon who had been superintendent of the Aboriginal establishment at Flinders Island in 1843 and later supervised the transfer of Aborigines from there to Oyster Cove in 1847. He was interested in natural history and Aboriginal languages and customs.[26] As secretary of the Royal Society of Van Diemen's Land, he played an active part in soliciting items for the Great Exhibition.

In 1851, there were 33 Aboriginal people still alive at Oyster Cove and who, apart from occasional forays into the bush and to Hobart, were confined there (fig. 12).[27] It is likely that Milligan obtained the objects from these people. Unaware of the people remaining at Oyster Cove, a London journalist, while admiring the workmanship of the brilliant shell necklaces, described the

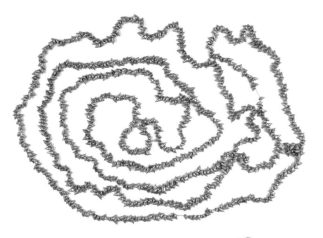

14.
Shell necklace
Displayed at the Great Exhibition, London, 1851

Probably Oyster Cove, Tasmania, before 1851
Maireener shell (*Phasianotrochus irisodontes*), fibre;
L. 2000 mm
British Museum, London
Oc1851,1122.4 Exh. BM
Donated by Joseph Milligan

display in London as a 'a melancholy tribute paid in the Van Diemen's Land Department to its now extinct Aborigines' who 'ought not to have been hunted down'.[28] After the exhibition closed, Milligan donated some of these objects to the Museum: a model canoe (see fig. 34, p. 56), a basket (fig. 13), two shell necklaces (fig. 14) and the only kelp water container that has survived from earlier times (fig. 15).

People out of country

When new circumstances prevailed, Aboriginal people and Torres Strait Islanders expanded their realm of engagement with outsiders in travelling beyond their own lands. As described earlier (see p. 154), Bungaree accompanied Flinders and King around Australia, and Aboriginal people from northern Australia travelled to Indonesia with fishermen in the nineteenth century. The crew of HMS *Fly* noted in 1846 that 'the natives of Port Essington are very fond of going abroad to see the world, and the Malays, having a great dread of them in general, are glad to humour them.'[29] Neinmal (d. before 1852), a man from Port Essington who assisted John MacGillivray in collecting objects, voyaged as far as Sydney, Singapore and Java as he 'begged so hard I could not refuse him',[30] and a Tasmanian Aboriginal woman, Woretemoeteryanner (*c.* 1795–1847), travelled on a whaling ship to Mauritius.[31]

A number of Aboriginal people, perhaps a hundred or more,[32] travelled to the UK in the late eighteenth and nineteenth century, with various motivations and levels of freewill. The first to visit were Bennelong (*c.* 1764–1813) and Yemmerawanne (*c.* 1774–1794), brought by Governor Phillip in 1792–5 who considered that they would provide 'much information' to the British.[33] In London, Bennelong and Yemmerawanne visited sites such as St Paul's Cathedral, the Tower of London and also the Parkinson Museum, which housed artefacts from Cook's voyages.[34] While Bennelong returned to Australia in 1795, Yemmerawanne died in the UK and is buried in the churchyard of St John the Baptist at Eltham.[35] Explorer Edward John Eyre (1815–1901) brought back Warrulan (*c.* 1836–1855), the son of Tenberry (1798–1855), an Aboriginal leader from South Australia. Ian Henderson has argued that Tenberry deliberately sent Warrulan as part of a long-term project to help negotiate with the settlers.[36] Reading Cemetery is the resting place of William Wimmera (*c.* 1841–1852). Having been taken from his dead mother's arms when she was violently killed in north-western Victoria, and subsequently becoming lost in Melbourne, he was taken in and brought to the UK by Reverend Septimus Chase (1819–1895) in 1851, but died at Reading aged eleven before he could be returned to his own people.[37]

15.
Kelp water container
This water container is made from the giant bull kelp, which grows in waters around Tasmania. Pulled from the water when wet, it quickly hardens as it dries. Tea tree is inserted through holes punched in the side of the kelp, and various fibres form a handle. Sand is used to fill the container as it dries to maintain the desired shape. From the 1990s, Tasmanian Aboriginal women began to remake items such as this. Although illustrations and photographs of this container have been published and, more recently, put online, few Aborigines have had the chance to see it in person in London. Beautifully crafted, showing fine knowledge of natural materials, it symbolises the fragility of the Aboriginal population of Tasmania in 1851, and its cultural regeneration today.

Probably Oyster Cove, Tasmania, *c.* 1851
Bull kelp (*Durvillaea potatorum*), tea tree wood, fibre;
H. 60 mm, L. 155 mm, D. 155 mm
British Museum, London
Oc1851,1122.2 Exh. BM
Donated by Joseph Milligan

16.
The first Australian cricket team to tour the United Kingdom
Standing, left to right (nicknames given in brackets): Jungunjinuke (Dick-a-Dick), Bonnibarngeet (Tiger), Unamurriman (Mullagh), C. Lawrence (coach), Yellana (Cuzens), Brimbunyah (Red Cap), Bullchanach (Bullocky), Jarrawuk (Twopenny). Seated, left to right: Grongarrong (Mosquito), Arrahmunyarrimun (Peter), W. Shepherd (occasional relief player), Brippoki (Dumas).

Trent Bridge, Nottingham, 1868

The first Australian cricket tour (1868)

Unlike the individual Aboriginal people noted above whose visits received little attention, the first Aboriginal people to gain widespread public awareness in the UK was a team of Aboriginal cricketers who toured in 1868, being the first Australian touring cricket team (fig. 16). Between May and October 1868, a group of thirteen cricketers, mostly from the state of Victoria, played matches at various towns in England. Before or after the cricket game, they displayed their traditional skills in throwing and dodging spears, boomerangs and clubs.[38] While these performances were popular with the public, members of the Marylebone Cricket Club were initially reluctant to host the players at Lord's as they deemed traditional displays, like other novelty displays such as pony races, unfitting to take place on that ground.[39] The cricket tour occurred not long after the publication of Darwin's *The Origin of the Species* in 1859. William Tegetmeier (1816–1912), a poultry fancier and correspondent of Charles Darwin, went to see them play. He subsequently took their physical measurements, arranged for three of them, including Jungunjinuke, to be photographed as three different physical 'types' and displayed their weapons in a small museum in the offices of *The Field* magazine.[40]

Jungunjinuke, or 'Dick-a-Dick', quickly developed a reputation for his skill and dexterity in dodging cricket balls thrown at him, which he would deflect with his spear and club, and only rarely being hit. During his time in England, he was noted not only for his cricketing skills, but also his style of fashionable dress, his Swiss clock and his ability to charm an audience.[41] A club used by Junjunjinuke has remained in the UK since that tour and, from 1947, been housed at the Marylebone Cricket Club (fig. 17). An old paper label stuck on the club is signed 'GWG', suggesting it passed through the hands of George W. Graham (1828–1886), the Sydney solicitor who was the co-promoter of the tour. The style of the club is typical of those from western Victoria, which are often referred to as 'leangles', used in fighting at close quarters. All members of the team returned to Australia, save for Bripumyarrumin ('King Cole') (d. 1868) who is buried in Meath Gardens in east London.

Human remains

In the nineteenth and early twentieth centuries, Australian Aboriginal people were often considered as the lowest order of mankind and thus their skeletons were prized by collectors.[42] Many, often recent, Aboriginal graves were dug up to collect skeletal remains. In Tasmania, where it was believed the Aboriginal people were soon to die out, human remains were highly sought after. Some individuals, such as William Lanne (*c.* 1835–1869) and Truganini (*c.* 1812–1876), knew their graves were in danger of being robbed once they died. These fears were well-founded as Lanne's body was dug up, various body parts taken, and his skull ended up at the University of Edinburgh.[43] Truganini's body was exhumed and her skeleton displayed for many decades at the Tasmanian Museum and Art Gallery until it was returned to the Aboriginal community for cremation in 1976.[44]

The British Museum holds few human remains from Australia as many remains were transferred to the Natural History Museum when it was separately located in the 1880s. The Museum has received several repatriation requests, including from Tasmania and the Torres Strait. A request to return two cremation ash bundles was made by the Tasmanian Aboriginal Centre (TAC) in 1985 but, until 2004 with changed legislation, the Trustees had no legal basis to consider this request.[45] In 2006, the Trustees agreed to return these two bundles, which had been collected by G.A. Robinson in the 1830s, as they were satisfied that their cultural and religious importance would outweigh public benefit if retained in the collection, provided they were subject to a mortuary disposal in accordance with Aboriginal tradition.[46]

A request by the Torres Strait Islands Repatriation Working Group on behalf of traditional owners was made in 2011 for the return of two ancestral remains that had been purchased from Islanders in 1888–9 by A.C. Haddon. The Islanders' submission to the Trustees stated that in relation to potential public benefit, science and human understanding should proceed on a basis of cooperation and consensus. They argued that 'Our ancestors' remains are a fundamental spiritual and cultural link to our past and that appropriating…

17.
Club belonging to Jungunjinuke
Jungunjinuke was a member of the first Australian cricket team to tour the United Kingdom in 1868.

Victoria, before 1868
Wood; L. 700 mm, W. 275 mm, D. 36 mm
Marlybone Cricket Club Museum, Lord's Ground, London
M 47.1 Exh. BM

ancestral remains violates the sanctity of the dead. We consider that there will be no spiritual peace until the dead are returned "to country" and have received their last rights in accordance with their traditions'.[47] The Trustees, much to the disappointment of Torres Strait Islanders, considered the evidence provided but in November 2012 declined the request, believing the way the remains had been collected did not represent an interruption to customary mortuary processes.[48]

Artwork produced today also reflects these difficult histories. The near-genocidal treatment of Aboriginal people in Tasmania is referenced in the T-shirt 'lutruwita [Tasmania] has a black history' given to the Museum by

18.
'lutrawita has a black history'
This t-shirt was given to the British Museum by representatives of the Tasmanian Aboriginal Centre in 2006 when they collected ancestral remains that were repatriated. 'Lutruwita' means Tasmania. 'Land Rights, Treaty, Stolen Generation, Compensation, Justice' is printed on the reverse.

Designed Tasmania, c. 2000–6
Cotton; H. 730 mm, W. 900 mm
British Museum, London
2013,2027.1 Exh. BM
Donated by Tasmanian Aboriginal Centre Inc.

19.
Tasmanian Aborigines and supporters leaving the Royal College of Surgeons in London with ancestral remains being repatriated back to Tasmania
Top, left to right: supporters Rikki Shields and Piers H. Gardener. Bottom, left to right: Sara Maynard and Caroline Spotswood.

London, 16 September 2009

the TAC representatives on the occasion of the repatriation of the burial bundles (fig. 18).

There are still many ancestral remains of Indigenous Australians in museums around the world. Some of these are of known individuals from the nineteenth century, such as Jandamarra whose head was removed after his killing and brought to the UK. Its whereabouts is still being investigated by his descendants.[49] Aboriginal people and Torres Strait Islanders continue to undertake research and negotiate to have remains still in museums in the United Kingdom and elsewhere returned home (fig. 19).

Missionary collecting

Missionary endeavour among Aboriginal and Torres Strait Islander people was undertaken by a variety of faiths from early colonial times. Objects in the British Museum derive from Quakers, Lutherans, Presbyterians, the Society for the Propagation of the Gospel, as well as from the London Missionary Society. Individual missionaries and different faiths had particular motivations for collecting.

Quakers James Backhouse (1794–1869) and George Washington Walker (1800–1859) travelled to the Australian colonies in 1832 at a time when the abolition of slavery was a topic of debate in Britain. They visited Van Diemen's Land (Tasmania) as part of a humanitarian enquiry into reports of Aboriginal women living in conditions akin to slavery among sealers.[50] They gathered the testimony of Aboriginal women, recorded a Tasmanian Aboriginal song and collected a hunting club on Flinders Island. On their return to Britain they gave evidence to the 1837 Select Committee on the Aboriginal Tribes (British Settlements). Backhouse died in York in 1869 and in 1921 the Yorkshire Philosophical Society Museum sold the club, along with other ethnographic objects, to the British Museum (fig. 22. p. 142).

Significant collections were assembled by the Anglican artist and teacher Henry James Hillier (1875–1958) from among Diyari people at Killalpaninna in northern South Australia and from Arrernte people at the Lutheran mission at Hermannsburg between 1893 and 1910. Hillier travelled back and forth from the UK several times. His mother, Sarah Hillier, appeared to act as his agent[51] and sold this material to the Museum over the period 1908–11. Hillier's own art depicting Aboriginal items shows a keen interest in the material he observed and his collection contains a broad range of object types.[52] This interest can be contrasted with the Lutheran missionaries at Hermannsburg who, although they made extensive studies of languages and traditions, forbade expressions of ceremonial life for those converted to Christianity, collecting sacred and other objects for sale.[53]

The Presbyterian Reverend J.R.B. Love, who lived among Worora people at Kunmunya Mission in the Kimberley region of Western Australia, donated objects to the British Museum in 1936. Love noted that 'the government of Western Australia does not forbid the export of these objects, but does forbid their export without official permission'.[54] He admired the skill in making spear heads and described collecting them as meaning 'really… nothing at all, beyond a pleasant interchange of tobacco and talk with our native men. The somewhat exasperating attitude of the Government departments makes such collecting less pleasant'.[55] The largest item sent was a raft but Love commented that 'unfortunately' the maker had '"improved" it by hammering some iron wire into the small ends of the poles. It is hard to get them without any "white-man" taint now' (fig. 20),[56] echoing beliefs of the time that objects with new materials lacked authenticity.

20.
Men on a raft near Kunmunya Mission
This raft and many other objects associated with Worora people were donated to the British Museum by the Reverend J.R.B. Love in 1936. Love greatly admired the workmanship of the objects he collected, but thought the use of wire on this raft rendered it less authentic.

J.R.B. Love (1889–1947), born County Tyrone, Ireland
Kimberley region, Western Australia, c. 1927–36
Gelatin silver print on paper; H. 105 mm, W. 141 mm
British Museum, London
Oc,B70.30

Love learnt the local language and wrote a detailed account of Aboriginal life and customs, which was published in his book *Stone Age Bushmen of To-day*.[57] For a film made by the amateur archaeologist and fellow Presbyterian H.R. Balfour (1875–1962), Love provided a detailed commentary. This was the first cinefilm presented to the Museum in 1935 but 'owing to the fact that it was taken in a Government Native Reserve, it cannot be shown commercially, and their [*sic*] is no provision for the display of films in the British Museum'.[58]

Prior to the arrival of Christianity (the 'Coming of the Light') in the Torres Strait with the missionaries from the London Missionary Society in 1871, the

21.
Head ornament
Made from a strip of dingo tail.
Collected by missionary teacher
William Kennett.

Torres Strait or Somerset, Cape York
Peninsula, Queensland, before 1870
Dingo tissue, fibre; L. 490 mm (including
ties), D. 30 mm
British Museum, London
Oc.6944
Donated by Sir Augustus Wollaston
Franks

22.
Photograph album, undated
This page comes from a photograph album
found in a house in Symondsbury, Dorset,
where missionary William Kennett returned
to teach. Images of the building at the bottom
and the person at centre left are copies of
images in Kennett's collection at the British
Museum.

Private collection

London-based Society for the Propagation of the Gospel sent a mission teacher, William Kennett (1840–1897), to Somerset, at the tip of Cape York Peninsula. Kennett travelled extensively in this area during his residence from 1867 to 1869. On a visit in June 1867 to Muralag (then Prince of Wales Island), Kennett noted his need to further the instructions of the Missionary Society in Torres Strait, 'to get a good canoe for our own use and to get any curiosities that fell in my way.'[59]

Kennett left Somerset when it became clear that the Queensland government would not continue to fund his work, and returned to England. He brought back a 'complete collection' of objects that were exhibited at the Manchester Missionary Exhibition in 1870, which curator Sir Augustus Wollaston Franks (1826–1897) purchased for the British Museum. Kennett noted: 'I am sorry that circumstances will not allow of my presenting them to the Christy collection but I have no objection to disposing of them' (fig. 21).[60] A local photograph album from Symondsbury in Dorset, where Kennett returned to live and teach, suggests he may also have brought back an Aboriginal person and a wallaby. Handwritten notes on the album state that the Aboriginal person was buried in the churchyard and the wallaby in the orchard, although these assertions have not been verified (fig. 22).

Financial hardship was also an incentive for collecting objects for other missionaries. Reverend Samuel Macfarlane from the London Missionary Society worked in Torres Strait from 1871 until 1886 and needed to support his wife and children when they returned to England in 1878.[61] He collected hundreds of natural history specimens and cultural items, including twelve spectacular turtle-shell masks from the island of Mabuiag. Macfarlane used the services of Edward Gerrard, a London taxidermist and clerk at the British Museum, to sell these objects, some of which came to the Museum and others to Dresden and Edinburgh.[62] Although Museum records note that the large crocodile mask (see fig. 97, p. 106) was made for Macfarlane, Jude Philp has suggested it may have been made for a ceremonial event before it was given to him, or Macfarlane could have commissioned it.[63]

Like Love in the Kimberley, Methodist missionaries in places such as Goulburn Island and Yirrkala took a genuine interest in and admired the cultural products they saw. They encouraged the production and marketing of art and craft to create a local economy and to change attitudes in southern Australia towards Aboriginal people.[64] There were also economic and social benefits to Yolngu people from participating in these developing markets, which built on long-term economic exchange experience with neighbours and outsiders. Missionaries such as Thomas Theodor Webb (1885–1948) and Edgar Wells (1908–1955) played a significant role in the early stages of the development of the market for contemporary Aboriginal art that emerged strongly in the 1970s.[65]

British Museum expedition to tropical Australia 1923–5

In 1923–5, the Natural History Museum organised a collecting expedition to northern Australia. The expedition had its impetus in a request from the Tasmanian Museum's curator, Clive Lord (1889–1933), in 1921. He was concerned that the fauna and flora of Australia were beginning to disappear before they could be properly studied and, as no Australian museum had the resources for a major expedition, he approached the Trustees of the British Museum to mount such an expedition. With a special grant allocated by His Majesty's Treasury, the Museum arranged the services of an Australian, George Hubert Wilkins (1888–1958), to lead it.[66]

The expedition began in Brisbane, traversed inland across north Queensland, and then west to Groote Eylandt, Milingimbi and adjacent areas in the Northern Territory. Although primarily focused on natural history specimens, the expedition also collected approximately 164 Aboriginal artefacts, mainly from locations in the Northern Territory (fig. 23).

Like nineteenth-century explorers before him, Wilkins relied on Aboriginal guides to assist him in his task. In north Queensland, he engaged an Aboriginal guide 'Johnny' to help him cross the Great Dividing Range (fig. 24). Aboriginal women played an important part in collecting for the expedition at the Goyder and King River Districts, whom he described as being 'most enthusiastic hunters' and 'more helpful than the men'.[67]

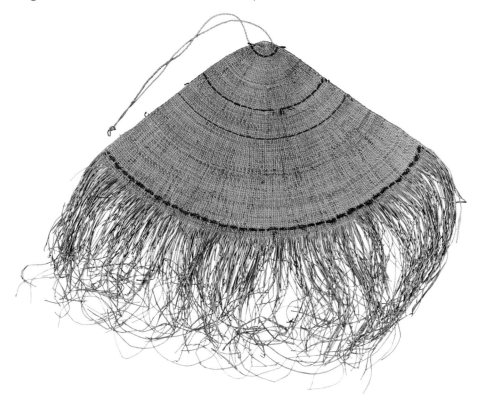

23.
Conical mat
Collected by George Hubert Wilkins.

Crocodile Islands, Northern Territory, before 1925
Fibre, wool, hair; L. 580 mm
British Museum, London
Oc1981,Q.1775

24.

George Hubert Wilkins and 'Johnny'

The photograph records the beginning of their trek across the Great Dividing Range, north Queensland, 1923. Many explorers and collectors were heavily dependent on Aboriginal guides to find their way, collect specimens and interact with other Aboriginal people.

Great Dividing Range, north Queensland, 1923
Photographer: unknown

At the time of Wilkins's visit to Arnhem Land, a mission had been recently established at Milingimbi in the Crocodile Islands and also at Groote Eylandt. At Groote, he noted the shyness and curiosity of the women, who used folded bark skirts to cover their bodies and that, after some hesitation, they exchanged them for dresses. He also witnessed and described certain stages of a ceremony held to commemorate the death of a young boy who had drowned. When it was finished and the ceremonial pole was still standing, Wilkins enquired what would be done with it and was told that, as the pole had served its purpose, they were willing to part with it 'but nothing would induce the mother to give up the feathered strings, though Olembek made me a similar set.'[68]

At a time in the 1920s and 1930s when punitive expeditions were still being mounted against Aboriginal people,[69] Wilkins developed an admiration for Aboriginal people and their culture that he contrasted with the 'absence of expressed desire for culture' in other Australians.[70] While the natural history specimens collected were divided between the Natural History Museum in London and the Queensland Museum in Brisbane, the ethnographic objects were exported and remain in the British Museum.

25.
Dance ornament

Tudu, Torres Strait, Queensland, before 1888
Wood, fibre, feather, cane, bamboo, natural pigment;
Diam. 620 mm
British Museum, London
Oc,89+.94 Exh. BM
Donated by A.C. Haddon

Memories and museums

In those localities where anthropologists returned to work regularly, some long-term relationships were formed that have had lasting consequences over generations. One such connection was a friendship between a Torres Strait Islander named Maino and anthropologist A.C. Haddon. Haddon is significant in British anthropology for his role in leading a major anthropological expedition to the Strait in 1898 and for publishing its extensive results.[71] Most of the many thousands of objects collected were deposited in the Cambridge Museum of Anthropology and Archaeology. Less well known is his earlier trip in 1888–9 from which many artefacts were deposited in the British Museum.

Some Islanders had an interest in actively engaging with Haddon to promote the memory of important ancestors. Kebisu (before 1840–1885) was a renowned warrior from the island of Tudu, who was widely influential from the southern coastal villages of the Fly River delta of Papua New Guinea down to Cape York in northern Australia. A descendant, Ned David (b. 1966), has described Kebisu as a 'man before his time': a great strategist, trader (or financier) through his control of pearl shell and a visionary for his people's future.[72] Family traditions also tell of Kebisu's father leading a flotilla of canoes in an encounter with Captain William Bligh (1754–1817) in 1792 and he is remembered as having the discerning eye of his totem, the crocodile, using the knowledge of shallow waters to strategic advantage.[73] His fame in battle was also acknowledged in a special dance performed by Islanders in 1954 during the visit of Her Majesty The Queen Elizabeth II to Cairns.[74]

Kebisu's son Maino (c. 1863–1939) was one of Haddon's chief informants. On a visit to Tudu in 1888, Haddon noted that Maino was very pleased to see him and they spent three days together: 'I got a great deal of information from him – especially as he warmed up towards the last…'.[75] Maino organised a dance for Haddon and also traded objects (figs 25–27): Haddon noted of this exchange in his diary:

> Although greatly against the grain Maino gave the headdress his father King Kabagi [Kebisu] used to wear when on the warpath and a boar's tusk's ornament he used to stick in his mouth to render his appearance yet more terrible. Like a true gentleman Maino did not let me know of his reluctance to part with these mementos [sic] of his famous father until the next day…. Still as we were such good friends he wanted me to have them and he also wanted them to be exhibited in a big museum in England where plenty of people could see his father's things.[76]

Haddon gave Maino 'what he wanted' in exchange: a small oval looking glass, 2 pocket knives, a blue bead necklace, 2 clay pipes and 11 sticks of tobacco.[77] Anita Herle has commented that although Haddon's intention was to trade fairly, there were political asymmetry and different value systems at work in this exchange.[78] Maino had earlier traded with Haddon a magnificent crocodile dance mask (fig. 28), which can be seen as a major investment in their relationship.[79]

The strategic relationships developed with outsiders continue in engagements by Torres Strait Islanders in the twentieth and twenty-first centuries. New generations of Torres Strait Islanders visit the museums in Cambridge and London from time to time to view, engage and be inspired by the collections. Although not readily accessible to all in the Torres Straits, Maino's objects can play a significant role in London too, as Ned David has commented:

'*he wanted them to be exhibited in a big museum in England where plenty of people could see his father's things*'
A.C. Haddon

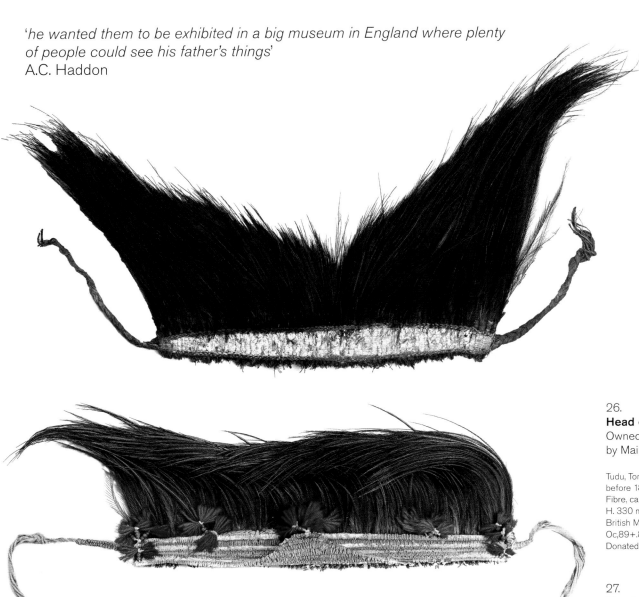

26.
Head ornament
Owned by Kebisu and traded by Maino with A.C. Haddon.

Tudu, Torres Strait, Queensland, before 1888
Fibre, cassowary feather;
H. 330 mm, W. 330 mm
British Museum, London
Oc,89+.80a Exh. BM
Donated by A.C. Haddon

27.
Head ornament
Owned by Kebisu and traded by Maino with A.C. Haddon.

Tudu, Torres Strait, Queensland, before 1888
Wool, glass, fibre, cassowary feather;
H. 145 mm, W. 255 mm
British Museum, London
Oc,89+.80.b Exh. BM
Donated by A.C. Haddon

28.
Crocodile mask
Made by Maino at Iama, who traded it
with A.C. Haddon at Tudu in 1888.

Maino (*c.* 1863–1939), Tudu and Yam
Tudu, Torres Strait, Queensland, before 1888
Wool, wongi (*Manilkara kauki*) wood, coral tree (*Erythrina*)
wood, hawksbill turtle (*Eretmochelys imbricata*) shell, resin,
pigeon feather, pandanus fibre, pigment, ochre, goa nut,
lime, iron, hibiscus (*Hibiscus tiliaceus*) wood and fibre, heron
feather, glass, cuscus (*Spilocuscus maculatus*) fur, cowrie
shell (*Bistolida brevidentata*), copper, coconut palm (*Cocos
nucifera*) wood and fibre;
H. 460 mm, W. 450 mm, L. 960 mm
British Museum, London
Oc89,+.73 Exh. BM
Donated by A.C. Haddon

these objects were given to Haddon for the very purpose
of telling everyone outside the Torres Strait that here is a
race of people, that continue to exist, that contribute to world
knowledge, that have a pride in their own history and stories.
That is what these objects are for. In this context, they serve
the very purpose they were given.[80]

In 1901, when the colonies of Australia federated to become the nation of
Australia, museums had been established in all states, yet objects from
Indigenous Australia continued to flow to London. Some were sent by various
state governments or exchanged for foreign items with museums in the UK

or other countries. The British Museum paid freight costs for artefacts sent and noted that for donors:

> it ought to be some small satisfaction of knowing that the names of donors figure prominently as benefactors to the national collection. I fear a great many native weapons are destroyed, instead of being carefully preserved as they should be – for it is quite certain that the memory of them is all that will remain in a generation or two.[81]

Ties to Britain were still strong and individuals continued to send objects to family in Britain or to offer material to the British Museum, where they understood their memories and their artefacts would be preserved. Items from Victoria River Downs and the Goyder River came from Captain Joseph Bradshaw (1854–1916) in the period 1902–5, from Daisy Bates (1863–1951) via the Empire Union Press in 1926, and from Northern Territory journalist Jessie Litchfield (1883–1956) in the 1920s. Litchfield advised that: 'If the goods I sent you are less than 10/- in value, please accept them as a gift, merely refunding postage… These parcels are very much in the way of experiment. Perhaps, if you do not need them, smaller museums may welcome them as presents'.[82]

Memories of and memorials to past places and people were also a motivation for some donors. Robert Christison from Lammermoor in central Queensland (see pp. 173–4) gave material to the Museum in 1901 and 1904, and his daughter Mary Montgomerie Bennett, later a strong advocate for Indigenous rights, donated further material in 1927 and 1953. Bennett had been born in the UK but went to Australia as a child and travelled back and forth several times.[83] Memories of the Aboriginal life they saw in Australia were kept alive in the UK by both a young Aboriginal girl brought back to live for a short time with the family[84] and by the display of Aboriginal artefacts at their family home in Burwell Park in Lincolnshire (fig. 29).

In 1927 Bennett published a sympathetic memoir of her father's life, *Christison of Lammermoor*, and in correspondence to the Museum before she returned to Australia, requested that the objects donated be recorded in her father's name: 'say, thus "from Mrs Bennett for her father Robert Christison"…That I did not use my opportunities to make a full collection of perfectly wrought implements is one of my regrets.'[85] For Aboriginal people from Lammermoor, they too had to keep their country in their memory, as many of them were removed from there by government officials to settlements in southern Queensland, making ongoing connections with country difficult.

In the later twentieth and twenty-first centuries, the British Museum has continued to acquire Indigenous Australian objects to ensure its collection reflects aspects of contemporary Indigenous life. In the 1960s and early 1970s, Indigenous items made for sale were often deemed inauthentic and

29.
Display of Aboriginal objects from Lammermoor
The setting is the entrance hall at Burwell Park, the Lincolnshire home of Robert Christison, who owned Lammermoor station.

Lincolnshire, 1911
Photographic print on paper; H. 160 mm, W. 200 mm
Townsville Library, Townsville
LC 929.2099437 CHRI

not collected by museums.[86] In the 1980s, under curator Michael O'Hanlon, the Museum became one of the first non-Australian museums to challenge received categories of what constitutes 'authenticity' in its acquisition of a major collection of acrylic canvases from Yuendumu (Northern Territory). Similarly, bark paintings were acquired from the 1980s and recognised for their artistic as well as ethnographic significance. Importantly, these acquisitions were made with the assistance of Australian anthropologists Howard Morphy and Luke Taylor and, more recently, by Lissant Bolton, who curated the exhibition *Baskets and Belonging: Indigenous Australian Histories* in 2011 for the Museum.[87]

In recent years, and particularly through the 'Engaging Objects' research project undertaken jointly with the National Museum of Australia and the Australian National University, Indigenous Australians have engaged with the museums' collections both in Australia and in London by way of critical and reflective discussions, new works of art, research and curation.[88] Through such collaborative work, the Australian collections have been reconsidered and researched, and new avenues of enquiry opened up for further mutual investigation in both countries.

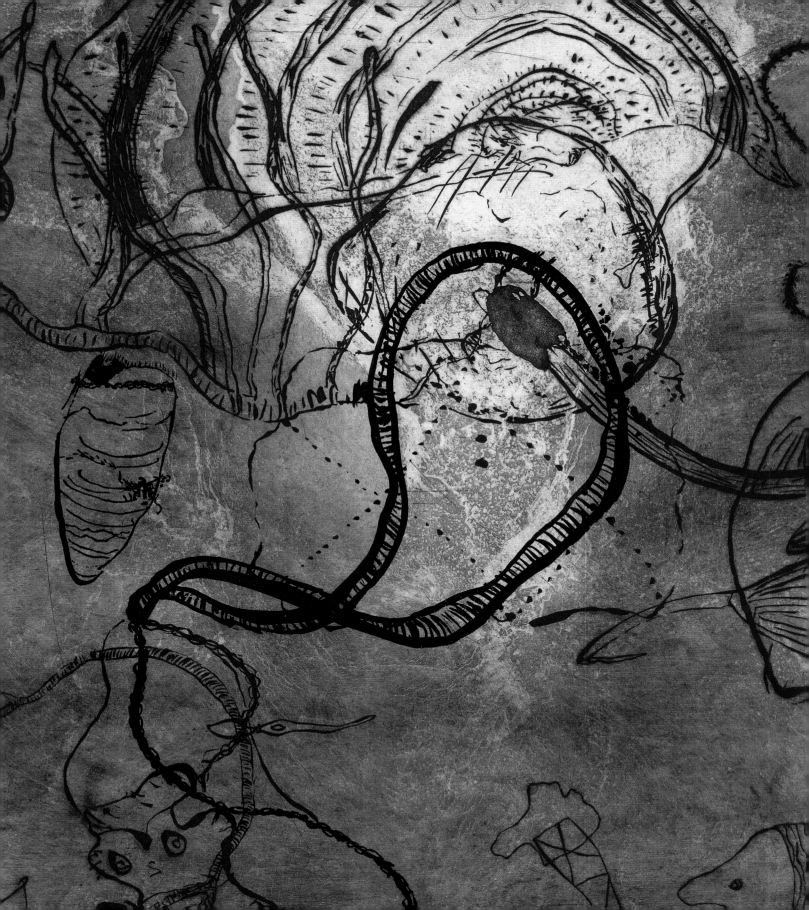

Drawing on country

Gaye Sculthorpe

The increasing engagement of Indigenous Australians with museums since the 1980s has resulted in transformation in museum practices and new and creative ways of working with museum artefacts. Knowledge of particular items and photographs has been increased through documentation by traditional owners, objects are being used as an important source of information in cultural projects, and contemporary artists have begun to interrogate museum collections and histories in their art practices.

Renewing meanings and forms

In south-east Australia, there has been a re-emergence of the art of making possum-skin cloaks and fibrecraft that has drawn heavily on museum objects. Basketry and other forms of fibrecraft fell from everyday use during the late nineteenth and twentieth centuries, with only a few individuals keeping the knowledge and skill alive. Connie Hart (1917–1993) was a Gundjitmara woman from western Victoria. She lived in and around her traditional country and later worked in a munitions factory during the Second World War and as a wardsperson in a Melbourne hospital.[1] As a young girl she remembered seeing her mother collecting rushes and making baskets but was not taught the technique. She recalls:

> No-one taught me to make baskets. I used to watch my mother
> do it and when she put her basket down and went outside,
> I'd pick it up and do some stitches. When I heard her coming
> back, I would shove it away real quick and run away. I was a
> great one for sitting amongst the old people because I knew

I was learning something just by watching them… They didn't want us to learn. My mum told me we were coming into the white people's way of living. So she wouldn't teach us. That is why we lost a lot of culture. But I tricked her. I watched her and I watched those old people and I sneaked a stitch or two.[2]

Decades later, at age sixty-five, after seeing a basketry eel trap collected in 1872 from Lake Condah exhibited in Museum Victoria, she was inspired to make a new one (fig. 1). Through Connie, and several other women in south-east Australia with such knowledge, fibrecraft has been revived and new forms are flourishing.

The use of possum-skin cloaks for warmth, as drums and funerary wrappings in south-east Australia was also once widespread, yet due to their fragility, only seven nineteenth-century cloaks remain in museum collections (fig. 2).[3] In 1999–2000, artists Lee Darroch (b. 1957) and Vicki Couzens (b. 1960) used two cloaks from Lake Condah and Echuca in Museum Victoria, Melbourne, as inspiration and references to make new cloaks and revive this practice. They have described first seeing the historic cloaks as like being in the presence of ancestors who, since then, have travelled with them, linking them to the land.[4] Cloaks are now worn for significant community events, and they are also used as baby carriers, for spiritual healing and sold as new works of art (fig. 3).[5]

In Tasmania, the art of making water containers from kelp and baskets from various plant fibres has also been revived during the last few decades. Although illustrations of kelp containers were made by French artists on early voyages to Tasmania, the only surviving kelp water container, housed in the British Museum, has been a key reference for contemporary Tasmanians (see fig. 15, p. 224). Similarly, Tasmanian baskets and shell necklaces surviving in museum collections are rare, and access to inspect those in museum collections in Tasmania and elsewhere has helped artists such as Lola Greeno (b. 1946), Colleen Mundy (b. 1940), Lenna Newson (1940–2005) and Verna Nichols (b. 1947) understand the original techniques. Patsy Cameron (b. 1947), a scholar and artist from north-east Tasmania, began making kelp water containers in the early 1990s. She has taken a keen interest in the earliest techniques of making containers, baskets and shell necklaces as documented or drawn by early explorers. In 2014 she visited the British Museum to see first-hand the necklaces, kelp container and baskets in the collection (fig. 4). She said of the experience: 'It's very emotional because I think about the spirits of the ancestors and the old women that made these precious objects; because when they made them they would have been all together talking. As Verna Nichols says "our baskets and little vessels like this are never empty, they are full of memories".'[6]

Aboriginal men in Victoria and Tasmania have in recent years similarly looked to museum collections to make new canoes. Artists such as Rex

1.
Connie Hart with her eel trap

Victoria, *c.* 1988
Museum Victoria, Melbourne
XP 3941

2.
Decorated possum pelt
This pelt, one of dozens that would make up a complete cloak, is a rare survival from the 19th century.

New South Wales, before 1868
Possum skin, natural pigment; W. 190 mm, L. 340 mm
British Museum, London
Oc.4571 Exh. BM
Donated by William Henry Blackmore

3.
On Country
Gunditjmara Elder Ivan Couzens wearing a decorated possum-skin cloak.

Thunder Point, Victoria, 2011
Photograph: Sarah Rhodes

Greeno (b. 1942), Brendon 'Buck' Brown (b. 1967) and Sheldon Thomas (b. 1970) in Tasmania and Steaphan Paton (b. 1985) in Victoria have experimented with materials and techniques to revive this almost lost art (fig. 5). In Tasmania and Torres Strait, no full-size canoes have survived, so model canoes are important in understanding the original manufacture and use.

In north Queensland near Cardwell, artists associated with the Girringun Art Centre have drawn on traditional artefacts such as fire-sticks and bicornual baskets to gain knowledge and inspiration for new works. As a child, Abe Muriata saw his grandmother making baskets from lawyer cane found in the rainforests, and as an adult began experimenting to make his own: 'I used to watch my old grandmother make them, but I wasn't actually taught by her. I taught myself by going to the museum and looking at the real... the old, the ancient artefact done by real master craftsmen. So I can say I've been taught by master craftsmen, rather than anything else.'[7] Muriata is now one of Australia's finest basket makers, represented in the collections of many museums, and one of the few men who make baskets (figs 6–7).

4.
Patsy Cameron examining Tasmanian baskets at the British Museum

British Museum, London, 2014

5.
Brendon 'Buck' Brown aboard the ningher canoe on the Derwent River
It was made for the Museum of Old and New Art's winter festival, Dark MOFO, 2014.

Hobart, Tasmania, 2014
Photograph: Rémi Chauvin / MONA

6.
Abe Muriata beginning a bicornual basket

Cardwell, Queensland, 2009
Photograph: Sarah Scragg

7.
Bicornual basket

Abe Muriata (b. 1952), Girramay
Cardwell, Queensland, c. 2012
Lawyer cane (*Calamus*), pigment; H. 410 mm, W. 480 mm,
D. 360 mm
National Museum of Australia, Canberra

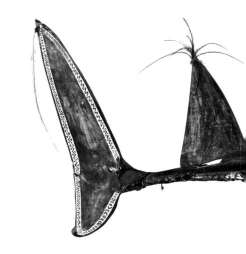

Torres Strait Islanders also innovate with new forms of art, based on traditional knowledge and techniques. Alick Tipoti, traditional name Zugub, is a Torres Strait Islander artist from the island of Badu who draws on his knowledge of cultural practices as well as museum objects in his artistic repertoire. Working first as a print maker and painter, since 2008 he has begun to create masks based on traditional designs but using new materials such as fibreglass. He has visited museum collections in the UK to examine masks, as there are few early examples in museums in Australia. In 2014, he crafted a mask based on one in the British Museum that he considers to be a masterpiece. Tipoti's mask represents a *kaygas*, a shovel-nosed shark, and is made from fibreglass, resin, wax, rope, shells, beads and raffia. It took many months to produce and during this time he visualised and dreamt about the finished work and its associated performances every night (figs 8–9).[8]

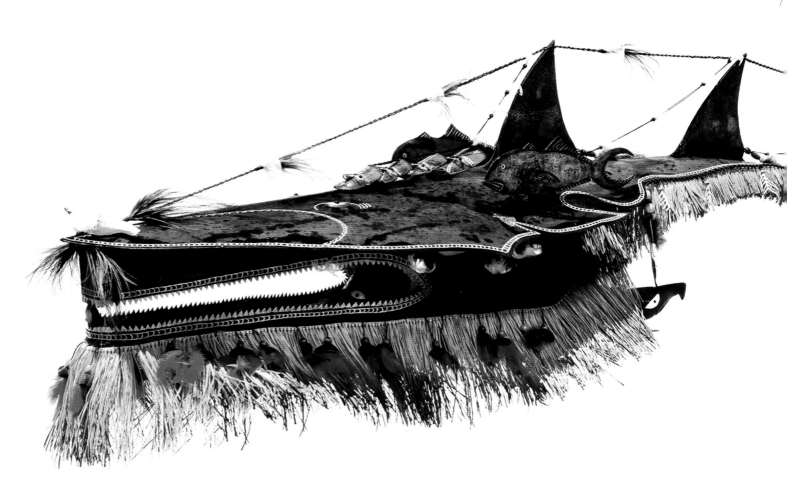

8.
Mask in the form of a shovel nose shark

Mabuiag, Torres Strait, Queensland, 1880s
Turtle shell, cassowary feather, feather, cowrie shell,
pearl shell, fibre, wood, wool, pigment; L. 1190 mm,
H. 470 mm, W. 670 mm
British Museum, London
Oc,+.3278
Donated by Sir Augustus Wollaston Franks

9.
Kaygasiw Usul (Shovel nose shark dust
trail reflected in the heavens as the Milky
Way)

Alick Tipoti (b. 1975), Kala Lagaw Ya
Badu, Torres Strait, Queensland, 2014
Fibreglass resin, wood, wax, rope, feather, shell;
H. 700 mm, W. 700 mm, L. 250 mm (approx.)
Private collection

Artists' reflections on museums

Contemporary Indigenous Australian artists have engaged with museums more generally to reflect on collections and past museum practices. In the period 2012–13, a number of artists were invited to visit the British Museum to view and respond to the Australian objects.[9] Their responses show the power of artists to see objects and museums as institutions in new ways and to consider the complex issues relating to representation, race relations, history and philosophy.

Judy Watson (b. 1959) is a Waanyi artist based in Brisbane who has long taken an interest in museum collections (fig. 10). Her work often critiques past museum practices such as collecting human remains. In 1997 she made a series of prints – titled *our bones in your collections*, *our hair in your collections* and *our skin in your collections* – reflecting on the placement of these materials in overseas museums.[10] After seeing hair-string skirts in the British Museum, she said: 'I looked at the hair colour and thought: "That's almost my colour. That could be my grandmother's mother's family, entwined

10.
museum piece

Judy Watson (b. 1959), Waanyi
Brisbane, Queensland, 1998
Lift-ground aquatint etching on paper;
H. 700 mm, W. 500 mm
British Museum, London
2009,7048.99
Donated by Australian Print Workshop

11.
The Promise

Julie Gough (b. 1965)
Hobart, 2011
Found chair, shadow casting LED light, kangaroo skin
silhouettes, H. 950 mm
Private collection

through there". The old people in our area used to say that they knew where you came from when they touched your hair.'[11] Watson's recent works also address museum practices of labelling objects and domestic paraphernalia found in collections.[12]

Julie Gough (b. 1965) from Tasmania often creates mixed-media installations that draw on detailed historical research and museum objects to make works that consider the difficult colonial histories of nineteenth century Tasmania and the impact of that past on people's lives today.[13] Her art has drawn on museum items such as the proclamation board (fig. 11, and see fig. 21, p. 140) and the kelp container (see fig. 15, p. 224). She has described her work as representing 'a claiming within a larger consideration of ways to involve nation, viewer and self in acknowledging our entangled histories'.[14]

Jonathan Jones (b. 1978) is a Wiradjuri/Kamilaroi artist and curator, based in Sydney, New South Wales. His work often uses light, a familiarity with which he developed from his grandfather's knowledge of electrical circuitry.[15] Cross-cultural intersections of Aboriginal and non-Aboriginal history and culture are common themes of his work.

After visiting the British Museum in 2013 and examining weapons from New South Wales, he developed a concept for an installation using light for the exterior of the Round Reading Room of the Museum, which reflects powerfully on the Museum and cultural knowledge (fig. 12):

> Based on a traditional Wiradjuri/Kamilaroi design from south-east Australia, this direct-to-wall light intervention encases the exterior of the British Museum's Reading Room with hundreds of fluorescent-light tubes. The artwork's pattern echoes the engraved line designs found on Wiradjuri and Kamilaroi shields, clubs and boomerangs that are housed in institutions such as the British Museum.
>
> Traditionally, for ceremonies and performances, the engravings on these objects would be infilled with white ochre, and in this way the fluorescent tubes of the proposed artwork trace the white ochre lines, remembering the hands of my ancestors. The layering of these designs onto the Reading Room comments on complex and entwined knowledge systems. Like words in books, these engraved designs are encoded, and layered with tradition, history and knowledge. They map country and community, speaking of ancestral actions and the energy these actions infused into the land.
>
> By scribing these designs directly on the wall with lights, this work comments on the establishment of the British Museum and the period of Enlightenment, which saw south-eastern Aboriginal communities stripped of their cultural material. By creating a sense of immersion – flooding the Great Court with

light – this work seeks to reinstate the immense knowledge inherent in engraved Wiradjuri and Kamilaroi objects, conveying their power to transmit this knowledge.[16]

Jones' work *untitled (Oc1894,-.279)* installed at the entrance to the *Indigenous Australia: enduring civilisation* exhibition at the Museum in 2015 developed from this concept. The site-specific light installation celebrates the engraved designs of a parrying shield from south-east Australia (see fig. 65, p. 77), which was collected before 1894 from the Macquarie River.

Similarly, Yolngu artists from north-east Arnhem Land, viewing the British Museum's Great Court and Round Reading Room for the first time in 2013, saw links and coincidences of that design with their own culture. Wukun Wanambi (b. 1962) walked into the Museum and within seconds had identified in the shape of the Round Reading Room a kind of *larrakitj* (memorial pole, see p. 116). Wanambi's *minytji* (clan design), which he paints on larrakitj, tells an ancestral story that strongly resonates with his experience at the Museum (fig. 13): 'The fish are swimming from creek to creek, river to river, searching for their destiny. Just like all these people from all over the world coming to the British Museum here. Everybody is searching for their own story.'[17]

12.
Concept for an installation in the Great Court of the British Museum
The design, using lights, echoes engraved lines on shields in the Museum's collection.

Jonathan Jones (b. 1978), Wiradjuri/ Kamilaroi
Artist's impression, 2014

13.
Bamarrungu

Wukun Wanambi (b. 1962), Marrakulu clan, Dhuwa moiety, Yolngu
Yirrkala, northeastern Arnhem Land, 2007
Natural pigment on hollowed stringybark log;
H. 1950 mm
Buku-Larrnggay Mulka Centre, Yirrkala
3267-Y, 11241

Yolngu artist Gunybi Ganambarr (b. 1973) sees an incredible alignment between the geometry of the architecture of the Round Reading Room and Great Court with the design of his Dhalwangu's clan area, *buyku* (fig. 14). The circular form of a fish trap in sunlit water is echoed by the shape of the Reading Room under the roof of the Great Court. The pattern depicted in the painting is a reflection of Yolgnu philosophy:

> The varying states and movement of sacred water is pivotal to Yolgnu philosophies. The journey of freshwater down river to meet the salt, the tidal ebb and flow, the rough and the calm are the basis or rhythm of sacred *manikay* (ritual song). One of the metaphorical overviews of this painting is the union between the different subgroups of the Dhalwangu clan in the ancestral cycle of regular fishtrap ceremonies they join together in celebrating. The last one of these was five years ago. These gatherings are ceremonial and political but also social and educational and of course productive of food. In effect without the unity of all those who live along the river the trap cannot be constructed and the resource cannot be secured. Sustenance through unity. The fishtrap is also metaphorically a harbour for the spirits of the land. The actual physical construction of the trap is sung and danced as it occurs in a tense of 'everywhen' and the participants are indistinguishable from the origin beings who also make this trap in the same place and manner.[18]

Ganambarr's painting is incised into the rubber of a conveyor belt discarded by a mine that was built on land against the will of the Yolngu (see p. 192). In employing rubber rather than bark, Ganambarr is the first Yolngu artist to break away from the convention of using natural media to represent such a sacred topic.[19]

The exhibition *Indigenous Australia: enduring civilisation* presented at the British Museum in London in 2015 and the subsequent showing of many of the objects in a related exhibition at the National Museum of Australia in 2015–16 will bring public attention to the significance of this early Indigenous Australian material. When the objects go back to Australia for exhibition, many Indigenous Australians will see them for the first time since they were collected in the late eighteenth and early nineteenth centuries. For some Indigenous Australians this will raise issues about access to items of their cultural heritage. For others, the exhibition in London will be an important moment to engage with an international audience about the place of Indigenous Australians in contemporary Australian society. That these museum objects continue to provoke topical debate, evoke wonder and engage with topics at the heart of Australian society is a testament to their enduring value.

14.
Buyku
Gunybi Ganambarr sees a synergy between this design, depicting a waterhole at Baraltja in his mother's clan country, and the geometry of the British Museum's Round Reading Room.

Gunybi Ganambarr (b. 1973), Ngaymil clan, Dhuwa moiety, Yolngu
Yirrkala, northeastern Arnhem Land, October 2011
Natural earth pigments on incised conveyor belt rubber;
H. 1250 mm, W. 540 mm
Kerry Stokes Collection, Perth, Australia

Notes

Introduction

1. W. Dampier, *A New Voyage Around the World: Volume 1 - The Seventh Edition*, London 1729, p. 464.

2. Ibid., p. 466.

3. B. Gammage, *The Biggest Estate on Earth: How Aborigines Made Australia*, Sydney 2012.

4. The research project was led by Professor Howard Morphy of the Australian National University. The other members were Dr Maria Nugent of the Australian National University, Dr Lissant Bolton of the British Museum, and Dr Ian Coates and Dr Michael Pickering of the National Museum of Australia. Dr John Carty was engaged as an anthropologist to document the process and write an ethnography of the research, community engagement and exhibition-making process.

5. The artists engaged were Julie Gough, Jonathan Jones, Elma Kris, Judy Watson, Wukun Wanambi and Ishmael Marika.

6. June Oscar, Bunuba woman, interview with National Museum of Australia, Fitzroy Crossing, Western Australia, 5 May 2013.

7. *Oxford English Dictionary*.

8. For example, J.R.B. Love, *Stone Age Bushmen of To-day: Life and Adventure Among a Tribe of Savages in North-Western Australia*, London 1936; and more recently, A.M. Duncan-Kemp, *People of the Grey Wind: Life with a Stone Age People*, Oakey 2005.

9. In 1848, near Melbourne, a colonist wrote to the editor of the *Geelong Advertiser* indicating his intent to dig up an Aboriginal 'idol' interred in the ground and send it to the British Museum, 'to convince many that the natives of Australia are not the last existing link between the animal and the man', *Geelong Advertiser*, 31 March 1848, p. 2.

10. A.C. Haddon (ed.), *Reports of the Cambridge Anthropological Expedition to Torres Straits*, Cambridge 1901–1935; W. Baldwin Spencer and F.J. Gillen, *Native Tribes of Central Australia*, London 1899; W. Baldwin Spencer, *Native Tribes of the Northern Territory*, London 1914.

11. See D. Thomson, *The Economic Structure and the Ceremonial Exchange Cycle in Arnhem Land*, Melbourne 1949; G.H. Wilkins, *Undiscovered Australia*, London 1928; W. Lloyd Warner, *A Black Civilization*, New York and London 1937.

12. S. Cane, *First Footprints: The Epic Story of the First Australians*, Crows Nest 2013, p. 3.

13. For a discussion of dating issues and oldest sites in Australia see ibid., pp. 66–7.

14. Ibid., pp. 66–8.

15. Ibid., pp. 92–6.

16. J. McCalman and R. Kippen, 'Population and Health', in A. Bashford and S. Macintyre (eds), *The Cambridge History of Australia, Volume 1: Indigenous and Colonial Australia*, Melbourne, 2013, pp. 294–5.

17. British Museum, *The Australian Aborigines*, London 1973, p. 12.

18. *Mabo* v. *Queensland (No. 2)* [1992] HCA23; 175 CLR1 (3 June 1992).

19. Estimates of Aboriginal and Torres Strait Islander Australians, June 2011 (release 20/08/2013) www.abs.gov.au/ausstats/abs@.nsf/mf/3238.0.55.001.

Chapter 1

1. Dispersal was used as a euphemism for shooting at and killing Aboriginal people in periods of conflict on the colonial frontier.

2. R.M. and C.H. Berndt, *Arnhem Land: its History and its People*, Melbourne 1954. The most detailed account of the history of Makassan contact in northern Australia is C. Macknight, *The Voyage to Marege: Macassan Trepangers in Northern Australia*, Carlton 1976.

3. M.J. Carter, 'North of the Cape and South of the Fly: the Archaeology of Settlement and Subsistence on the Murray Islands, Eastern Torres Strait', PhD thesis, James Cook University 2004, p. 63.

4. J. Falkenberg, *Kin and Totem; Group Relations of Australian Aborigines in the Port Keats District*, Oslo 1962.

5. Thomson 1949, op. cit.

6. 'We liken the flight of these spears to fine rain – rain just starting – and the bigger ones of similar form to heavy N.W. rain' (Donald Thomson's Field Notes, Museum Victoria, 1293 [1936]). Cited in H. Allen, 'Thomson's spears: innovation and change in Eastern Arnhem land projectile technology', in Y. Musharbash and M. Barber (eds), *Ethnography and the Reproduction of Anthropological Knowledge*, Canberra 2011, p. 79.

7. Ibid.

8. Ibid.

9. I. McBryde, 'Kulin greenstone quarries: the social contexts of production and distribution for the Mount William site', *World Archaeology* 16(2) (1984), pp. 267–85.

10. Thanks are due to Kim Akerman for his insightful contributions to this text.

11. H.R. Balfour, 'A native toolkit from the Kimberley District, Western Australia', *Mankind* 4(7), pp. 273–4.

12. K. Akerman, R. Fullager and A. Van Gijn, 'Weapons and Wunan: production, function and exchange of Kimberley points', *Australian Aboriginal Studies*, 2002(1) (Spring 2002).

13. D.J. Mulvaney and J. Kamminga, *Prehistory of Australia*, Washington DC 1999, p. 238.

14. P.P. King, *Narrative of a Survey of the Intertropical and Western Coasts of Australia: Performed Between the Years 1818 and 1822*, Adelaide 2012.

15. Eth Doc 909b, British Museum Archive.

16. Love 1936, op. cit., pp. 74–5.

17. Ibid., p. 75.

18. D.W. Carnegie, *Spinifex and Sand*, Victoria Park W.A. 1982 [1898], pp. 196–7.

19. Kim Akerman and Rodney Harrison have had a robust exchange on the question of for whom Kimberley points were produced at this time in Australian history. Harrison argues that the larger glass points that ended up in museum collections were made specifically for white trade, and were therefore more a product of a colonial fetish for the 'stone age' than functional objects. Akerman has strongly rebutted these arguments with evidence that glass points were ongoing features of Kimberley men's suite of objects used for hunting, fighting and exchange. For a summary of these arguments, see K. Akerman, '"Missing the point" or "What to believe" – the theory or the data: rationales for the production of Kimberley points', *Australian Aboriginal Studies* 2 (2008), pp. 70–9. See also: 'On Kimberley points and the politics of enchantment', *Current Anthropology* 48(1) (February 2007), pp. 133–4.

20. Akerman 2008, op. cit., p. 71.

21. J. and E. Treganza, *Ngintaka*, Adelaide 2014.

22. For the most detailed account of the archaeology of Central Australia see M. Smith, *The Archaeology of Australia's Deserts*, Cambridge 2013.

23. Moiety refers to the division of a society into two halves. Many Australian Aboriginal societies are divided into two moieties based on descent through the father. A person belongs to his or her father's moiety and has to marry a person belonging to the opposite moiety. Often the whole world is divided on the basis of moiety with the land, animals and spirit world being associated with one moiety or the other. The concept of moiety underpins people's understanding of the nature of the world.

24. P. Jones, 'Flinders Ranges ochre', in V. Donovan and C. Wall (eds) *Making Connections: A Journey Along Central Australian Aboriginal Trading Routes*, Brisbane 2004, pp. 70–9.

25. Ibid.

26. Ibid.

27. Carter 2004, op. cit, p. 4.

28. R. Jones, 'Fire stick farming', *Australian Natural History* 16, (1969), pp. 224–48.

29. R.G. Kimber and M. Smith, 'An Aranda ceremony', in D.J. Mulvaney and J.P. White (eds), *Australians to 1788*, Broadway 1987, p. 233.

30. S.J. Hallam, *Fire and Hearth: A Study of Aboriginal Usage and European Usurpation in South-western Australia*, Canberra 1975.

31. Gammage 2012, op. cit.

32. Ibid., p. 7.

33 Thomson 1949, op. cit., p. 14.

34 Kimber and Smith 1987, op. cit.

35 J. Flood, *The Moth Hunters: Aboriginal Prehistory of the Australian Alps*, Canberra 1980.

36 B. Meehan, *Shell Bed to Shell Midden*, Canberra 1982.

37 D.F. Thomson, 'A new type of fish trap from Arnhem Land Northern Territory of Australia', *Man* 38 (1938), pp. 193–8.

38 An excellent account of the Victorian eel traps including extracts from Robinson's journal is provided by I. McNiven and D. Bell, 'Fishers and farmers: historicising the Gunditjmara freshwater fishery, western Victoria', *The La Trobe Journal* 85 (May 2010), pp. 83–105.

39 K. Saunders, quoted in *The People of Budj Bim: Engineers of Aquaculture, Builders of Stone House Settlements and Warriors Defending Country by the Gunditjmara People with Gib Wettenhall*, Victoria 2010, p. 18.

40 P. Memmott, *Gunyah, Goondie and Wurley: The Aboriginal Architecture of Australia*, St Lucia 2007.

41 N. Patterson, *Tjanpi Desert Weavers*, South Yarra, Australia 2012, p. 127.

42 'Dilly bag' is Australian English for a net bag or other carry bag.

43 Quoted in L. Bolton, *Baskets and Belonging: Indigenous Australian Histories*, London 2011, p. 34.

44 P. Clarke, *Australian Plants as Aboriginal Tools*, New South Wales 2012.

45 Thomson 1949, op. cit., p. 34.

46 Ibid., p. 57.

47 B.J. Cundy, 'Formal variation in Australian spears and spearthrower technology', *BAR International Series* (1989), p. 546.

48 R. Carter, in *Bunjilaka: The Aboriginal Centre at Melbourne Museum*, Melbourne 2000, p. 16.

49 C. Cooper, 'South-eastern shields', in *Treasures of the Museum: Museum Victoria, Australia*, Melbourne 2004, p. 81.

50 R.B. Smyth, *The Aborigines of Victoria: with Notes Relating to the Habits of the Natives of Other Parts of Australia and Tasmania Compiled from Various Sources for the Government of Victoria*, Cambridge 1878, p. xxvii.

51 *Lines in the Sand: Botany Bay Stories from 1770*, Hazelhurst 2008, p. 15. The name Cooman/Goomun has been recorded in only one source, and has not yet been corroborated.

52 http://southseas.nla.gov.au/journals/cook/17700429.html.

53 D. Baker, *The Civilised Surveyor, Thomas Mitchell and the Australian Aborigines*, Melbourne 1997, pp. 101–28.

54 Ibid. p. 109.

55 J. Lydon, *Eye Contact, Photographing Indigenous Australians*, Durham and London 2005.

56 S. Atkinson, in F. Edmunds and M. Clarke, *Sort of Like Reading a Map: A Community Report on the Survival of South-east Australia Aboriginal Art Since 1834*, Darwin 2009, p. 7.

57 It should be noted that despite their association with Australia, boomerangs (by different names) were used by many peoples across the globe. The returning boomerang is, however, unique to Australia.

58 P. Jones, *Boomerang: Behind an Australian Icon*, Adelaide 2004, p. 32.

59 W.B. Spencer (ed.), *Report on the Work of the Horn Scientific Expedition to Central Australia*, London 1896. It is worth noting that although Spencer and Gillen are commonly credited with coining the phrase 'Dream Time' they themselves did not initially use it much. It was used only three times in the Horn Expedition report, and does not occur at all in their major work, *The Native Tribes of Central Australia*. For more on this historical emergence of the term, see H. Morphy, 'From empiricism to metaphysics: in defence of the concept of the dreamtime', in T. Bonyhady and T. Griffiths (eds), *Prehistory to Politics: John Mulvaney the Humanities and the Public Intellectual*, Melbourne 1996, pp. 163–89.

60 K.K. Wallace and J. Lovell, *Listen Deeply: Let these Stories In*, Alice Springs 2009, p. 21.

61 W.H. Stanner, 'The Dreaming', *The Dreaming & other Essays*, Melbourne 2009, p. 57.

62 E. Alberts, quoted in *The People of Budj Bim* 2010, op. cit., p. 7.

63 S. Cane, *Pila Nguru: the Spinifex People*, North Fremantle 2002, p. 91.

64 Ibid., pp. 91–2. See also D.J. Mulvaney, *Prehistory of Australia*, revised edition, Ringwood 1975; and J. Flood, *The Archaeology of the Dreamtime*, Sydney 1983.

65 Cane 2002, op. cit., p. 91.

66 M. Kerinaiua and A. Puruntatameri, *Ngirramini Ngini Murtankala*, Nguiu, Bathurst Island 1989.

67 Mulvaney 1975, op. cit., p. 138.

68 See, for example, M. Nugent, *Captain Cook Was Here*, Port Melbourne 2009, pp. 117–27; D. Bird Rose, *Ned Kelly Died for our Sins*, Underdale 1988; A. Redmond, 'Captain Cook meets General Macarthur in the Northern Kimberley: Humour and ritual in an Indigenous Australian life-world', *Anthropological Forum* (18)3 (2008), pp. 255–70.

69 L. Barwick, 'Song as an Indigenous art', in M. Neale and S. Kleinert (eds), *The Oxford Companion to Aboriginal Art and Culture*, Melbourne 2001, pp. 328–35.

70 J. Ryan and K. Akerman, *Images of Power: Aboriginal Art of the Kimberley*, Melbourne 1993, p. 12.

71 Yolngu today note that the sculpture was present before, and during, Donald Thomson's visit in the 1930s, and has been continuously maintained since at least that time.

72 J.M. Bowler et al., 'New ages for human occupation and climatic change at Lake Mungo, Australia', *Nature* 421 (20 February 2003), pp. 837–40.

73 Recent statistics suggest that Indigenous men and women in Australia are expected to live, on average, approximately 10 years less than their non-Indigenous counterparts. Australian Bureau of Statistics, *Life Tables for Aboriginal and Torres Strait Islander Australians, 2010-2012*, Canberra 2013.

74 For a detailed exploration of these issues across Australia, see K. Glaskin, M. Tonkinson, Y. Musharbash and V. Burbank, *Mortality, Mourning and Mortuary Practices in Indigenous Australia*, Farnham 2008.

75 S. Anderson and R. Apuatimi, *Tiwi Pima Art: Bathurst and Melville Islands*, Nguiu 1987, p. 5.

76 B. David and I. McNiven et al., outline and summarise these different contexts in which turtle-shell masks have been known to be used on different islands in the Torres Strait, in 'Archaeology of Torres Strait turtle-shell masks, the Badu Cache', *Australian Aboriginal Studies* 1 (2004), p. 19.

77 A.C. Haddon (ed.), *Reports of the Cambridge Anthropological Expedition to Torres Straits* vol. IV, Cambridge 1912, p. 927.

78 J. Philp, 'KRAR: nineteenth century turtle-shell masks from Mabuyag collected by Samuel McFarlane', in I.J. McNiven and G. Hitchcock (eds), *Goemulgal: Natural and Cultural Histories of the Mabuyag Islands, Zenadth Kes (Torres Strait)*, *Memoirs of the Queensland Museum – Cultural Heritage Series* 8(1), forthcoming, pp. 101–28.

79 Ibid., p. 109.

80 J. Carty, 'Rethinking Western Desert Abstraction', in Stephen Gilchrist (ed.), *Crossing Cultures: The Owen and Wagner Collection of Contemporary Australian Aboriginal Art at the Hood Museum of Art*, Hanover 2012, pp. 105–18.

81 H. Morphy, 'From Dull to Brilliant: the aesthetics of spiritual power among the Yolngu', in J. Coote and A. Shelton (eds), *Anthropology, Art and Aesthetics*, Oxford 1992, pp. 181–208.

82 See P. Sutton (ed.), *Dreamings. The Art of Aboriginal Australia*, New York and Ringwood 1988; V. Johnson (ed.), *Papunya Painting: Out of the Desert*, Canberra 2008; and T. Smith, *Transformations in Australian Art: the Twentieth Century – Modernism and Aboriginality*, vols 1 and 2, Sydney 2002.

83 A conception ancestor – a place, animal or Dreaming linked with the moment one's spirit is understood to have entered one's mother – is among the most important associations in desert identity. See also F. Myers, 'Aesthetics and practice: a local art history of Pintupi painting', in M. Smith Boles and H. Morphy (eds), *Art From the Land: Dialogues with the Kluge-Ruhe Collection of Aboriginal Art, Charlottesville*, University of Virginia 1999, pp. 245–56; Johnson 2008, op. cit., p. 113.

84 Central Australian historian Dick Kimber has noted that, at this one Yumari site, there are 'at least five levels of interpretation, of which at least three are increasingly "deep" secret-sacred men's law.' *Friendly Country - Friendly People: an Exhibition of Aboriginal Artworks from the Peoples of the Tanami and Great Sandy Deserts*, Alice Springs, N.T. 1990.

85 Myers 1999, op. cit., p. 254.

86 J. Carty and A. French, 'Art in Central Australia: refigured ground', in J. Anderson (ed.), *The Cambridge Companion to Australian Art*, Melbourne 2011, pp. 122–42.

87 Myers 1999, op. cit., p. 254.

88 Ibid.

89 Ibid., p. 256.

90 These arguments have been developed at greater length in Carty and French 2011, op. cit.

91 Buku Larrngay Mulka catalogue documentation, 2131X, 2002.

Chapter 2

1 W. Eisler, *The Furthest Shore: Images of Terra Australis from the Middle Ages to Captain Cook*, Cambridge 1995, p. 69.

2 P. Sutton, 'Stories about Feeling: Dutch-Australian Contact in Cape York Peninsula, 1606–1756', in P. Veth, P. Sutton and M. Neale (eds), *Strangers on the Shore: Early Coastal Contacts in Australia*, Canberra 2008, pp. 36–42.

3 W. Dampier, *A New Voyage Around the World: The Journal of an English Buccaneer* (London 1998), pp. 218–9, cited in S. Konishi and M. Nugent, 'Newcomers, c. 1600–1800', in Bashford and Macintyre Volume 1, 2013, op. cit., pp. 49–50.

4 N. Thomas, 'European incursions 1765–1880', in P. Brunt et al., *Art in Oceania: A New History*, London 2012, p. 274.

5 J.V.S. Megaw, '"There's a hole in my shield…": a textual footnote', *Australian Archaeology* 38 (1994), pp. 35–7; N. MacGregor, 'Australian bark shield', in N. MacGregor, *A History of the World in 100 Objects*, London 2010, pp. 580–5; Nugent 2009, op. cit., pp. 40–2.

6 All quotes from James Cook's and Joseph Banks's journal accounts are taken from *South Seas: Voyaging and Cross-Cultural Encounters (1760–1800)*, http://southseas.nla.gov.au.

7 Thomas 2012, op. cit., pp. 271–4; Nugent 2009, op. cit., pp. 88–91.

8 S. Williams cited in 'Once were warriors', *Sydney Morning Herald*, 11 November 2002.

9 See N. Thomas, *Discoveries: The Voyages of Captain Cook*, London 2003.

10 Nugent 2009, op. cit.

11 Sutton 2008, op. cit., pp. 50–4; S.J. Hallam, 'A view from the other side of the western frontier: or "I met a man who wasn't there…"', *Aboriginal History*, 7(2) (1983), pp. 140–1.

12 P. Seed, *Ceremonies of Possession: Europe's Conquest of the New World*, New York 1995.

13 For a fuller discussion, see H. Reynolds, *The Law of the Land*, 2nd edn, Melbourne 1992, pp. 9–18. See also: B. Attwood, 'Law, history and power: the British treatment of Aboriginal rights in land in New South Wales', *Journal of Imperial and Commonwealth History* 42(1) (2014), pp. 171–92.

14 E. Christopher and H. Maxwell-Stewart, 'Convict transportation in global context, c. 1700–88', in Bashford and Macintyre Volume 1, 2013, op. cit., pp. 68–90.

15 Cited in D. Bird Rose, 'The saga of Captain Cook: morality in Aboriginal and European law', *Australian Aboriginal Studies* 2 (1984), p. 32.

16 M. McKenna, 'The history anxiety', in A. Bashford and S. Macintyre (eds), *The Cambridge History of Australia, Volume 2: The Commonwealth of Australia*, Melbourne 2013, p. 562.

17 R. Gibson, *26 Views of the Starburst World: William Dawes at Sydney Cove 1788–91*, Perth 2012, pp. 9–11. For a recent fictionalised account, see K. Grenville, *The Lieutenant*, Sydney 2008.

18 I. McBryde, '"…to establish a commerce of this sort" – Cross-cultural exchange at the Port Jackson settlement', in J. Hardy and A. Frost (eds), *Studies from Terra Australis to Australia*, Canberra 1989, p. 174.

19 G. Karskens, *The Colony: A History of Early Sydney*, Sydney 2009, p. 4.

20 http://foundingdocs.gov.au/resources/transcripts/nsw2_doc_1787.pdf.

21 T. Shellam, *Shaking Hands on the Fringe: Negotiating the Aboriginal World at King George's Sound*, Perth 2009, p. 30. For a recent fictionalised account, see K. Scott, *That Deadman Dance*, Sydney 2010.

22 Governor Stirling, Report, March 1827, cited in T. Stannage, *The People of Perth: A Social History of Western Australia's Capital City*, Perth 1979, p. 28.

23 From a description of the Talbot collection in the 'Acquisitions Ethnographical 1835-1839', Department of Africa, Oceania and the Americas Archive, British Museum. The entry includes a listing of this collection, titled 'Implements used by the Natives in the neighbourhood of the Swan River, collected by S Neil Talbot Esq. in 1838 and presented by him to the British Museum'.

24 P.G. Spillett, *Forsaken Settlement: An Illustrated History of the Settlement of Victoria, Port Essington, North Australia, 1838–1849*, Sydney 1972.

25 Ibid., p. 73.

26 J. Huxley (ed.), *T.H. Huxley's Diary of the Voyage of the HMS Rattlesnake*, London 1935, p. 364.

27 J. Boyce, *Van Diemen's Land*, Melbourne 2009, p. 261.

28 Arthur to Goderich, 10 January 1828, *Historical Records of Australia*, series 3, vol. 5, Sydney 1921–3, pp. 26–9, cited in Boyce 2009, ibid., p. 262.

29 L. Ford and D.A. Roberts, 'Expansion, 1820–50', in Bashford and Macintyre Volume 1, 2013, op. cit., pp. 121–48 (p. 144).

30 T. Banivanua Mar and P. Edmonds, 'Indigenous and settler relations', in Bashford and Macintyre Volume 1, 2013, op. cit., pp. 342–66 (pp. 346–9); Boyce 2009, op. cit., pp. 261–78. For a recent fictionalised account, see R. Wilson, *The Roving Party*, Sydney 2011.

31 L. Ryan, *Tasmanian Aborigines: A History Since 1803*, Sydney 2012, pp. xix, 144, 146.

32 J. Boyce, 'Towlangany: to tell lies', in R. Perkins and M. Langton (eds), *First Australians*, Melbourne 2010, pp. 43–76. See also: J. Boyce, 'Fantasy Island', in R. Manne (ed.), *Whitewash: On Keith Windschuttle's Fabrication of Aboriginal History*, Melbourne 2003, pp. 17–78.

33 Frankland to Arthur, 4 February 1829, cited in P. Edmonds, '"Failing in every effort to conciliate": Governor Arthur's proclamation boards to the Aborigines, Australian conciliation narratives and their transnational connections', *Journal of Australian Studies*, 35(2) (June 2011), pp. 201–18 (p. 204).

34 Edmonds 2011, op. cit., p. 201.

35 D. Manderson, 'Not yet: Aboriginal people and the deferral of the Rule of Law', *Arena* 29 (2008), pp. 219–72 (p. 228).

36 Ibid., p. 224.

37 Edmonds 2011, op. cit., p. 213.

38 Boyce 2009, op. cit., pp. 279–313. See also: Ryan 2012, op. cit.

39 Boyce 2009, op. cit., p. 294.

40 Reynolds 1995, op. cit., p. 168.

41 L. Russell, *Roving Mariners: Australian Aboriginal Whalers and Sealers in the Southern Oceans, 1790-1870*, Albany 2012.

42 Reynolds 1995, op. cit., p. 168.

43 Reynolds 1995, ibid., p. 7.

44 A. Curthoys and J. Mitchell, '"Bring this paper to the good governor": Indigenous petitioning in Britain's Australian colonies', in S. Belmessous (ed.), *Native Claims: Indigenous Law Against Empire 1500–1920*, Oxford 2012, pp. 182–203.

45 Petition to 'Her Majesty Queen Victoria, the Queen of England and Van Diemans [sic] Land etc etc etc' from 'the Free Aborigines Inhabitants of Van Diemans [sic] Land now living upon the Flinders Island in Basses Straits etc etc etc', February 1846, transcribed in Reynolds 1995, op. cit., pp. 7–9. Holograph copy held in The National Archives, Kew, CO 280/195.

46 H. Kolenberg, 'Introduction', in T. Brown and H. Kolenberg *Skinner Prout in Australia 1840-48*, Hobart 1986, p. 8.

47 See, for instance, Elisabeth Findlay, 'Peddling prejudice: a series of twelve profile portraits of Aborigines of New South Wales', *Postcolonial Studies*, 16(1) (2013), pp. 2–27.

48 H. Kolenberg 1986, p. 8.

49 Gaye Sculthorpe, 'Weep bitterly: the life of Tanganutara', unpublished paper. Copy in possession of author.

50 'LOCAL', *The Courier* (Hobart), 29 December 1847, p. 2. Mrs Dandridge, wife of the Oyster Cove Superintendent, was Prout's daughter. Truganini was being cared for by Dandridge at her house when she died. Thanks to Ian Coates for these references and details.

51 J. Boyce, *1835: The Founding of Melbourne and the Conquest of Australia*, Melbourne 2011.

52 R. Broome, *Aboriginal Victorians: A History Since 1800*, Sydney 2005, pp. xxiii and xxiv.

53 B. Attwood, *Possession: Batman's Treaty and the Matter of History*, Melbourne 2009, p. 29.

54 Broome 2005, op. cit.; Attwood 2009, ibid.; Boyce 2011, op. cit.

55 For full text, see http://www.nma.gov.au/engage-learn/schools/classroom-resources/multimedia/interactives/batmania_html_version/transcript_of_the_batman_land_deed.

56 Attwood 2009, op. cit.; D. Barwick, *Rebellion at Coranderrk*, Canberra 1998; R. Kenny, 'Trick or treats? A case for Kulin knowing in Batman's treaty', *History Australia*, 5(2) (2008), pp. 38.1–38.14.

57 Attwood 2009, op. cit., p. 42.

58 Kenny 2008, op. cit., p. 38.7.

59 L. Ford and D.A. Roberts, 'Expansion 1820–1850', in Bashford and Macintyre Volume 1, 2013, op. cit., pp. 142–8.

60 A. Lester and F. Dussart, 'Trajectories of protection: protectorates of Aborigines in early 19th century Australia and Aotearoa New Zealand', *New Zealand Geographer* 64 (2008), pp. 205–20 (p. 210).

61 T. Banivanua Mar, 'Imperial literacy and indigenous rights: Tracing transoceanic circuits of a modern discourse', *Aboriginal History* 37 (2013), pp. 1–28 (p. 14).

62 For detailed accounts of politics at Coranderrk, see Barwick 1998, op. cit.; B. Attwood, *Rights for Aborigines*, Sydney 2003, pp. 3–30.

63 List provided by Office of the Central Board for the Protection of Aborigines accompanying gifts forwarded to London, 18 June 1863, The National Archives, Kew, CO309/63. Most discussions draw only on newspaper reports, which did not include specific details about the allocation of the objects by the Coranderrk people to particular members of the royal family. This list indicates that objects were given according to status, age and gender.

64 M. Nugent, '"The queen gave us the land": Aboriginal people, Queen Victoria and historical remembrance', *History Australia*, 9(2) (2012), pp. 182–200.

65 'Illuminated address to Graham Berry from William Barak and Coranderrk Residents, 1886', 2008.0037.0001, National Museum of Australia. See also: B. Attwood, *Rights for Aborigines*, Sydney 2003, p. 3.

66 J. Ryan, 'Barak: A singular artist', in National Gallery of Victoria (ed.), *Remembering Barak*, Melbourne 2003, p. 12.

67 C. Cooper, 'Remembering Barak', in ibid., p. 15.

68 See, for example, M. Davis, 'Encountering Aboriginal knowledge: explorer narratives on north-east Queensland, 1770 to 1820', *Aboriginal History* 37 (2013), pp. 29–50.

69 F. Driver and L. Jones, *Hidden Histories of Exploration: Researching the RGS-IBG Collections*, London 2009.

70 See, for instance, K. Scott and H. Brown, *Kayang and Me*, Fremantle 2005, p. 51; M. Langton, 'Out from the shadows', *Meanjin* 65(1) (2005), pp. 55–64.

71 T. Flannery (ed.), *Terra Australis: Matthew Flinders' Great Adventures in the Circumnavigation of Australia*, Melbourne 2000, p. 34.

72 Ibid., p. 123.

73 B. Douglas, 'The lure of texts and the discipline of praxis: cross-cultural history in a post-empirical world', *Humanities Research*, XIV(1) (2007), pp. 11–30 (p. 19).

74 F.D. McCarthy, quoted in K.V. Smith, *King Bungaree: A Sydney Aborigine Meets the Great South Pacific Explorers, 1799-1830*, Sydney 1992, p. 109.

75 P.P. King, *Narrative of a Survey of the Intertropical and Western Coasts of Australia, 1818–1822*, London 1827, Facsimile Edition, Libraries Board of South Australia, Adelaide 1969, p. 47.

76 Major T.L. Mitchell, *Three Expeditions into the Interior of Eastern Australia; with Descriptions of the Recently Explored Region of Australia Felix and of the Present Colony of New South Wales*, vol. II, 2nd edn, London 1839, Facsimile Edition, Library Board of South Australia, Adelaide, 1965, p. 35.

77 Mitchell 1839, vol. 1, op. cit., p. 111.

78 Ibid., p. 127.

79 Ibid., p. 173.

80 Ibid., p. 247.

81 Flannery 2000, op. cit., p. 44.

82 Mitchell 1839, vol. 1, op. cit., p. 288.

83 Ibid., p. 293. See also: B. Buchan, 'Traffick of empire: trade, treaty and *terra nullius* in Australia and North America, 1750-1800', *History Compass* 5(2) (2007), pp. 386–405.

84 D. Carnegie, *Spinifex and Sand: A Narrative of Five Years' Pioneering and Exploration in Western Australia*, London 1898, Chapter VIII, http://adc.library.usyd.edu.au/data-2/p00122.pdf.

85 Letter from Roe to his brother William, 6 June 1821, Mitchell Library. Thanks to Tiffany Shellam for this reference.

86 P.A. Clark, *Aboriginal Plant Collectors: Botanists and Aboriginal People in the Nineteenth Century* Sydney 2008; T. Shellam, '"Manyat's sole delight": travelling knowledge in western Australia's southwest, 1830s', in D. Deacon, P. Russell and A. Woollacott (eds), *Transnational Lives: Biographies of Global Modernity, 1700–Present*, London 2010, pp. 121–32.

87 Shellam 2009, ibid., pp. 147–53.

88 Mitchell 1839, vol. 1, op. cit., p. 109; Mitchell 1839, vol. II, p. 128.

89 Entry in British Museum register of 'Acquisitions Ethnographical 1835–1839'.

90 D. Collins, *An Account of the English Colony in New South Wales*, London 1802, quoted in Smith 1992, op. cit., p. 30.

91 King 1827 [1969], vol. II, op. cit., p. 67.

92 J.S. Roe to his father, 28 September 1821, Battye Library. Thanks to Felix Driver for this reference and these insights.

93 Konishi and Nugent, in Bashford and Macintyre Volume 1, 2013, op. cit., p. 66.

94 Mitchell 1839, vol. 1, op. cit., pp. 71–2.

95 J.A. Mills, 'Davidson, John Ewen (1841–1923)', *Australian Dictionary of Biography*, National Centre of Biography, Australian National University, http://adb.anu.edu.au/biography/davidson-john-ewen-5902/text10051. See also: 'A Sugar Pioneer', *Cairns Post*, 14 December 1923, p. 9.

96 R. Evans, 'Across the Queensland frontier', in Bain Attwood and S.G. Foster (eds), *Frontier Conflict: The Australian Experience*, Canberra 2003, pp. 63–75 (p. 63).

97 Diary of J.E. Davidson 1865–1868, Unpublished MS Davidson Collection No. 1570, Royal Historical Society of Queensland, cited in Report prepared by Ian Coates, 'Encounters Project: British Museum Objects from the Cardwell Region', National Museum of Australia, November 2012, p. 61.

98 Davidson 1865–8, p. 101, cited in Coates 2012, op. cit., p. 61.

99 Evans 2003, op. cit., p. 71.

100 Ibid., p. 69.

101 T. Griffiths, 'The language of conflict', in Attwood and Foster 2003, op. cit., pp. 135–49 (p. 138).

102 A. Palmer, *Colonial Genocide*, Adelaide 2000, cited in Evans 2003, op. cit., p. 68. See also: T. Roberts, *Frontier Justice: A History of the Gulf Country to 1900*, Brisbane 2005.

103 Evans 2003, p. 68. See also: J. Richards, *The Secret War: A True of the Queensland's Native Police*, Brisbane 2008.

104 Davidson 1865–8, pp. 55–56., cited in Coates 2012, op. cit., p. 61.

105 Rogers, Colonial Office Minute, 29 January 1866, National Archives, Kew, CO 234/16, 57333, cited in Evans 2003, op. cit., p. 66.

106 Evans 2003, op. cit., p. 70.

107 C.H. Ord to C.H. Read, Keeper, British Museum, letter 6 October 1899, Department of Britain, Europe and Prehistory Archive, British Museum.

108 H. Pedersen and B. Woorunmurra, *Jandamarra and the Bunuba Resistance*, Broome 1995.

109 George Phillips to C.H. Ord, letter 29 February 1896, Western Australian Archives.

110 Duncan Ord, C.H. Ord's grandson, interview with the National Museum of Australia, 18 March 2014.

111 June Oscar, Bunuba woman, interview with the National Museum of Australia, 5 May 2013.

112 Dr C. Clement, Submission to National Museum of Australia Review of Exhibitions and Public Programs, Canberra n.d.: http://www.nma.gov.au/__data/assets/pdf_file/0015/2409/Dr_Clement.pdf.

113 In addition to Attwood and Foster 2003, op. cit., see S. Macintyre and A. Clarke, *The History Wars*, Melbourne 2003; R. Manne 2003, op. cit.

114 K. Windschuttle, 'Doctored evidence and invented incidents in Aboriginal historiography', in Attwood and Foster 2003, op. cit., pp. 99–112 (pp. 106–7).

115 Clement n.d., op. cit. See also: C. Clement, 'Mistake Creek', in R. Manne 2003, op. cit., pp. 199–214.

116 Cited in P. Daley, 'What became of the Mistake Creek Massacre?', Global Mail, 2 July 2013.

117 Banivanua Mar and Edmonds 2013, op. cit., p. 359.

118 Ibid., p. 359. See also: P.A. Smith, 'Station camps: legislation, labour relations and rations on pastoral leases in the Kimberley region, Western Australia', Aboriginal History 24 (2000), pp. 75–97; R. Foster, 'Rations, co-existence, and the colonisation of Aboriginal labour in the South Australian pastoral industry, 1860-1911, Aboriginal History 24 (2000), pp. 1–26.

119 See, for instance, A. McGrath, Born in the Cattle: Aborigines in Cattle Country, Sydney 1987.

120 For details of this case, see: http://www.atns.net.au/agreement.asp?EntityID=775.

121 N. Green and S. Moon, Far From Home: Aboriginal Prisoners of Rottnest Island 1838–1931, Perth 1997.

122 For details about 'Lallan Yering, son of Mum-jet', see I. Clark and F. Cahir 2009, http://prov.vic.gov.au/publications/provenance2009/the-case-of-peter-mungett. For a recent history of Aboriginal prisoners in the nineteenth century, see K. Harman, Aboriginal Convicts: Australian, Khoisan and Maori Exiles, Sydney 2012.

123 For a discussion of colonial policing of Aboriginal people, see M. Finnane, 'Law and regulation', in Bashford and Macintyre Volume 1, 2013, op. cit., pp. 391–413 (pp. 406–8).

124 Western Australia 4 & 5 Vic. No. 21, s. 1, An Act to Constitute the Island of Rottnest a Legal Prison (1841), cited in M. Finnane and J. McGuire, 'The uses of punishment and exile: Aborigines in colonial Australia', Punishment and Society 3(2) (2001), pp. 279–98 (p. 286).

125 P. Edmonds, '"We think that this subject of the native races should be thoroughly gone into at the forthcoming exhibition": The 1866–67 Intercolonial Exhibition', in K. Darian-Smith, R. Gillespie, C. Jordan and E. Willis (eds), Seize the Day: Exhibitions, Australia and the World, Melbourne 2008, pp. 04.1–04.21 (p. 04.8).

126 A. Haebich and S. Kinnane, 'Indigenous Australia', in Bashford and Macintyre Volume 2, 2013, op. cit., pp. 332–57 (p. 338).

127 Ibid.

128 Ibid.

129 D.R. Byrne, 'Nervous landscapes: race and space in Australia', Journal of Social Archaeology, 3(2) (2003), pp. 169–93.

130 Human Rights and Equal Opportunity Commission (HREOC), Bringing Them Home: Report of the National Inquiry into the Separation of Aboriginal and Torres Strait Islander Children from their Families, Sydney 1997. For a recent detailed history of the practice, see A. Haebich,

Broken Circles: Fragmenting Indigenous Families 1800–2000, Fremantle 2000.

131 M. Nugent, Botany Bay: Where Histories Meet, Sydney 2005.

132 See N. Peterson, 'Early 20th century photography of Australian Aboriginal families: Illustration or evidence?', Visual Anthropology Review, 21(1) and (2) (2006), pp. 11–26 (p. 18).

133 J. Lydon (ed.), Calling the Shots: Aboriginal Photographies, Canberra 2014.

134 Attwood 2003, op. cit., p. 32.

135 J.T. Patten and W. Ferguson, 'Aborigines claim citizen rights! a statement of the case for the Aborigines Progressive Association', The Publicist, Sydney 1938, p. 5, cited in R. McGregor, Indifferent Inclusion: Aboriginal People and the Australian Nation, Canberra 2011, p. xi.

136 Florence Rutter, in Daily Graphic, 29 July 1950, quoted in J.E. Stanton, Nyungar Landscapes: Aboriginal Artists of the South-West: the Heritage of Carrolup, The University of Western Australia, Berndt Museum of Anthropology, Occasional Paper no. 3, 1992, p. 20.

137 Ezzard Flowers 2005, see http://www4.colgate.edu/scene/sept2005/artists.html.

138 Attwood 2003, op. cit., p. 59.

139 Ibid., p. 74.

140 L. Hall and J. Mahar, 'How Willie Wombat charmed the Block', Sydney Morning Herald, 20 January 2010, http://issuu.com/first_nations_telegraph/docs/william_cooper___s_original_1937_pe.

141 McGregor 2011, op. cit., p. 34.

142 Ibid., p. 37.

143 Ibid., p. xii.

144 Ibid., p. xi.

145 National Museum of Australia's Collaborating for Indigenous Rights 1957–1973 website, http://indigenousrights.net.au/civil_rights/albert_namatjira_and_citizenship,_1958–59.

146 D. Lockwood, 'The rise and fall of Albert Namatjira', Herald (Melbourne), 8 October 1958, cited on ibid.

147 D. Thomson, The Aborigines and the Rocket Range, Rocket Range Protest Committee, Melbourne 1947, p. 1, cited in S. Davenport, P. Johnson and Yuwali, Cleared Out: First Contact in the Western Desert, Canberra 2005, p. 19.

148 H. Goodall, 'Colonialism and Catastrophe: Contested Memories of Nuclear Testing and Measles Epidemics at Ernabella', in K. Darian-Smith and P. Hamilton (eds), Memory and History in Twentieth-Century Australia, Melbourne 1994, pp. 55–76 (p. 57).

149 Kunmanara Cooper, quoted in M. Knights, Irrunytju Arts, Wingellina 2006, p. 42.

150 Goodall 1994, op. cit., p. 57.

151 Davenport, Johnson and Yuwali 2005, op. cit., p. 46.

152 A short film, Contact, directed by Bentley Dean and Martin Butler and based on the book Cleared Out: First Contact in the Western Desert, was produced in 2010.

153 B. Attwood and A. Markus, The 1967 Referendum: Race, Power and the Australian Constitution, Canberra 2007, p. 3.

154 Attwood 2003, op. cit., p. 263.

155 V. Lingiari cited in Attwood 2003, op. cit., p. 274.

156 For an account of the NSW freedom ride, see A. Curthoys, Freedom Ride: A Freedom Rider Remembers, Sydney 2002.

157 Darlene Johnson [dir.], The Redfern Story, Samson Productions, 57 mins, 2014.

158 McGregor 2011, op. cit., p. 168.

159 http://www.aiatsis.gov.au/fastfacts/AboriginalFlag.html.

160 McGregor 2011, op. cit., p. 168.

161 H. Reynolds, The Law of the Land, 2nd edn, Melbourne 1992 [1987], p. 186.

162 Ibid., p. 187.

163 Ibid., p. 188.

164 Mark Anderson on behalf of the Spinifex People v. State of Western Australia [2000] FCA 1717.

165 Cited in I. Chance, Kaltja Now: Indigenous Arts Australia, Adelaide 2001, p. 38.

166 S. Cane has produced the definitive study of the Spinifex people and their native title case: Cane 2002, op. cit.

167 Note also that spinifex (Triodia), which proliferates in the Great Victoria Desert, is a spiky grass, adapted to fire, which has many uses for desert people. Central among these is the resin they produce, which can be processed with heat to become a hard-setting glue crucial to the production of desert tools.

168 S. Furphy, 'Our civilisation has rolled over thee': Edward M. Curr and the Yorta Yorta case', History Australia 7(3) (2010), pp. 54.1–54.16.

169 See A. Massola, 'A Victorian Aboriginal bark drawing in the British Museum', The Victorian Naturalist 75(8) (December 1958), pp. 124–7.

170 R.E. Johns's original notebooks are held at Museum Victoria.

171 See: Museums Board of Victoria v. Rodney Carter [2005], Federal Court of Australia, 645. For differing views of this case see P. Fung and S. Wills, 'There's So Much in Looking at those Barks: Dja Dja Wurrung Etchings 2004–05', in C. Healy and A. Whitcomb (eds) South Pacific Museums, Melbourne 2006, pp. 11.1–11.16; and E. Willis, 'History, Strong Stories and New Traditions: The Case of "Etched on Bark 1854"', History Australia 4(1) (2007), pp.13.1–13.11.

172 G. Murray cited in R. Usher, 'Petition calls for return of Koori etchings', The Age (Melbourne), 27 May 2004.

173 Letter from Graeme Atkinson, Chairperson, Dja Dja Wurrung Clans Aboriginal Corporation to Gaye Sculthorpe, Curator and Section Head, Oceania, Department of Africa,

Oceania and the Americas, British Museum, 30 September 2014.

174 For reference to this quote, see: http://www.aph.gov.au/Parliamentary_Business/Bills_Legislation/bd/bd0506/06bd067, accessed 10 October 2014. Dawn Casey is an Aboriginal woman from north Queensland. Her tenure as Director of the National Museum of Australia coincided with the 'history wars'.

175 T. Griffiths, *Hunters and Collectors: The Antiquarian Imagination in Australia*, Melbourne 1996.

Chapter 3

1 Information on the Museum's modern Acquisition Policy is available on the Museum website http://www.britishmuseum.org/pdf/Acquisitions%20policy%20July%202013%20FINAL.pdf.

2 British Museum Ethnography Register, 10 February 1798. These arrows have not been identified in the collection.

3 See generally N. Chambers, *Joseph Banks and the British Museum: The World of Collecting 1770–1830*, London 2007 (especially Chapter 2 Ethnography), pp. 11–18. The Museum Register records on 18 October 1771: 'A curious collection of weapons, utensils, & manufactures of various sorts, sent from the Hota Hita and other newly discovered islands in the South Seas, and from New Zealand made by Captain Cook: from the Lords of the Admiralty'; and on 23 October 1778: 'A collection of artificial curiosities from the South Seas Islands: from Joseph Banks, Esq.'

4 C. McCreery and K. McKenzie, 'The Australian colonies in a maritime world', in Bashford and Macintyre Volume 1, 2013, op. cit., pp. 560–84 (p. 568).

5 M. Nugent 2009, op. cit., p. 42.

6 M. Flinders, 30 October 1802, *A Voyage to Terra Australis: Undertaken for the Purpose of Completing the Discovery of that Vast Country, and Prosecuted in the Years 1801, 1802, and 1803, in His Majesty's Ship the Investigator*, Vol. 2, London 1814, p. 110.

7 T. Shellam, *Shaking Hands on the Fringe*, Crawley 2009, p. 184.

8 Ibid., p. 185.

9 See illustrations in P.P. King, *Narrative of a Survey of the Intertropical and Western Coasts of Australia Performed Between the Years 1818–1822*, London 1827.

10 J. Lahn, '"The 1836 Lewis Collection and the Torres Strait turtle-shell mask of Kulka", from loss to reengagement', *Journal of Pacific History*, 48(4), pp. 386–408 (p. 389).

11 G.B. Kempthorne, 'A narrative of a voyage in search of the crew of the ship "Charles Eaton", performed in the year 1836', *Transactions of the Bombay Geographical Society* VIII(1849), p. 219.

12 Ibid., p. 224.

13 R. Bayliss, 'The travels of Joseph Beete Jukes, F.R.S.', *Notes and Records of the Royal Society of London*, 32(2) (March 1978), p. 206.

14 See D.R. Moore, *Islanders and Aborigines at Cape York. An Ethnographic Reconstruction Based on the 1848-1850 'Rattlesnake' Journals of O.W. Brierly and Information he Obtained from Barbara Thompson*, Canberra 1979.

15 T. Rattler to I. Coates, National Museum of Australia, March 2014, personal communication.

16 R.W. Copping, *Cruise of the Alert: Four Years in Patagonian, Polynesian and Mascarene Waters (1878–1882)*, London 1883, p. 192.

17 *South Australian Gazette and Colonial Register*, 23 June 1838, p.1.

18 For example, *South Australian Gazette*, 23 June 1838; *Hobart Town Courier*, 6 April 1838; *Perth Gazette & W.A. Journal*, 16 March 1839.

19 *Hobart Town Courier*, 20 April 1838, p. 4.

20 British Museum 'Acquisitions – Ethnographical 1835–1839'.

21 *Launceston Examiner*, 19 July 1848, p. 2.

22 T.L. Mitchell, *Origin, History and Description of the Bomerang [sic] Propeller*, London 1853.

23 P. Hoffenberg, *An Empire on Display: English, Indian and Australian Exhibitions from the Crystal Palace to the Great War*, London 2001, pp. 131–2.

24 L. Douglas, 'Representing colonial Australia at British, American and European international exhibitions', *Re-collections*, 3(1) (March 2008), p. 16.

25 For an account of Christy and his relationship with British Museum curator A.W. Franks, see H.J. Braunholtz, 'Ethnography since Sloane', in W. Fagg (ed.), *Sir Hans Sloane and Ethnography*, London 1970, pp. 38–9. See also, J.C.H. King 'Franks and Ethnography', in M. Caygill and J. Cherry, *A.W. Franks. Nineteenth-Century Collecting and the British Museum*, London 1997, pp. 136–59.

26 W.G. Hoddinott, 'Milligan, Joseph (1807–1884)', *Australian Dictionary of Biography*, National Centre of Biography, Australian National University, http://adb.anu.edu.au/biography/milligan-joseph-2456/text3283.

27 L. Ryan, *Tasmanian Aborigines: A History Since 1803*, Sydney 2012, p. 259.

28 E. Willis, 'Exhibiting Aboriginal industry: a story behind a "re-discovered" bark drawing from Victoria', *Aboriginal History* 27 (2003), pp. 39–58 (p. 50).

29 J. Beete Jukes, *Narrative of the Surveying Voyage of HMS Fly: During the Years 1842–1846*, Vol. 1, London 1847, p. 359.

30 J. MacGillivray, *Narrative of the Voyage of HMS Rattlesnake*, Vol. 1, London 1852, p. 155.

31 M. Walter and L. Daniels, 'Personalising the history wars: Woretemoeteryanner's story', *International Journal of Critical Indigenous Studies* 1(1) (2008), pp. 35–44.

32 Estimates from historians; personal communication.

33 K. Fullagar, 'Bennelong in Britain', *Aboriginal History* 33 (2009), pp. 31–51 (p. 31).

34 Ibid., p. 39.

35 Ibid., p. 40.

36 I. Henderson, 'Planetary lives: Edward Warrulan, Edward John Eyre, and Queen Victoria', *English Studies in Africa* 57(1) (2014), pp. 66–80, DOI: 10.1080/00138398.2014.916910.

37 H. Scholefield, *A Short History of William Wimmera. An Australian Boy who Sailed from Melbourne April 1 1851, Died at Reading March 10 1852*, Cambridge 1853.

38 J. Mulvaney and R. Harcourt, *Cricket Walkabout.The Australian Aborigines in England*, Sydney 1988.

39 D. Sampson, 'Strangers in a Strange Land. The 1868 Aborigines and Other Indigenous Performers in Mid-Victorian Britain', PhD thesis University of Technology, Sydney 2000, p. 221.

40 Ibid., p. 213.

41 Ibid., p. 367.

42 See H. McDonald, *Human Remains: Dissection and its Histories*, Carlton 2005.

43 Ryan 2012, op. cit., p. 267.

44 Ibid., p. 269–70.

45 British Museum Act 1963, esp. Sections 3(4) (Keeping and Inspection of Collections) and 5 (Disposal of Objects); and section 47 Human Tissue Act 2004 (Power to De-accession Human Remains). The Trustees' policy on the application of section 47 Human Tissue Act may be found at: http://www.britishmuseum.org/about_us/management/human_remains/policy.aspx. See also A. Fletcher, D. Antoine and J.D. Hill, *Regarding the Dead: Human Remains in the British Museum*, Research Publication 197, Trustees of the British Museum, London 2014.

46 British Museum, Minutes of Trustees Meeting, March 2006.

47 The Torres Strait Islander Traditional Owners Submission to the Board of Trustees of the British Museum. Claim for the Repatriation of Two Torres Strait Islander Ancestral Remains, 31 May 2011, p. 10.

48 British Museum, Minutes of Trustees Meeting, November 2012.

49 J. Oscar and C. Cressida Fforde, personal communication.

50 For a detailed analysis of this Quaker visit to Bass Strait, see P. Edmonds, 'Collecting Looerryminer's "testimony": Aboriginal women, sealers and Quaker humanitarian anti-slavery thought and action in the Bass Strait Islands', *Australian Historical Studies* 45(1) (2014), pp. 13–33.

51 I. Coates, 'A Report on British Documents relating to Aboriginal Collections held by the Museum of Mankind, London, United Kingdom. A Report to AIATSIS', July 1995, p. 5.

52 See P. Jones, *Ochre and Rust. Artefacts and Encounters on Australian Frontiers*, Adelaide 2007, p. 262–3.

53 For a discussion of the influence of Lutheran missionaries at Hermannsburg, see ibid., pp. 305–35.

54 Love to Braunholtz, letter 11 March 1936, Eth Doc 909b, British Museum.

55 Love to Braunholtz, letter 27 July 1936, British Museum.

56 Love to Braunholtz, letter 11 March 1936, British Museum.

57 Love 1936, op. cit.

58 Letter to the editor of *The Times*, I7 February 1935, p. 10. See also British Museum Eth Doc 900, and press clippings including the *Observer*, 24 March 1935.

59 Extract from journal of W. Kennett, 4 June 1867, in letter of 1 October 1867. From Articles and letters relating to the English Carpentaria Association, 1867–1957 – National Library of Australia MS 5952.

60 Kennett to A.W. Franks, letter 4 January 1869, Britain, Europe and Prehistory Archives, British Museum.

61 J. Philp forthcoming, op. cit., p. 109.

62 Ibid., p. 111.

63 Ibid., p. 113.

64 See H. Morphy, *Becoming Art. Exploring Cross-Cultural Categories*, Sydney 2008.

65 Ibid., pp. 32 and 54.

66 G.H. Wilkins, *Undiscovered Australia. Being an Account of an Expedition to Tropical Australia to Collect Specimens of the Rare Native Fauna for the British Museum 1923–1925*, London 1928, pp. 265–6.

67 Ibid., p. 168.

68 Ibid., p. 187.

69 B. Wilson and J. O'Brien, "To infuse an universal terror": a reappraisal of the Coniston killings', *Aboriginal History* 27 (2003), pp. 59–78; D. Thomson, *Donald Thomson in Arnhem Land*, Melbourne 2003.

70 Wilkins 1928, op. cit., p. 15.

71 For analysis of the work of Haddon's 1898 expedition, see A. Herle and S. Rouse (eds), *Cambridge and the Torres Strait: Centenary Essays on the 1898 Anthropological Expedition*, Cambridge 1998.

72 N. David, interview with G. Sculthorpe, British Museum, 16 July 2014.

73 N. Sharp, *Stars of Tagai. The Torres Strait Islanders*, Canberra 1993, p. 23.

74 *Cairns Post*, 11 March 1954, p. 5.

75 A.C. Haddon, Journal 1888–9, p. 66. Envelope 1029, Haddon Papers, Cambridge University Library, p. 64.

76 Ibid., p. 66.

77 A.C. Haddon *Head-hunters: Black, White and Brown*, London 1901, p. 178.

78 A. Herle, 'Objects, agency and museums: continuing dialogues between the Torres Strait and Cambridge', in L. Peers and A.K. Brown (eds), *Museums and Source Communities: A Routledge Reader*, London and New York 2003, pp. 194–207 (p. 197).

79 N. McKinney, 'Maino and the crocodile dance mask', *Pacific Arts Journal* 12(2) (2012), pp. 45–50 (p. 47).

80 N. David, interview with G. Sculthorpe, British Museum, 16 July 2014.

81 C.H. Read, letter to C.H. Ord, 13 November 1899, Letterbook, Britain, Europe and Prehistory Archives, British Museum.

82 J. Litchfield, letter to H. Joyce, British Museum, 2 June 1925, British Museum Eth Doc 907.

83 G.C. Bolton and H.J. Gibbney, 'Bennett, Mary Montgomerie (1881–1961)', *Australian Dictionary of Biography*, National Centre of Biography, Australian National University, http://adb.anu.edu.au/biography/bennett-mary-montgomerie-5212/text8773.

84 M. Cryle. 'A "fantastic adventure": reading Christison of Lammermoor', *Journeys Through Queensland History. Landscape, Place and Society*, Proceedings of the Professional Historians Association Queensland Conference, St Lucia 2009.

85 M.M. Bennett to Braunholtz, letter 11 June 1927, British Museum.

86 H. Morphy, *Aboriginal Art*, London 1998, p. 374.

87 Bolton 2011, op. cit.

88 Gaye Sculthorpe, curator of the exhibition *Indigenous Australia: enduring civilisation* at the British Museum in 2015 is a descendant of Tanganutara, see p. 146.

Chapter 4

1 C. Hart, Biography, Design & Art Australia Online www.daao.org.au/bio/connie-hart/biography.

2 C. Hart as told to A. Jackomos, A. and D. Fowell, 'Three basket makers: Thelma Carter, Connie Hart, Grace Cooper Sailor', in A. Jackomos and D. Fowell (eds), *Living Aboriginal History of Victoria*, Cambridge 1991, pp. 72–7.

3 Two cloaks are in Museum Victoria, Melbourne; the others are in museums in the USA, Italy, Britain and Germany. The 'cloak' in Britain is a single pelt of decorated possum skin from New South Wales.

4 V. Couzens and L. Darroch, 'Possum skin cloaks as a vehicle for healing in Aboriginal communities in the south-east of Australia', in S. Kleinert and G. Koch (eds), *Urban Representations: Cultural Expressions, Identity and Politics*, Canberra 2012, pp. 63–8.

5 V. Couzens, 'Kooramook yakeen: possum dreaming. Culture Victoria', 2011, www.cv.vic.gov.au/stories/possum-skin-cloaks/11483/kooramook-yakeen-possum-dreaming.

6 P. Cameron, interview with G. Sculthorpe, British Museum, June 2014.

7 A. Muriata – Basket Craftsman. http://aatv.atsiphi.com.au/index.php?option+com (part of the State Library of Queensland's *Storylines Project*, 2009).

8 A. Tipoti, email communication to British Museum, 13 July 2014.

9 The artists were Julie Gough, Jonathan Jones, Elma Kris, Judy Watson, Wukun Wanambi and Ishmael Marika.

10 J. Watson and L. Martin-Chew, *blood language*, Melbourne 2009, p. 172.

11 J. Watson, interview with Hetti Perkins, *Art and Soul*, Melbourne 2010, p. 68.

12 See D. Young (ed.), *Written on the Body*, Brisbane 2014.

13 See juliegough.net/artist-statement/.

14 Ibid.

15 A. White, *Jonathan Jones*, Auckland 2010.

16 J. Jones, email communication to British Museum, July 2014.

17 Wukun Wanambi, 2013, personal communication. An exhibition of Wanambi's larrakitj was displayed at the British Museum in 2015.

18 Information supplied by Buku-Larrnggay Mulka Centre, Yirrkala, February 2014.

19 Ibid.

Further reading

The following publications are intended as a selected list of titles the authors think are particularly useful for those wishing to learn more about Indigenous Australia and the themes covered in this book. Other more specific references are given in the Notes on pages 256–62.

K. Akerman with J. Stanton, *Riji and Jakuli: Kimberley Pearl Shell in Aboriginal Australia*, Darwin 1994.

J. Altman, *Crossing Country: the Alchemy of Western Arnhem Land Art*, Sydney 2004.

B. Arthur and F. Morphy (eds), *Macquarie Atlas of Indigenous Australia*, Ryde 2005.

B. Attwood and A. Markus, *The 1967 Referendum: Race, Power and the Australian Constitution*, Canberra 2007.

A. Bashford and S. Macintyre (eds), *The Cambridge History of Australia*, Volume 1 & Volume 2, Port Melbourne and New York 2013.

L. Bolton, *Baskets & Belonging: Indigenous Australian Histories*, London 2011.

J. Boyce, *Van Diemen's Land*, Melbourne 2008.

J. Boyce, *1835: The Founding of Melbourne and the Conquest of Australia*, Melbourne 2011.

A.M. Brody, *Larrakitj*, West Perth 2011.

R. Broome, *Aboriginal Australians: A History Since 1788*, Crows Nest 2010.

S. Cane, *Pilu Nguru: The Spinifex People*, North Fremantle 2002.

S. Cane, *First Footprints: The Epic Story of the First Australians*, Crows Nest 2013.

N. Chalmers, *Joseph Banks and the British Museum*, London 2007.

I.D. Clark and F. Cahir (eds), *The Aboriginal Story of Burke and Wills: Forgotten Narratives*, Collingwood 2013.

I. Clendinnen, *Dancing with Strangers: Europeans and Strangers at First Contact*, Melbourne 2003.

S. Davenport, P. Johnson and Yuwali, *Cleared Out: First Contact in the Western Desert*, Canberra 2005.

F. Edmonds with M. Clarke, *Sort of Like Reading a Map: a Community Report on the Survival of South-east Australian Aboriginal Art since 1834*, Casuarina 2009.

J.J. Field, *Written in the Land: The Life of Queenie McKenzie*, Melbourne 2008.

G. Foley, A. Schaap and E. Howell (eds), *The Aboriginal Tent Embassy: Sovereignty, Black Power, Land Rights and the State*, London 2014.

B. Gammage, *The Biggest Estate on Earth: How Aborigines Made Australia*, Sydney 2011.

J. Gough, *Tayenebe: Tasmanian Aboriginal Women's Fibre Work*, Hobart 2009.

L. Greeno and J. Gough, *Cultural Jewels*, Surrey Hills 2014.

T. Griffiths, *Hunters and Collectors: The Antiquarian Imagination in Australia*, Cambridge 1996.

A. Haebich, *Broken Circles: Fragmenting Indigenous Families 1800–2000*, Fremantle 2000.

L. Hamby, *Containers of Power: Women with Clever Hands*, Sydney 2010.

J. Hardy, J.V.S. Megaw and M.R. Megaw, *The Heritage of Namatjira*, Port Melbourne 1992.

A. Herle and S. Rouse (eds), *Cambridge and the Torres Strait: Centenary Essays on the 1898 Anthropological Expedition*, Cambridge 1998.

J. Isaacs, *Tiwi: Art/History/Culture*, Melbourne 2012.

P. Jones, *Boomerang: Behind an Australian Icon*, Kent Town 1996.

C. Keeler and V. Couzens (eds), *Meerreeng-an, Here is My Country: the Story of Aboriginal Victoria Told Through Art*, Melbourne 2010.

S. Kleinert and M. Neale (eds), *The Oxford Companion to Aboriginal Art and Culture*, Oxford 2000.

J. Lydon (ed.), *Calling the Shots: Aboriginal Photographies*, Canberra 2014.

C. Macknight, *The Voyage to Marege: Macassan Trepangers in Northern Australia*, Carlton 1976.

H. Morphy, *Aboriginal Art*, London 1998.

H. Morphy, *Becoming Art: Exploring Cross-cultural Categories*, Sydney 2008.

J. Mulvaney, and R. Harcourt, *Cricket Walkabout: The Aboriginal Cricketers of the 1860s*, Blackburn South 2005.

J. Mulvaney and J. Kamminga, *Prehistory of Australia*, St Leonards 1999.

F. Myers, *Painting Culture: The Making of an Aboriginal High Art*, Durham 2002.

National Museum of Australia, *Yiwarra Kuju: The Canning Stock Route*, Canberra 2010.

M. Nugent, *Botany Bay: Where Histories Meet*, Sydney 2005.

M. Nugent, *Captain Cook Was Here*, Cambridge and Melbourne 2009.

E. Osborne, *Throwing Off the Cloak: Reclaiming Self-Reliance in Torres Strait*, Canberra 2009.

H. Pedersen and B. Woorunmurra, *Jandamarra and the Bunuba Resistance*, Broome 2011.

H. Perkins and H. Fink (eds), *Papunya Tula: Genesis and Genius*, Sydney 2004.

R. Perkins and M. Langton (eds), *First Australians: An Illustrated History*, Melbourne 2008.

Queensland Art Gallery, *Story Place: Indigenous Art of Cape York and the Rainforest*, Brisbane 2003.

Queensland Art Gallery, *The Torres Strait Islands: a Celebration*, Brisbane 2011.

H. Reynolds, *Fate of a Free People*, Camberwell 2004.

J. Ryan with K. Akerman, *Images of Power: Aboriginal Art of the Kimberley*, Melbourne 2004.

L. Ryan, *Tasmanian Aborigines: A History Since 1803*, Sydney 2012.

A. Sayers, *Aboriginal Artists of the Nineteenth Century*, Melbourne 1994.

K. Scott, *That Deadman Dance*, Sydney 2010.

N. Sharp, *Stars of Tagai: The Torres Strait Islanders*, Canberra 1993.

T. Shellam, *Shaking Hands on the Fringe: Negotiating the Aboriginal World at King George's Sound*, Crawley 2009.

R.B. Smyth, *The Aborigines of Victoria: with Notes Relating to the Habits of the Natives of Other Parts of Australia and Tasmania Compiled from Various Sources for the Government of Victoria*, New York [1878] 2009.

L. Taylor, *Seeing the Inside. Bark Paintings in Western Arnhem Land*, Oxford 1996.

P. Veth, P. Sutton and M. Neale (eds), *Strangers on the Shore*, Canberra 2008.

J. Watson and L. Martin-Chew, *Judy Watson blood language*, Carlton 2009.

M. West (ed.), *Yalangbara: Art of the Djang'kawu*, Darwin 2008.

G. Wettenhall and the Gunditjmara people, *The People of Budj Bim: Engineers of Aquaculture, Builders of Stone House Settlements and Warriors Defending Country*, Mollongghip Victoria 2012.

Websites

Australian Institute of Aboriginal and Torres Strait Islander Studies: www.aiatsis.gov.au

British Museum Collection Online: www.britishmuseum.org /research/collection_online/search.aspx

National Film and Sound Archive, Canberra, Digital Learning Resources: dl.nfsa.gov.au/tag/Indigenous+Australia

National Museum of Australia Collections: www.nma.gov.au/collections/collection-explorer

Acknowledgements

This book is both a record of the exhibition *Indigenous Australia: enduring civilisation* at the British Museum (23 April–2 August 2015) and a stand-alone publication drawing on the background knowledge of the various authors. The scope for the exhibition and publication was developed by Gaye Sculthorpe. Although the individual chapters and features of this book were authored as indicated, all the authors provided comment on each other's chapters and we would like to acknowledge this useful input. Much of the collection information from the archives of the Museum was sourced and collated by Ian Coates of the National Museum of Australia as part of a curatorial exchange between staff from the two museums, and the other authors would like to acknowledge his background research.

Many Aboriginal people and Torres Strait Islanders commented on parts of the text, allowed quotes to be used, assisted with information, discussed objects or visited the collections and provided insights. These include: Eileen Alberts, Damein Bell, Patsy Cameron, Rodney Carter, Ned David, Mick Harding, Vic McGrath, Sara Maynard, Gary Murray, Bernard Namok Jnr, June Oscar, Lorraine Pridgham, Zoe Rimmer, Laddie Timbery, Shayne Williams and Peter Yu.

Various community organisations and art centres also provided information or other assistance, often at short notice. These include: Kade MacDonald and Will Stubbs at Buku Larrngay Mulka Arts Centre at Yirrkala; Amanda Dent and Ian Baird from Spinifex Arts; Daniel Kennedy and Liz Martin of Injalak Arts; Aven Noah and Doug Passi of Mer Prescribed Body Corporate; Valerie Keenan of Girringun Arts; Terence Whap on behalf of traditional owners of Mabuiag; Marshall Arts; and staff of the Tasmanian Aboriginal Centre. Graham Atkinson, Di Smith and Barbara Huggins of the Dja Dja Wurrung Clans Aboriginal Corporation also provided useful input.

Many colleagues both in Australia and the United Kingdom generously provided information or comment on various objects or text. These include: Kim Akerman, Lindy Allen, Bain Atwood, Peter Bindon, Sandra Bowdler, Scott Cane, Ian Clark, Carol Cooper, Jeremy Coote, Felix Driver, Maureen Fuary, Louise Hamby, Rachael Handley, Ian Henderson, Anita Herle, Philip Jones, Frances Morphy, Jude Philp, Tiffany Shellam, Luke Taylor and Sarah Yu.

The National Museum of Australia interviewed dozens of people in many Aboriginal and Torres Strait Islander communities across Australia. Although too numerous to mention here, we thank all these individuals for providing insights and comments about the collection.

Within the British Museum, the authors would particularly like to thank Claudia Bloch, senior development editor, The British Museum Press, for her excellent work, ably assisted by Axelle Russo-Heath as picture researcher, and Kate Oliver senior production controller. The book has been beautifully designed by Will Webb. Rachael Murphy, project curator for the exhibition, was exemplary in her role. She assisted in innumerable ways including keeping track of all objects, liaising with photography, assisting with research, drafting all captions and arranging many permissions. Museum photographer Mike Row took most of the images of Museum objects and the results of his work can be seen in the quality of images depicted. Other Museum staff who commented or assisted in other ways include: Rosemary Bradley, Caroline Cartwright, Tony Doubleday, Monique Harter, J.D. Hill, Joanna Lister, Antony Loveland and Hannah Thomas. Several postgraduate students volunteered time or information, including Sarah Florender, George King and Daniel Simpson. Other staff of the Oceania section assisted at various stages including Polly Bence and Natasha McKinney, and Jill Hasell in facilitating access to the collection.

The exhibition project manager was Jane Bennett, senior project manager, and 3D and graphic design was by James Norton and Bridget Allison of nortonallison Ltd. Other members of the core exhibition team include: Olivia Bone, Helene Delaunay, Julia Evans, Jessica Hunt, Philip Kevin, Stewart Marsden, Rebecca Penrose, Julianne Phippard, Anita Sheth, Ian Taylor and Rachael Utting. We would also like to acknowledge: David Bilson, Hannah Boulton, Phil Carley, Graham Dunkley, Nicola Elvin, Dan Ferguson, Stuart Frost, Kathryn Havelock, Sukie Hemming, Caroline Ingham, Joanna Mackle, Jill Maggs, Shelley Mannion, Carolyn Marsden-Smith, Olivia Rickman, Jennifer Suggitt, Patricia Wheatley and Jonathan Williams.

Lenders to the exhibition include: the British Library; Marylebone Cricket Club Museum, Lord's Ground; Museum of Archaeology and Anthropology, University of Cambridge; Museum Victoria, Melbourne; National Museum of Australia; Pitt Rivers Museum, University of Oxford; and SOAS Library, University of London. We thank the institutions and their staff for agreeing to and facilitating these loans.

The visits of the contemporary Indigenous artists who were fellows on the 'Engaging Objects' research project were made possible by a research grant from the Australian Research Council facilitated by John Carty.

While the views in the book are those of the authors only, we would like to acknowledge the numerous Aboriginal people and Torres Strait Islanders who have generously shared their knowledge and experiences with us over many years. We trust that readers will be inspired to learn more of the regional histories and personal narratives found across Australia from the general overview that we have provided in this book.

Illustration credits

The publisher would like to thank the copyright holders for granting permission to reproduce the images illustrated. Every attempt has been made to trace accurate ownership of copyrighted images in this book. Errors and omissions will be corrected in subsequent editions provided notification is sent to the publisher.

Unless otherwise stated below, copyright in photographs belongs to the institution mentioned in the caption.

Photographs of British Museum objects are © The Trustees of the British Museum, courtesy of the Department of Photography and Imaging. Registration numbers and donor information for British Museum objects are included in the image captions. Further information about the Museum and its collection can be found at britishmuseum.org.

Objects included in the exhibition *Indigenous Australia: enduring civilisation* at the British Museum from 23 April to 2 August 2015 are marked Exh. BM in the image captions.

Endpapers
Front: Painting on a rock shelter on the Arnhem Land plateau. It is believed to depict *Genyornis*, a large flightless bird, which once lived in Arnhem Land. It may be over 45,000 years old.
Western Arnhem Land, Northern Territory, 2010
Photograph: Robert Gunn
© Jawoyn Association

Back: This rock shelter includes art which dates from about 15,000 years ago to about 1940. More recent images depicted include Makassan fishermen, missionaries, bicycles, rifles, a biplane and WWII era ships.
Djulirri, Western Arnhem Land, Northern Territory
Photograph: Paul Taçon
© Paul Taçon, Griffith University

pp. 10–11: Map, Martin Brown

Chapter 1
p. 20 and fig. 103: National Museum of Australia
Fig. 1: Photo M. Gebicki/Getty Images
Fig. 3: © The British Library Board
Fig. 6: National Museum of Australia
Fig. 9: Map, Martin Brown
Fig. 16: © Diana James. Courtesy of the Canning Stock Route Research Project, Australian National University
Fig. 28: © Jenny Chang/ the Martu Ecological Anthropology Project (R. Bliege Bird, D.W. Bird and B.F. Codding)
Fig. 29: National Library of Australia
Fig. 31: © Pitt Rivers Museum, University of Oxford

Fig. 36: Courtesy Thomson Family and Museum Victoria
Fig. 37: © the artist's estate c/o Bula'bula Arts, Ramingining
Fig. 38: © Tyrell Collection, Museum of Applied Arts and Sciences, Sydney
Fig. 39: © Museum der Kulturen Basel
Fig. 40: Courtesy Thomson Family and Museum Victoria
Fig. 42: Robert Harding Picture Library / Ashley Cooper
Fig. 53: Reproduced by permission of the artist courtesy Rebecca Hossack Art Gallery
Fig. 75: National Museum of Australia
Fig. 76: From *Pila Nguru – The Spinifex People* © Scott Cane 2002, Published by Fremantle Press, Western Australia
Fig. 77: Courtesy of Spinifex Arts Project
Fig. 78: © the artists, courtesy of Spinifex Arts Project
Fig. 79: © the artist's family; image courtesy Pitt Rivers Museum, University of Oxford
Fig. 80: Courtesy Museum Victoria
Fig. 81: © John Carty
Fig. 82 and fig. 106: Reproduced by permission of the artist © Buku-Larrnggay Mulka Centre www.yirrkala.com
Fig. 84: © Sahyma Lachman
Fig. 88: © Peter Eves
Fig. 90: © Margie West
Fig. 91: © Howard Morphy
Fig. 95: © John Carty
Fig. 100: © the artists, courtesy of the Spinifex Arts Project
Fig. 101: © the artist's estate
Fig. 102: Reproduced by permission of the artist © Buku-Larrnggay Mulka Centre www.yirrkala.com
Fig. 105: National Gallery of Australia, Canberra
Fig. 107: Getty images Photo by Pool JO SYDNEY 2000, with permission of the IOC and Donny Wollagoodja

Chapter 2
p. 121 and fig. 5: © Vincent Namatjira
Fig. 2: Museum of Archaeology and Anthropology, University of Cambridge
Fig. 3: © The British Library Board
Fig. 4: © The British Library Board
Fig. 6: © Michael Cook
Fig. 7: SOAS Library
Fig. 10: Map, Martin Brown. Source: Alan Atkinson and Marian Aveling, *Australians 1838*, Sydney 1987, p. xvii
Fig. 19: Auscape/ UIG/ Gettyimages
Fig. 20: The National Archives of the UK
Fig. 21: Museum of Archaeology and Anthropology, University of Cambridge
Fig. 24: The National Archives of the UK
Fig. 27: © The British Library Board
Fig. 28: bpk / Ethnologisches Museum, Staatiche Muzeen zu Berlin
Fig. 30: National Museum of Australia
Fig. 31: National Gallery of Australia, Canberra and the National Library of Australia, Canberra Rex Nan Kivell Collection
Fig. 32: © Pitt Rivers Museum, University of Oxford
Fig. 33: National Library of Australia

Fig. 34: © Ian Rolfe Photography
Fig. 41: From P.P. King, *Narrative of a Survey of the Intertropical and Western Coasts of Australia*, John Murray, 1827
Fig. 45: © Dan Proud Photography
Fig. 46: Sourced from the collection of the State Library of Western Australia and reproduced with the permission of the Library Board of Western Australia
Fig. 48: State Records Office of Western Australia
Fig. 49: Courtesy Museum Victoria
Fig. 50: National Museum of Australia
Fig. 62: © Juno Gemes Archive
Fig. 69: © Legend Press
Fig. 70: National Library of Australia
Fig. 71: © the artist c/o Martumili artists
Fig. 72: Image courtesy of the Yirrkala Art Centre and Parliament House
Fig. 73: National Museum of Australia
Fig. 74: State Library of New South Wales Courtesty Tribune/SEARCH foundation
Fig. 76: Photo George Serras, National Museum of Australia
Fig. 81: Courtesy of Spinifex Arts Project
Fig. 82: Victor France Photographic
Fig. 83: Victor France Photographic
Fig. 87: Fairfax syndication/ THE AGE NEWS Picture by CRAIG ABRAHAM

Chapter 3
p. 210 and fig. 12: National Library of Australia
Fig. 2: National Library of Australia
Fig. 6: State Library of New South Wales, Sydney
Fig. 9: © Sonia M Photography
Fig. 11: © The British Library Board
Fig. 16: With permission from Trent Bridge, Nottinghamshire. Source: J. Mulvany and R. Harcourt, *Cricket Walkabout: the Australian Aborigines in England*, Melbourne, 1988
Fig. 17: Marylebone Cricket Club
Fig. 19: © Courtesy of Sara Maynard and Tasmanian Aboriginal Centre
Fig. 22: Private collection
Fig. 24: Source: G.H. Wilkins, *Undiscovered Australia*, London 1928
Fig. 29: CityLibraries Townsville, Local History Collection

Chapter 4
p. 242 and fig. 10: reproduced by permission of the artist
Fig. 1: Courtesy Museum Victoria
Fig. 3: Sarah Rhodes/Culture Victoria
Fig. 5: Rémi Chauvin/MONA
Fig. 6: Sarah Scragg, courtesy National Museum of Australia
Fig. 7: National Museum of Australia
Fig. 9: © Alick Tipoti
Fig. 11: © Julie Gough
Fig. 12: © Jonathan Jones
Fig. 13: Image courtesy of the artist, Yirrkala Art Centre and Niagara Galleries, Melbourne
Fig. 14: © Gunybi Ganambarr

Index

Page numbers in *italics* refer to figures and captions. Abbreviations used: BM (British Museum), NSW (New South Wales), NT (Northern Territory), Qld (Queensland), SA (South Australia), Tas (Tasmania), Vic (Victoria), WA (Western Australia).